Bicycle
Odyssey

AN AROUND-THE-WORLD JOURNEY
OF INNER AND OUTER DISCOVERY

CARLA FOUNTAIN

BALBOA.PRESS
A DIVISION OF HAY HOUSE

Copyright © 2020 Carla Fountain.
www.CarlaFountain.com

All rights reserved. No part of this book may be used or reproduced by any means, graphic, electronic, or mechanical, including photocopying, recording, taping or by any information storage retrieval system without the written permission of the author except in the case of brief quotations embodied in critical articles and reviews.

Balboa Press books may be ordered through booksellers or by contacting:

Balboa Press
A Division of Hay House
1663 Liberty Drive
Bloomington, IN 47403
www.balboapress.com
844-682-1282

Because of the dynamic nature of the Internet, any web addresses or links contained in this book may have changed since publication and may no longer be valid. The views expressed in this work are solely those of the author and do not necessarily reflect the views of the publisher, and the publisher hereby disclaims any responsibility for them.

The author of this book does not dispense medical advice or prescribe the use of any technique as a form of treatment for physical, emotional, or medical problems without the advice of a physician, either directly or indirectly. The intent of the author is only to offer information of a general nature to help you in your quest for emotional and spiritual well-being. In the event you use any of the information in this book for yourself, which is your constitutional right, the author and the publisher assume no responsibility for your actions.

Any people depicted in stock imagery provided by Getty Images are models, and such images are being used for illustrative purposes only.
Certain stock imagery © Getty Images.

Cover Photo by Steen Brogaard

Print information available on the last page.

ISBN: 978-1-9822-5616-6 (sc)
ISBN: 978-1-9822-5618-0 (hc)
ISBN: 978-1-9822-5617-3 (e)

Library of Congress Control Number: 2020919256

Balboa Press rev. date: 10/06/2020

With deep gratitude, I dedicate this book to my parents and to my partner in this wonderful adventure, Dermot Begley.

One's destination is never a place, but a new way of seeing things.

—Henry Miller

Contents

Note to Readers...xiii
Hippos in the Night...xv

PART 1 • The Beginnings

1 Introduction.. 1
2 Trip Preparation 4

PART 2 • Europe—History Comes Alive

3 England—Literary Haunts 11
4 Scotland—A Homecoming 16
5 France, Spain, and the North—Castles, Food, and Friends 27

PART 3 • Africa—No One Sacrificed a Goat in Our Honor

6 Kenya—Following the Pan-African Highway........................... 43
7 Uganda—Into the Unknown 63
8 The Swahili Coast.. 96
9 Lamu Island—Our Dark Night of the Soul........................... 102

PART 4 • India—Down the Rabbit Hole

10 Bombay and Goa...113
11 Karnataka—A Week of Festivals 121
12 The Karnataka Coast and Inland to Mysore 134
13 Civil Unrest and into Tamil Nadu 146
14 A Hospital Stay 157

15 Kodaikanal—Bliss in the Hill Stations 162
16 Coming Down the Mountain 173
17 Kerala—The Backwaters and Rest 179
18 Madras and Calcutta 186

PART 5 • Nepal—Touching the Sky

19 Kathmandu Valley and Trekking 195

PART 6 • Thailand—Temples and Monks

20 Bangkok 207
21 Chiang Mai to the Northeast—Hill Tribes and Buffalo 211
22 Ko Samet 233

PART 7 • Vietnam—A Warm Welcome

23 Saigon—A Cyclist's City 239
24 The Mekong Delta 250
25 Hue—Imperial Festivals 267
26 The Central Coast 273

PART 8 • Singapore and Bali—Winding Down

27 Singapore—A Pause 289
28 Bali—Blessings and Balm 292

Afterword 311
Budget and Sample of Expenses 315
Trip Itinerary 317
Packing List 325
Acknowledgments 329

Note to Readers

I have changed the names of many of the people we met to protect their privacy. Indian cities underwent name changes after our travels. In this memoir, I chose the names in use at the time of our travels. I provide the current name at the first mention of each city that has been changed since our trip. Chapter titles retain the use of the city name at the time of our visit to that city.

Hippos in the Night

In the moonless night, I zipped open our tent a few inches to investigate the sounds of munching and soft footfalls that surrounded us. We were the only ones in a tent on a wide expanse of green lawn by the lake at Fisherman's Camp near Lake Naivasha, Kenya. My heart froze when I saw that the sounds came from several large hippopotami grazing around our flimsy shelter. Two of them turned to look in my direction, and their eyes glinted back at me, red in my flashlight. I quickly moved the beam, not wanting to irritate them. God knows what they would do if they felt threatened. I could make out the huge, black hulks of their bodies as they slowly moved around us. Apparently, hippos come out of the lake at night to graze. Now we understood why the campground was so well manicured and deserted, apart from us.

But I urgently had to go to the bathroom, and the night was still young. Near the equator, the sun rises and sets at about six o'clock in the morning and six o'clock in the evening, which gives an even twelve hours of daylight and darkness. We had a long way to go before dawn. I roused Dermot to come with me and hold the flashlight so I would be safe; at least we would be together if the hippos attacked. Mission accomplished, we zipped up tight in our tent and nervously settled into our sleeping bags with only a millimeter of canvas sheeting separating us from curious hippopotami.

We slept fitfully that night and woke at dawn to find the lawn empty. The hippos had made their way back to the lake to submerge their massive bodies. Only their ears and noses peeked above the surface. We had set out on our bicycle odyssey to be close to nature, to see the creatures in Africa, and to meet people. We hadn't bargained on encountering wild animals at night only inches away from our tent.

How did we get here?

PART 1
• The Beginnings

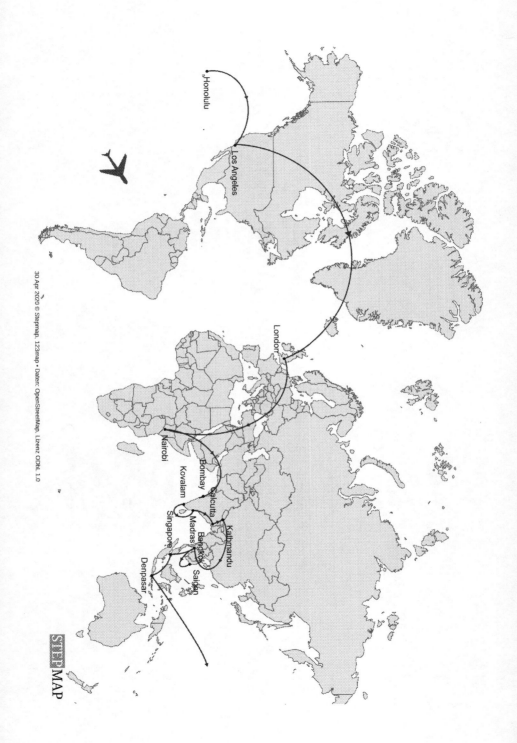

1

Introduction

In the summer of 1991, my husband, Dermot Begley, and I quit our teaching jobs, packed up everything in our house, and rented our home to three Pasadena Art Center students for a year so we could take an around-the-world bicycle trip. When I tell people Dermot and I are no longer married, they usually nod and say, "Yes, travel is hard on a relationship." But they don't understand that we traveled well together. We spent five years planning, poring over maps and guidebooks, reading all the travel adventure books we could get our hands on, and saving money. We structured a skeleton itinerary by figuring out the best time of year to travel through each area of the world on our list. All told, we bicycled about seven thousand miles and had only fifty flat tires.

This trip tested our determination, patience, faith, and fortitude. It pushed us to our physical and emotional limits. We learned many lessons along the way about ourselves and the world, such as to trust in serendipity; to be open to the unexpected; to welcome detours to magical, hidden places; and to be adaptable. We savored, and were grateful for, chance encounters with exceptional people, who opened our eyes to new possibilities and shared their human kindness with us. We cherished those warm connections we made along the way. We also discovered that we needed very few material possessions to be happy and live well.

Dermot and I first met in the late seventies when a college friend invited me home for dinner. Her younger brother bounced into the room with his flaming red hair, raving about his favorite punk rock group, the Sex Pistols. Five years later, when we met again, we realized we had a lot in common. I had recently returned from a homestay in Mexico, where I had gone to sharpen my Spanish language skills. My speaking proficiency had grown rusty after a long absence from Spain, where I had lived for three years as a child. Dermot had spent the last four years in Mexico, where he traveled, lived, and studied. We both loved adventure, art, languages, and exploration.

Dermot's colorful family was a sharp contrast to my own. His house rang with lively conversations and political debates. His mother was a writer. His father, the most colorful of all, did impersonations of George C. Scott as General Patton in motivational speeches for companies. He engaged anyone in political discourse who would listen. My parents were more conservative, subdued, and concerned about appearances. Time spent with the Begley family was exciting, stimulating, and freeing. Dermot was a nonconformist with a rebellious streak and a question-authority side I found thrilling. His personality helped push me out of my shell. A photo I took of him with his bicycle pointed the other way down a one-way street sums up his attitude. With our shared interests in travel, languages, and art, plus his passion and zest for life and adventure, we quickly fell in love.

By this time, I was working as an assistant film editor for National Geographic Films. When I wasn't at the office, I yearned to make my own documentary. Pulling together my resources and courage, I took time off to make a documentary on St. Elmo Village, an artist community in Los Angeles. Dermot helped me with the project and soon became the associate producer. He assisted with camerawork and interviews. He and a friend of his wrote and recorded the music for the film. Our documentary was nominated for an Emmy award, and Dermot found a distributor for the film. After that experience, we started a company to videotape oral histories.

I had always bicycled on short rides for recreation but never for more than five miles. When Dermot and I started dating, he invited me to go on longer bike rides. We ventured out on a few ten- to twenty-mile rides around the Palos Verdes Peninsula and Griffith Park in Los Angeles. As we biked, he told me stories about his travels by bicycle through Mexico, Belize, and Scotland after he graduated from high school.

I loved the feeling of freedom I experienced with the wind on my whole body as I rode. The slow pace enabled me to observe the details of the terrain around me. I was both invigorated and calmed as I used my muscles while surrounded by nature. The entire experience forced me to be fully present. It became meditative.

Not long after, we began regularly bicycling all over Los Angeles. I started to bike the six miles to and from work almost every day. I believed that if the destination was under six miles, I should use my bicycle and leave the car at home. On the weekends, we challenged ourselves. We mountain biked in the San Gabriel Forest above our house in Altadena, through the Angeles Forest, across Catalina Island, down the coast to San Diego, and in the mountains around Santa Barbara. We also completed a few metric century rides (one hundred kilometers) and a century ride (one hundred miles). For longer vacations of two or three weeks, we planned bicycle trips up the coast of Maine and into Canada to see the autumn leaves; around the islands of Hawaii, Oahu, and Jamaica; down the Oregon and Northern California coast all the way to San Francisco; and around the San Juan Islands off the coast of Washington. Bicycling became my preferred method of seeing the world.

2

Trip Preparation

I became an avid reader of books about bicycle travel adventure. I befriended a woman named Irene, who had traveled extensively. Irene and her boyfriend had bicycled throughout India and Nepal for several months. She lent me *Full Tilt* by Dervla Murphy, an Irishwoman who spent a year alone traveling from Dublin to Nepal on a one-speed bicycle. I read the late Barbara Savage's *Miles from Nowhere* and grew excited about the possibility of taking our own extended bicycle journey. Irene connected us with her friends Bruce Junek, Tass Thacker, and Bernard Magnouloux. All three had also journeyed around the world by bicycle. As I devoured their books, *The Road of Dreams* by Bruce Junek and *Travels with Rosinante* by Bernard Magnouloux, I started to research and plan a trip of our own.

Dermot and I were able to talk to Bruce and Tass a few days before our trip. They were helpful, and they encouraged us. They stressed that if a person was resourceful and planned well, very little money was needed to do such a trip. In his book, Bernard wrote that he had spent about $12,000 on his five-year journey. Dermot and I spent more than that in our eleven months of travel, although we have different ideas on the cost of the trip as well as different memories about the trip. Every adventure is as unique as the individual, even if you travel side by side. In this recounting, I can only be true to my memories and try to include the ones Dermot shared with me almost three decades later.

BICYCLE ODYSSEY

On our journey, we wanted to combine our interests in both the slow travel of bicycling and documentary film. We decided to set out equipped with a Hi8 camera and ten hours of tape. Hi8 was the smallest and highest-quality tape to use at the time. We planned to document our trip and interview people in different parts of the world as we journeyed. The odyssey would blend our passions for film, travel, and bicycling.

Dermot's parents were from England and Scotland. We wanted to visit his ancestral homeland and see his relatives on our trip. Because of the Middle Passage and slavery, my African heritage was untraceable to a specific country (that has changed recently with DNA testing). I had longed to visit sub-Saharan Africa, and Kenya was the country we could work into our itinerary.

We bought round-the-world tickets: Los Angeles to London, London to Nairobi via Moscow, Nairobi to Bombay, Bombay to Goa, Trivandrum to Madras, Madras to Calcutta, Calcutta to Kathmandu, Kathmandu to Bangkok, Bangkok to Singapore, Singapore to Denpasar, Denpasar to Biak, Biak to Honolulu, and Honolulu to Los Angeles. That was the skeleton of our trip. The highlights and magical gems lay hidden in between those cities. Travel by bicycle gives a personal view of the villages and hamlets that might not even be on a map. You meet people at tea stands by the side of the road in little places where no one else stops except for locals and other bicyclists.

At that time, the least expensive tickets could be found through a consolidator. A tiny, attractive ad in the *Los Angeles Times* offered what we were looking for. I called and spoke to the owner, who had a mellifluous, baritone voice. When he said Mombasa, Varanasi, and Irian Jaya, the words reverberated with a rich, exotic tone. As he said the names of the cities, excited chills filled me. After we discussed the plans and time frame, he helped me make an itinerary of flights. I wrote out a check and mailed it to the company, which was located in San Francisco.

CARLA FOUNTAIN

Big mistake! We waited and waited and waited for the tickets. Dermot and I had both already resigned from our teaching jobs with the Los Angeles Unified School District. The house was almost empty, and we had our tenants picked out and ready to move in with a one-year lease signed. But we didn't have our tickets! Dermot's mother, who had worked in the travel business, was appalled that we had sent a check to a consolidator. Apparently, they had a bad reputation at the time. She said we should have handed them the check with one hand as we took the tickets with the other. With two weeks to go before the trip and still no tickets, Dermot decided we should drive up to San Francisco and confront the man with the baritone voice in person. We had purchased travel insurance from a separate company when we bought our tickets. That proved to come in handy before we even left the country.

Determined and nervous, we left home at dawn and drove up to San Francisco, arriving by late afternoon. We went straight to the consolidator's office. The man in question, who was as good looking as his telephone voice had suggested, made a joke and chided us for being so anxious about our tickets. He handed us the tickets for the first leg of the trip (Los Angeles to London) and part of the last leg (Nairobi to Bombay and on). But he left out our London-to-Nairobi ticket, which was an important piece. He had also booked the wrong dates for our last leg and had ticketed our final leg a few months too early. He explained that he needed to zip out to the airport for the rest of the tickets and would be right back. His secretary invited us to wait with her in the office.

We waited most of the afternoon, but he never came back. Evening arrived. The young secretary had to go home and needed to close the office. She told us that her boss had been acting bizarre lately and that she was working with him only so she could get her own round-the-world tickets.

We checked into a hotel and returned to the office the next day. The door was locked, and no one answered our calls. Ever. The trip insurance made good on our claim, though, and we breathed a sigh of relief. Unfortunately, we didn't get the anticipated flight on Aeroflot

6

with a stopover in Moscow on our way from London to Nairobi. We had been looking forward to seeing the newly opened-up Russia. Instead, when the insurance took care of us (after multiple assertive phone calls from Dermot), we received an upgrade—we flew straight from London to Nairobi on British Airways. We were able to finish our air travel plans with no extra expense, as well as correct the dates on the last leg of the trip.

The stress of preparation took its toll. I started to break out in red, itchy blotches that raced over my body, disappeared, and then reappeared in another spot. The irritation kept me awake at night. I was exhausted from lack of sleep and worry. I consulted a doctor. I hoped to get a prescription for an antianxiety medication to calm my nerves, but the doctor repeatedly asked me whether I had eaten any new foods. He was certain the blotches were caused by a food allergy and not nerves. Finally, we narrowed the problem down to the new, inexpensive vitamins I had recently purchased for the trip or the chicken I had introduced into my diet after having been a vegetarian for five years. (I will explain later in the story why I started eating chicken again.) A few days after eliminating both the new vitamins and the chicken, I was back to normal. Dermot and I were both healthy and in top physical condition for the trip.

We had no personal cell phones in 1991, no cyber cafés or portable computers to send a quick e-mail home, and no ATMs outside the United States we could use. Plus, most places we traveled to didn't take credit cards. We plotted out our trip so we could check into an American Express office once a month. Our family knew our itinerary, and they wrote to us in care of different American Express offices. In the major cities where we touched base, we picked up our mail from home and purchased American Express Travelers Cheques, which we cashed at local banks as we traveled. Our parents and families waited for long stretches without news, and I'm sure they worried terribly about us. We tried to call home about once a month to connect with them.

CARLA FOUNTAIN

As our plane took off, the anxiety melted away. The previous month had been a nightmare of organization and endless lists. My stress dissipated as we cut ties with the earth. We carried with us everything we needed, and nothing more could be done to prepare. I sighed, relaxed, settled into my seat, and wrote in my journal.

> July 7, 1991
>
> I've regained my sense of pleasure and delight in life. During the past three weeks, I worried that I was losing my ability to see the beauty and joy around me. I was so stressed out preparing for the trip. Panic and anxiety overwhelmed me. The day would be gorgeous, but I'd feel terrible. Now a great weight has been lifted. I will go onward, explore, be alert, and learn!

PART 2

• Europe—History Comes Alive

July 8 to September 14, 1991

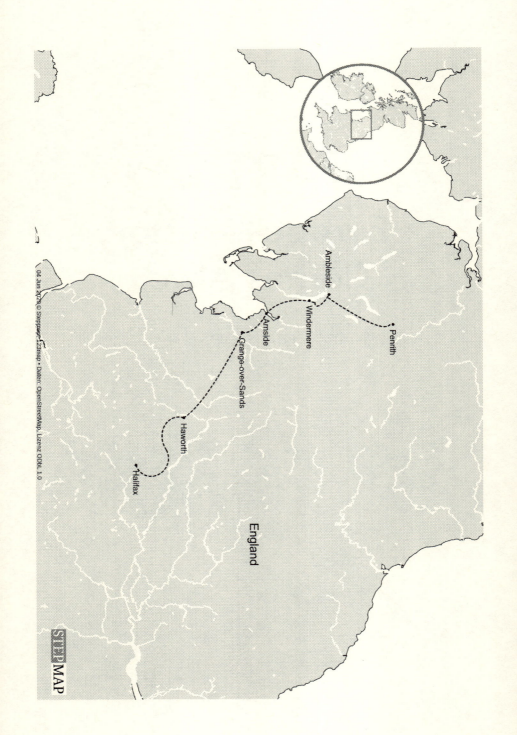

3

England—Literary Haunts

Dermot received a big smile and a hearty "Welcome home!" when he showed immigration officials his passport at Heathrow Airport. Although he had an American passport, his place of birth was Bridge of Allan, Scotland. When I followed after Dermot, the same immigration officer glared at me while he questioned me about my travel plans. He wanted to make sure I planned to leave the country after my trip there. We cleared immigration, unpacked our bikes from their containers, assembled them, and bicycled off. That was the only time we needed to break down our bicycles for a flight and reassemble them upon arrival. On every subsequent flight, the baggage attendants wheeled the bikes into the luggage compartment. They were our checked bag allowance. We carried our panniers, the saddlebags that attached to the front and rear racks of our bicycles, onto flights as carry-on luggage. They held all our other possessions.

This first leg of our journey was important to Dermot. He had grown up in Sierra Madre, California, but his mother had traveled back to her hometown in Scotland to give birth to him. He had toured Scotland by bicycle after high school and wanted to share the Highlands with me as well as explore areas he had never seen: the Outer Hebrides, Iona, and the Lake District National Park in England. Dermot's father had grown up in Yorkshire, and we wanted to see Dermot's grandmother, who resided there.

CARLA FOUNTAIN

We had reserved a room at a house in London for $166 a week. The room was on a quiet, residential street near Clapham South, where we explored and rested for a few days before heading out to the Lake District and continuing north to Yorkshire and Scotland. The stress of getting ready for this extensive trip and facing all the obstacles we needed to overcome before leaving had exhausted us. We crashed after a hearty breakfast of eggs and chips. It took days to get over jet lag, which, combined with a sudden onset of hay fever from all the unfamiliar pollen in the air, left us groggy for a week.

Once fully rested, we enjoyed exploring London. Dermot knew the area fairly well from previous visits. On the third day, we decided to get out of the city and bicycle to Kew Gardens. The traffic and fumes of the city were hard to take during our bicycle ride there. Kew Gardens was lush, green, and filled with flowers, but the pollen wreaked havoc on our systems. I had never suffered from hay fever before, and it hit me hard. For the return trip home, we decided to take the tube to avoid traffic.

As we rushed toward the train with our bicycles, we heard a shout. "Hello! Out with you! Hello! Just what do you think you're doing here?"

Dermot and I looked at the station guard who had yelled at us. Although we stopped to acknowledge him, he continued to blast us.

"Hello! Who allowed you in? And at rush hour! Get out and cycle! Get out and cycle!"

Pushed out of the station by the belligerent guard, we braved our way home using a compass. We avoided most major streets and saw a lovely part of residential London. We arrived at the flat tired, hungry, and covered in soot, with a resolution never to bike in London again, at least not on main streets. The cyclists we saw in London were road warriors. They wore filter masks against the car fumes and boldly darted and squeezed between cars and trucks like professionals. We had thought we were tough cyclists back home on the streets of Los Angeles, but the cyclists in London left us in awe.

We left the bikes at the flat the rest of our time in London and took the tube to Highgate Cemetery, my favorite cemetery in the world so far. The grounds are also a nature reserve. We strolled the winding paths, overgrown with plants and wildflowers, and admired the Gothic tombs covered in creeping ivy and vines. Highgate opened in 1839 and was popular in the Victorian era. Karl Marx is among the notable people buried there, and we came upon several people paying homage to him at his grave site.

We spent another afternoon at Tate, a collection of four separate art galleries. When Dermot told the museum staff that the painter Augustus John was his great uncle, they pulled out drawings and watercolors from the archives for him. The family resemblance in the self-portraits was striking.

Our first real day of cycling was July 18. We left London by train to avoid the worst of the city. We exited the train once we reached the countryside. I slipped into my toe harnesses and pedaled off. The toe harnesses enabled us to pedal more efficiently, covering more ground with less effort. The action of cycling involves not only pushing down on the pedal but also pulling up, which uses more of the various leg muscles. We covered thirty-five miles that first day. Exhilaration swept through me. Mist filled the sky, and rain fell softly at times. The clean, fresh air cleared our heads. We cycled along gently rolling hills and down narrow country lanes bordered with thick vegetation. At one point, dozens of bleating sheep blocked the road and milled about. Two highly trained sheepdogs responded to the shepherd's whistles and kept the flock in order while we all waited for a train to pass.

In Halifax, we visited Derm's paternal grandmother. He wanted to videotape her and record her oral history. She delighted in telling us stories about her past, the hardships of World War II, her work, and her fun times on vacation at Blackpool with friends in the summers. After our visit with her, we stayed the night with friends of the family. They treated us like royalty; they brought us tea in bed, made us nourishing meals, and took us out for fish and chips.

We biked through the melancholy moors in Yorkshire. At Haworth in West Yorkshire, we visited the Brontë sisters' home, now a museum, which is the site of *Jane Eyre* and *Wuthering Heights*.

Our itinerary led us north to the Lake District National Park, a mountainous region known for its lakes and forests. Hill Top was home to Beatrix Potter, author of *The Tale of Peter Rabbit* and many other well-known children's books. William Wordsworth, Samuel Taylor Coleridge, and other poets had also resided in the Lake District in the early 1800s. We set up our tent to face the lake near Ambleside and Windermere, and gazed out, drinking it all in. Imagine stepping inside a painting by Constable or Turner! The visit to the Lake District was Dermot's father's suggestion. It stands out for me as the most beautiful spot we visited in England. The Lake District is part of Britain's National Trust for environmental and heritage conservation. Since we could visit many impressive historical properties in the National Trust, we decided to purchase a membership to use throughout our trip. Traveling through England and Scotland transported us into the worlds of many of the authors we had grown up reading.

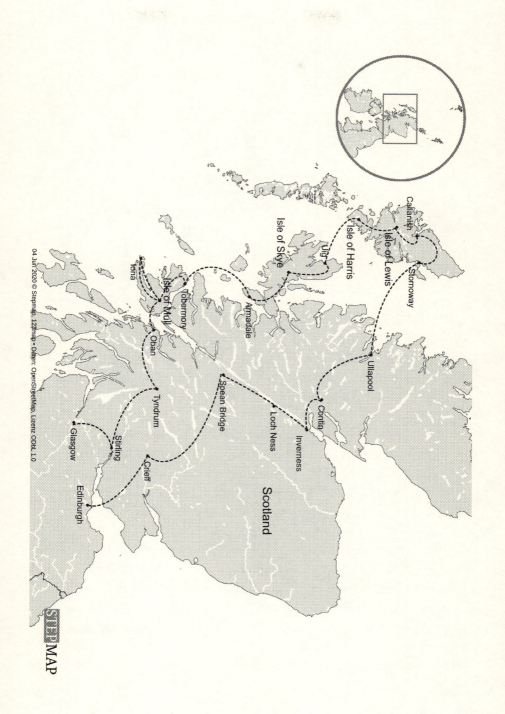

4

Scotland—A Homecoming

July in Scotland was chillier than expected, so we piled on all the warm clothes we had brought with us. A revolutionary, waterproof, and breathable material called Gore-Tex had come out on the market. Because of the rain, we layered jackets and pants made out of it for warmth. The big highlights of each day's cycling were tea breaks with scones or biscuits to warm and fuel our bodies. We averaged fifteen miles per the tea and bread.

The terrain was deceptive. Our bodies had the endurance to ride many miles in a day, but forty miles in Scotland often included numerous hills and strong headwinds. When we stopped to rest, the midges—tiny bugs that swarmed and delivered a nasty bite—attacked any exposed skin, leaving itchy welts that were by no means small.

We had trained as much as we could before the trip on the trails in the mountains above our house in Altadena, even going up to the peak of Mount Wilson and back—a climb of four thousand feet on dirt switchbacks. But nothing can completely prepare you for the journey of bicycling every day for miles. We developed new muscles and built stamina on this first leg of our travels across the Scottish Highlands. When we asked a Scot about the terrain up ahead, he answered with "fairly flat." We learned that this response translated to "hilly" in our language.

We journeyed on to visit Dermot's cousins in Buchlyvie. We stayed with them for a few days and enjoyed home-cooked meals and a family ambiance.

I rose early our first morning there, and stepped into the kitchen to get some tea. Dermot's cousin, Marge, was already up.

"Good morning, Carla!" Steam from the iron rose up around Marge's face as she beamed at me.

I glanced at the neat pile of freshly ironed clothes beside her. "Good Morning! But you didn't need to iron our clothes. I hate putting you out like that."

"Nonsense. I'm just drying them this way. I hung them in front of the Aga last night so the warmth would help. This gets the last bit of damp out. They'll be ready for when you set off after breakfast."

This was the first time someone had ironed my T-shirts. I usually just pulled them out of the dryer at home and folded them. Marge had offered to put our clothes in the wash the day before. She had hung them on the line in the garden before moving them inside when a soft rain started to fall.

I studied the large, cast iron Aga's many doors with interest. The cooker held pride of place in the kitchen and kept it cozy.

Marge followed my gaze. "Aye, that's the Aga. Have you not seen one before?"

"No, I've read about them, though."

CARLA FOUNTAIN

"They're wonderful. We use them a lot here in Scotland. Agas are very energy efficient. They keep the kitchen nice and warm, help dry the clothes, and we use them for cooking. They stay lit with a low intensity heat." Marge opened one of the oven's doors to show me the soft glow of the flame inside.

"It's lovely!"

"There now, that's the last one." Marge handed me the neat pile of clothes. "Is Dermot up yet? We'll be eating breakfast soon."

"Thank you!" I hugged the warm pile of clothes to my chest. The sweet clean scent was soothing. "I'll tell him and come back in a minute to help you."

We ladled out steaming oatmeal for our breakfast. "What are your plans for today?" Marge asked.

Dermot slurped his hot tea. "We're bicycling to Bridge of Allan so I can show Carla my birthplace. I was born in a castle, you know!"

Marge's husband, Angus, snorted. "You and everyone else born that year. Airthrey Castle was the maternity clinic back then."

I squeezed Dermot's arm. "It makes for a good story, though," I said.

Marge brought out a large plate of bacon and eggs. "I hope you also plan to visit Stirling Castle. Our great King Robert the Bruce took back the castle after his victory against the English at the Battle of Bannockburn in 1314. The castle is impressive. It sits high on a huge volcanic rock."

Dermot added an egg and toast to his plate but skipped the bacon. "Of course! That's such an important part of Scottish history. I read that a few historians in the 1300s and 1400s even speculated that the legendary King Arthur held court at the castle."

18

We enjoyed our stay with the cousins and their warm hospitality. Before we moved on, we reassessed our luggage. The extra panniers in the front made climbing the steep Scottish hills difficult. We culled our gear and sent home two boxes, which included the travel guitar, the retractable defense stick, and a few other items. With only two panniers each, cycling was easier. As for the defense stick, our wits and quick thinking would prove to be a much more effective defense method later on in our journey.

After we said our goodbyes, we rode through magnificent, green landscapes. Yet a deep heaviness filled me at times. Perhaps the skies, low and gray, and the cold, damp weather brought me down. Perplexed by my mood change, I wrote in my journal.

> July 23, 1991
> We've started our cycling trip to the Highlands. The sky has been overcast for the past two days. As we biked out of the Stirling area toward Mull this morning, it began to rain. The ride is fine in the rain because the dampness keeps me cool as I climb the steep Highland hills. But when I stop pedaling, I feel depressed.

Much later, I suspected that the cause lay deeper. This land had seen numerous battles and heavy loss of life in the bloody wars for independence. A mournfulness hung over the moors as heavy as the clouds in the skies.

Before boarding the ferry from Oban to the Isle of Mull, we searched for the cottage where Dermot's family friend Grace had grown up. The modest cottage sat on a garden site overlooking the bay. Grace was a dear lady I had met a few times in Pasadena. Dermot had known her all his life, and they had a close relationship. She spoke with a charming

Scottish accent and told me stories about her encounters with the wee people or fairies in her garden when she was little.

Grace possessed strong psychic abilities, so she rattled us when, during our last visit before the trip, she told Dermot in her heavy accent, "She's going to leave you, Dermot, and sooner than you think!" (I had left the room at that point.) Yes, as with any relationship, we experienced conflicts and problems. But the shared dream of realizing our around-the-world bicycle trip kept us together.

We cycled across the Isle of Mull to board the ferry for Iona. The island enchanted us as soon as we docked, and my feeling of melancholy lifted. The mist descended, and turquoise water lapped the pink rocks in the harbor. We wandered down narrow roads with no traffic. Sheep grazed in vibrant fields bordering the lanes.

Cozily tucked into a bed-and-breakfast, we rested after a meal of grilled, freshly caught wild salmon and a hot Gaelic coffee, which—if you haven't tasted one—is generously laced with whiskey. I soaked in a soothing, steamy bath and heard the sheep bleating outside in the fields. A soft, warm bed welcomed us instead of the hard, cold ground. The next day we cycled around the island and toured the medieval Iona Abbey, founded in 565 when the monk Columba came across the sea from Ireland to spread Christianity to Scotland. Monks had created the Book of Kells there, and many kings are entombed in the abbey, even King Arthur, according to legend.

Rain pelted us during the entire sixty miles to Tobermory. Soaked through, I fumed in silence as we slogged on. *What's the point of this? I could be in France now where the weather is warm. I could be sitting at a café in the sun. Dermot has such a do-or-die attitude. He's on some kind of quest. I understand that he wants to connect with his heritage, but I thought he was satisfied with seeing his grandmother and his cousins. He said he needs to "feel the land"! And the midge bites! And the sogginess!*

Luckily, the only hostel in town had two last-minute cancellations, so we were able to stay there and didn't have to camp. They let us in as the storm hit its peak. The dreary hostel lacked shower facilities and smelled of ripe hiking boots and damp, musty clothes and bodies. I started getting the blues again with all the damp and the gray.

I scowled when I picked up my shoes and socks from the floor in the morning. "They're still wet! I'm so tired of the rain. Why don't we just stay somewhere for a day until the weather changes?"

Dermot glared at me. "This is Scotland! It rains. Deal with it."

His harsh tone set me on edge and escalated my bad mood. "I don't know why we have to force ourselves to slog through this downpour." I stuffed the rest of my damp clothes into my panniers and stomped out of the room to make coffee.

Dermot found me in the kitchen and put his arm around my shoulder. "I'm sorry, babe. I don't like the rain either. We just have to get through this weather front. I know you'll love the Isle of Skye. I really want to share Scotland with you."

I sniffed back tears. "Okay, and I appreciate it. I'm just so tired and cold all the time here."

When the sun came out, my spirits soared again. I was amazed at how much the weather affected my mood. The Isle of Skye shone a brilliant emerald in the sun as we pulled into the harbor on a ferry. An hour into our ride, we ran into Duncan, an acquaintance from the boat who also bicycled. He was a Scot who dearly loved the countryside.

Duncan paused his photography to wave us over by the side of the road. He pointed to the cottage across from us. "Look!" he said. "This

CARLA FOUNTAIN

is a black house, a traditional Hebrides one-story dwelling made with stone walls and a thatched roof. You don't find many of these anymore."

"Why is it called a 'black house'?" I asked.

"The black houses didn't have chimneys, so smoke from the hearth blackened the ceiling and walls with soot."

Dermot took a swig of water. "I remember seeing many more thatched stone cottages on my trip through Scotland in the 1970s. People have rebuilt to have modern conveniences."

"Yes, they have. I've biked most of Scotland. This weekend I'm exploring Skye again. Since you have the time, I suggest you keep going north and take the ferry at Uig to the Isles of Lewis and Harris. You must see the Callanish Standing Stones."

I offered Duncan a piece of chocolate. "Thank you, Duncan! I look forward to that."

We biked up the coast to Uig, another sixty-mile day we hadn't planned on, but the ride glided by as we took in the beauty of the Cuillin Mountains. The long, undulating hills and the sunshine made for a more pleasant day. We camped out in Uig so we could take the ferry in the morning.

Immediately off the boat, we climbed a steep two thousand feet. Although we were exceptionally tired, we managed to make it to the Callanish Standing Stones on the Isle of Lewis. I gazed in awe at the solid blocks of stone that had stood for thousands of years. As night began to fall, I pressed my palm to the stone's rough surface, which still held warmth from the sun. I thought about the history. *What rituals took place here? What were the people like who participated?* I closed my eyes and listened to the stones in silence.

We camped nearby in a field and tucked behind a hill out of sight so we could see the stones under the moonlight and photograph them at dawn. Sheep grazed nearby, frisking and frolicking about while they investigated us. No one was around for miles except for a lonely cottage a short distance from the site.

From Stornoway on the Isle of Lewis, we took a ferry to Ullapool on the main island. Traffic was sparse on the roads. The summer daylight extended past ten o'clock in the evening. With our stronger, more conditioned muscles, we biked easily and hit a good rhythm. I loved the green all around us, which felt exotic and fresh after years of living in dry, brown Southern California. We glided by grand estates, castles, and fields of cattle.

Even though we followed the main road down from Inverness, there was minimal traffic. About five miles after Inverness, an inexplicable mournfulness fell over me in spite of the stunning nature and the occasional stately castle. I thought I suffered alone. Decades later, Dermot shared the melancholy that had swept over him during our ride through Scotland. I've since learned that we traveled right beside the area of the famous Battle of Culloden. Our spirits must have picked up on the sadness that permeated the land from so many souls who had lost their lives there. Highlanders had rebelled against the English for decades in the Jacobite risings during the early eighteenth century. On April 16, 1746, Scottish clans fought in support of Prince Charles Edward Stuart so he could regain the throne. The battle was fierce, bloody, and short. The Highland clansmen lost almost two thousand men in the hour-long battle against the better-equipped English, who lost only fifty men. That was the Highlanders' last battle.

We stopped at Loch Ness but didn't see Nessie, the famous Loch Ness Monster—a creature locals consider to be more than a myth. We looked out over the still loch waters and talked with a man working by the side of the road.

CARLA FOUNTAIN

"Hello! Have you come to see Nessie then? She hasn't shown herself today," the friendly man said.

"Have you ever seen Nessie?" I asked.

He took off his cap and scratched his head. "Aye, many times I've caught a glimpse of her. You should have been here yesterday. My neighbor Isla looked out the window as she was cleaning," he said as he pointed to the house by the loch. "She said she saw a hump of Nessie's back come right up out of the water."

Loch Ness, with a depth that surpasses the oceans surrounding the United Kingdom, was connected to the ocean at one time. Over the years, scientific investigations using sonar in the dark mysterious loch have yielded large animate objects. Not a single ripple disturbed the surface for us, though.

We headed south along the loch. A few miles before the village of Spean Bridge, my bicycle wobbled. *Flap, flap, flap.* The unmistakable sound and feel of a tire puncture brought me to a sudden stop.

"Wait! I've got a flat tire!" I called out to Dermot, who was several yards ahead of me.

He coasted back and scowled. "Another one! We bought these special tires that were supposed to be puncture resistant." He flopped onto a rock to rest while I struggled with the tire repair.

My hands fumbled with the tire levers as I removed the tire from the rim.

"You're not doing it right. You need to use the—"

"I *know* how to change a flat tire!" I cut him off and fumbled some more.

Dermot got up and reached for the tire. "Let me do it."

"No! I know how to this!" I jerked the tire back, knocking over the rest of my tools. Tears spilled from my eyes, and I burst into sobs.

Dermot had taught me how to change a flat tire. *Why would we disagree about that?* The argument reflected deeper, unresolved issues. We had experienced problems in our relationship before the trip. But we had smoothed them over to go on this bicycle journey. We had never addressed the real root of the problems and suppressed the negative feelings. All those feelings came bubbling up to the surface and erupted over a flat tire. No one but the cows witnessed our squabble. Quarrels like this were exhausting and left me drained. We resolved our disagreement after a while, changed the tire together, and continued on. This trip meant too much for us to abandon it now.

After camping for many nights in dampness so cold that it penetrated our bones, we found comfort in Edinburgh, where we treated ourselves to a hotel. A soft duvet with a crisp, cotton sheet covered the bed. We slept in luxury with a fluffy pillow under our heads. For two days, we explored the city and devoured as much good food as we could. Bicycling burned up a tremendous number of calories, so we were always enthusiastic about the next meal. On our last evening, Dermot wanted to see the Royal Edinburgh Military Tattoo—a bagpipe, drum, and dance extravaganza with fireworks on the esplanade of the Edinburgh Castle. Thousands of us gathered to watch the pageantry and playing as the band members marched out in traditional kilts in all their finery. I would have preferred to attend a cozy *ceilidh*, an intimate gathering of Scottish folk music, traditional dancing, and storytelling. But compromise is a good part of any relationship, so we attended the Tattoo that night.

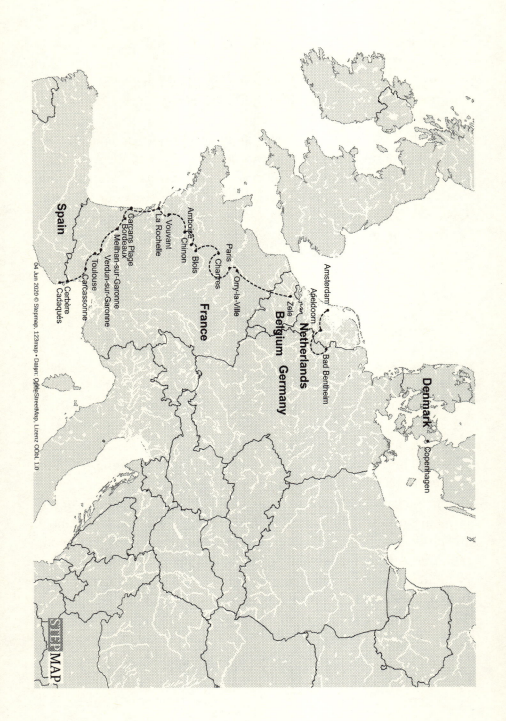

5

France, Spain, and the North— Castles, Food, and Friends

We took a flight to Paris from Edinburgh. I hadn't been there since 1979 when I studied in France for a year. I wanted to show Derm the city, but I was disoriented. On our first night in the city, I sprawled out on the bed with my journal and a pen in my hand.

> August 9, 1991
>
> I am so hungry to see all my old haunts that I want to do everything at once. But I don't recognize much of Paris anymore. I keep getting lost, and the weather is sweltering. Dermot isn't enjoying this as much as I had hoped he would. I am overcome with fatigue and want to weep. What did I expect? That old friends would pop out of the woodwork? That they would be sitting at the same cafés? I've been away for thirteen years. "You can't go home again" echoes in my head.

But I found my friend Brigitte the next day, and she was free. She invited us to stay with her at her mother's house for two nights. On one of the nights, we all met the author Bernard Magnouloux and his wife, Françoise, for dinner in their village outside Paris.

27

CARLA FOUNTAIN

Dermot helped himself to another piece of baguette. "We want to buy a copy of your book and have you sign it. It will be fun to read again as we travel."

Françoise ladled more stew on our plates. "Please eat up! I know what a big appetite bicycling gives. You burn more calories than you are able to take in. How long do you plan to be gone on your trip?"

"Mmm, Françoise, this stew is delicious." I used a piece of bread to soak up the sauce. "We planned for one year with our round-the-world tickets. It's not the five-year journey that Bernard took." I paused for a bite. "But who knows? Maybe our plans will change." I caught Dermot's eye and smiled.

"Make sure to come back and see us when you return to France," Bernard said. "Then we'll tell you about our own adventures. We're planning to bicycle the Arctic Circle in Finland in January."

To leave Paris, we took the metro and the Réseau Express Régional (the commuter rail service that links Paris to the suburbs) out of town as far as we could to avoid the traffic. We started cycling at Saint-Martin d'Étampes past brown fields of mown hay, waving barley, tall oats, and yellow sunflowers. In addition to the secondary roads, France has a wonderful system of even smaller roads only the local villagers use. These are the roads we chose for our trip in France. They are the thinnest lines on a detailed map and are called "departmental roads." We bicycled past a village every three to ten miles. Our plans were fluid, and we were open to a variety of routes depending on what caught our interest, the people we met, the weather, and the road conditions. Our only constraint was the time frame for the flights that connected each leg of our trip every month or two. We gave ourselves two months in Europe to play with before we returned to London to catch our flight to Nairobi.

Our first destination was the cathedral in Chartres. We spent an afternoon in and around the glorious medieval cathedral, marveling at the 167 stained-glass windows in its Gothic interior. The Chartres

Cathedral, home to a Black Madonna (Notre Dame de Pilar), is one of several pilgrimage sites throughout Europe with Black Madonna figures. We walked around the labyrinth on the floor of the cathedral, following the footsteps of pilgrims who had walked it for hundreds of years. This was a good start on our journey through France.

We continued on toward the Loire. Bicycling the Loire Valley was a dream. The land was fairly flat with dense forests on either side of the road. Every so often, a stately château broke up the ride and begged us to visit. We easily bicycled over one hundred miles a day, still managed to tour a château or two, and ate well. With the long summer days, we packed two days of cycling into one. Our legs and stamina were strong after Scotland. In France the days were warmer, and the sun shone during our entire month there. Campgrounds were plentiful with amenities, such as hot showers, clean toilets, swimming pools, and even little stores. We met other campers from all over Europe and enjoyed talking with them about travel and life.

The châteaux of Blois, Amboise, and Chinon impressed us, but my favorite château was Chambord, which Leonardo da Vinci had helped design. I had visited Chambord many years ago, but bicycling up to the château was an entirely different sensation. I hadn't realized that the grounds were so enormous and surrounded by woods full of deer, wild boar, and other animals. Before our visit inside, we took out our cameras and fanny packs with our money and passports, and locked the fully loaded bikes together. We did this at every stop without a problem.

After the Loire, we headed to the Atlantic coast and cycled to La Rochelle. We were invited to lunch by family friends, Lewis and Joëlle, at their house in Rochefort, where they had retired after living in California. Family and friends always took such good care of us on the trip when we stopped to see them. Joëlle pulled out maps and talked to us about the different directions we could take. We could go south to Bordeaux and then east into the Dordogne region or southeast through Toulouse and down to Spain. We ended up traveling south through the sandy pine forest of Les Landes along the Atlantic coast all the way to

Lacanau. At times we rode along the clean, lengthy beaches with clear water lapping the sand. But our mood fell when we came across World War II bunkers, and we reflected on the tragic past of the war. We camped at Soulac-sur-Mer and swam in the crisp Atlantic Ocean. This area of Les Landes made for quiet, peaceful, and effortless riding. We rode on for another day through the pine forest and stayed at Carcans Plage for the night. With a candle lantern hanging above me, I put my thoughts on paper.

August 24, 1991

> I feel more in the present now. My melancholy is gone. The scent of the pine forest, the warmth of the sun, and the bike paths free of traffic make my spirit soar. I'm excited to be discovering parts of France I didn't know before. If I come back and live in France, I'll visit this area again to meditate in the pine forest and enjoy the delightful beaches.

We had thought we would follow the road all the way to Spain on the Atlantic side, but we decided to cut inland across France and make our way to the Mediterranean.

On our way to Bordeaux, we found a bike path on a converted train line. A day without traffic was soothing. We hummed along the peaceful bike path through the forest for forty-five miles in the hot and humid weather. Few other people traveled on the path, so we felt far, far away from the world. After picnicking in the tall grass under the shade of swaying pine trees, we stretched out and dozed, happily lulled to sleep by the drone of cicadas.

In the city of Bordeaux, we had no choice but to stay at a hotel. Workers from Spain filled the restaurant next door. Because we both spoke Spanish, Dermot and I could talk and relate to people instead of me having to be an interpreter. Dermot, the more gregarious of the two of us, started to feel frustrated in France because he didn't speak the language.

BICYCLE ODYSSEY

From Bordeaux, we followed the Garonne River to Toulouse. In the middle of the bustling city of Toulouse, we found the Canal du Midi bike path and escaped the traffic. The Canal du Midi was an engineering feat that linked the Atlantic Ocean to the Mediterranean Sea in the seventeenth century and was one of the greatest constructions of that time. Tall French plane trees, native to eastern Europe, lined the banks and created cool shade. We welcomed the peaceful respite of cycling for two days along the banks of the canal. Our lungs appreciated the break from cars and exhaust. As we followed the Garonne River and the canal, we stayed in quiet campgrounds surrounded by nature near Verdun-sur-Garonne, Meilhan-sur-Garonne, and Molleville. We had planned to follow the canal all the way to the Mediterranean, but we diverted to see the walled city of Carcassonne instead.

The approach to the medieval citadel of Carcassonne took our breath away. The settlement, located on a strategic hill, had once controlled the crossroads from the Atlantic to the Mediterranean. The Celts built a fort on the site in 500 BC. The Romans conquered Gaul in 100 BC and built a stronger fort. (A portion of that structure remains as part of the castle now.) The Visigoths made the fort stronger in AD 453. The Counts of Toulouse fortified it even more in AD 1067. And in 1209 the French kings built the outside wall around the fort to defend the border with Spain. After surviving many sieges throughout history, Carcassonne stands as the largest walled city in Europe.

We stayed in a hostel inside the citadel and enjoyed meeting other people and talking to them about their adventures. Along the streets of the citadel, theater groups reenacted medieval life with dances, music, and pageantry. At night, the bulk of the tourists left. We walked the quiet, dark streets as if in a dream, getting a feel for what life must have been like over the ages in Carcassonne.

We decided to go south into Spain and ended up traveling down the Mediterranean coast all the way to Cadaqués. The road followed long, dramatic climbs and descents from the Pyrenees Mountains. Dermot was thrilled to be able to speak Spanish in the little towns where we

CARLA FOUNTAIN

camped. For our last two nights, we stayed in Cadaqués, the town where Salvador Dalí had lived and worked from 1930 to 1982. The entire town paid homage to Dalí, and we enjoyed our exploration of this Spanish treasure. We camped on the cliffs above the Mediterranean, not far from Dalí's house with its egg motifs. We swam and floated in the sea below the cliffs. For our final night in Cadaqués, we treated ourselves to a nice restaurant dinner with paella and sangria.

Dermot poured us a second helping of sangria from the pitcher we had ordered. "This is delicious!"

"Yes, it is!" I agreed. "Wait until you taste the paella. You'll love it."

I was on my third glass when the room started tilting. I had tasted sangria when I lived in Spain as a teenager, but I didn't realize they always gave us a very light concoction that was more carbonated water and juice than wine. This grown-up sangria contained not only wine but also high-octane liqueur. My five years as a non-alcohol-drinking vegetarian had left me ill equipped for that strong combination.

"The walls are moving … Oh, no … this sangria was too strong for me! I need to leave. I don't think I can even eat the paella. See if you can get it to go." I cradled my head in my hands and focused on breathing to combat the sudden waves of nausea.

Dermot helped me back to our tent, and I slept with a bucket beside me that night. The next morning, we biked to Llançà to catch the train. I dug out medicine for my headache and climbed the steep hill out of Cadaqués on wobbly legs. Those fourteen miles were some of the most miserable for me on the first portion of our trip.

In Llançà, we caught the train to the Spanish border city of Portbou and biked to Cerbère to catch the train on the French side. At that time, France and Spain operated different rail gauges. We exited the train on one side of the border, walked several yards, and boarded another train to continue on in the other country. Travelers packed the overnight train to Paris, and we couldn't find any seats in the second-class compartment. Dermot decided to upgrade our tickets to first class so we could rest. We were grateful for the cool air-conditioning and the space to stretch out and sleep.

We took the train back to Paris so we could bicycle north from there through Belgium, Holland, and Germany. Our final destination was Denmark. This time in the City of Lights, I found my bearings and showed Derm my favorite haunts for three days. I had been an exchange student in the summer of 1973 and stayed with a French family outside of Lyon. The family now lived in Paris, but they were all away on vacation except for François. François, my French brother, had been a small boy in 1973. In 1991, he was all grown up and producing television shows. We met him at his production office for a coffee. He worked with a fun, creative group of people at the newly formed Canal+.

Another day, we wandered into my favorite bookstore, Shakespeare and Company, as they hosted their traditional Sunday tea in the upstairs library. I used to visit the bookshop often when I lived in Paris. An exciting, eclectic mix of people gathered upstairs. The highlight was meeting the owner, George Whitman, who had opened the bookshop in 1951. We didn't have tea since they had run out of cups. But we had a wonderful time talking with people. Ted Jones, a well-known poet I had heard speak in the '70s, gave a reading at the end of the tea.

We met Isabelle, who filled us in on the history of the bookstore. "I love this place. I'm staying in Paris for six months while I write. My first week in the city, George let me stay in a room above the shop while I sorted things out. It's very inspiring to be here, knowing that so many creative spirits worked and lived between these walls for a spell."

"Like who?" Dermot asked.

CARLA FOUNTAIN

"James Baldwin, Anaïs Nin, and Henry Miller for starters!" Isabelle said.

I picked up a copy of Hemmingway's *A Moveable Feast*. "I have a classmate who dropped out of our graduate program to write her novel. She stayed here for a while also. George is really helpful to aspiring writers. He only asked that she read a book every day, help out in the shop, and write a one-page autobiography."

We paid for our books and left. Strolling arm and arm, we walked for hours through the streets, enjoying the city's romantic ambiance.

On our last evening in Paris, I wrote long into the night by the glow of my flashlight.

> September 2, 1991
>
> These past two days have been marvelous. The first day, we strolled down the Rue Moufftard in the misty rain and bought food at the market. I visited old haunts. A few places have changed their names: the cinema where a friend worked when I lived here and the café where I used to meet friends for afternoon espressos and long conversations. The café was closed today. Do my old friends from university still hang out there? What are their lives like now?
>
> I am glad we came back to Paris before we left France. I'm relieved that I found my bearings here. I reconnected with a few more people, met new ones, and made fresh memories. One day, I would like to return and live here again.

When we left Paris, we took public transport to Orry-la-Ville in the Oise, which was as far as we could go by the Réseau Express Régional so we could avoid traffic. From there we biked north through France and Belgium. To compensate for all the money we had spent in Paris, we camped in forests along the road. One evening in Belgium, a farmer gave us permission to camp in his field but warned us about the pigs.

Later that night we slumbered, lost deep in our dreams.

"Squeal, snort, squeal!" Loud animal noises and pounding feet jolted us awake.

"What's that?" I asked.

"The pigs! He warned us about pigs!"

"It's a herd of wild pigs! They're running around the tent!" I trembled. "What if they rip through the canvas?"

Thank goodness we didn't have a cache of food to tempt them. The pigs ran a few laps around our tent and took off, their grunts fading into the distance. Wild camping also meant no running water and no showers for a few nights. But the bicycling was splendid. Happiness and a sense of adventure for the ride filled me.

Every now and then, we came upon fields of graves from the battles in World War I and World War II. Dermot was drawn to these cemeteries. He became quiet and pensive as he walked through the lines of white headstones. He pondered what his life would have been like had he been born in another time. He might have fought in one of those wars and perhaps died on the battlefield as well. Decades later, we learned that Dermot had family members who lay at rest in the graves of Belgium. A generation of cousins before him had gone to war here and never returned to Scotland.

We cycled over two hundred miles from Paris to Zele (on the border of Belgium and Holland). To save time, we took a train the rest of the

CARLA FOUNTAIN

way into Amsterdam. We stepped off the train, uncertain where to go next for a place to stay.

Noticing our hesitation, a young man honed in on us. "Are you looking for a place to stay? I have rooms to rent at my apartment. I can take you there. It's not far from the city. Everything in Amsterdam is expensive. This will save you money."

We rode thirty minutes on another train. "How much farther is your apartment?" I asked.

"Don't worry! We're almost there."

The enterprising man had crammed each of his extra bedrooms with two sets of bunk beds. The apartment was clean, and he gave us breakfast every day. We were happy even though the lodging was a distance from the city center. We used it as our base to explore Amsterdam for several days.

Holland was a cyclist's dream country with a well-developed system of *fietspaden* (cycling paths). Dermot had cycled through this area before and wanted me to experience bicycling in Holland. I enjoyed people watching. Whole families on a single bike went to the market for produce and flowers. The father pedaled, the mother sat on the rear bike rack, and a child rode in the front basket. An elegant lady glided by in hose and pumps. Her purple, crushed velvet coat flowed out behind her. A bouquet of flowers graced the basket on her handlebars. A man rode by with his grandmother perched on the back rack.

I loved Amsterdam. We wandered for hours, taking in the beauty of the houses along the canals and stopping in cozy coffee shops for steaming cups of hot chocolate.

Our visit to Anne Frank's house was an intensely emotional experience that left me speechless. Her diary, which I had read several times, hit me even harder as I walked through the house where she lived

BICYCLE ODYSSEY

and hid during World War II. Dermot and I sat outside on a bench in silence afterward and digested the tour.

Dermot stared off into the canal and cleared his throat. "I'm hoping on this trip that we'll connect with people who have positive answers to the questions we want to ask. I want to meet individuals who see the beauty in all humans ... who see that we are all more equal than unequal."

I nodded and wiped my eyes. "People spend their time trying to understand the differences in races and cultures. Our commonalities are much greater."

He squeezed my hand. "I'm afraid that until we understand that, more atrocities such as the one that Anne Frank suffered will continue to happen."

Another poignant moment occurred on our canal tour. We glided along peacefully, looking at the attractive waterfront houses and boats. Our tour guide pointed out the merchants' houses with gable stones that depicted the various trade goods they sold. We passed the usual merchants: butchers, bakers, tailors, and so forth. But my heart fell when I saw the bronze sculpture of an African on the house of a wealthy slave trader. Much of the wealth still visible in those gorgeous seventeenth- and eighteenth-century homes came from money made in the slave trade by the Dutch West India Company.

We cycled out into the countryside toward Apeldoorn, a town lodged in Dermot's memory from a previous bicycle trip. The city was modern, but the countryside had old-fashioned traditions. When we stopped for a snack, an elderly woman in a long, traditional dress and a lace head covering made a phone call in a telephone booth next to us. She was straight out of the eighteenth century.

From Apeldoorn, we bicycled across the countryside toward Germany. Before we arrived at the border, we stopped in a bike shop to purchase a bell. We stayed in the shop for an enjoyable two hours while the owner fixed our lights and made other adjustments. He was a master bicycle mechanic. The Dutch cater to bicyclists' needs since their society utilizes bicycles so much. The shop was a treat, and we bought a few other supplies.

We crossed the German border and rode to Bad Bentheim to take a train to Denmark. Because of our afternoon spent at the bicycle shop, night fell before we reached our destination. But our newly repaired headlights helped us travel through the forest in the pitch darkness. "Hoo, hoo, hoo." Owls called out to us from the dense growth by the side of the road. No vehicles drove past us. After an hour, we thought we were lost and contemplated setting up camp in the woods. *Whoosh.* A lone car passed us. The headlights illuminated a sign for Bad Bentheim. The town was three miles away, so we continued.

We waited at the deserted station until the wee hours of the morning for our train. While we bode our time, we dozed on benches by our bikes. A loud, stern voice jolted us awake. "Was machen Sie hier?" (What are you doing here?) a guard asked. My sleepy brain dredged up the German long ago buried there, and I was able to explain that we were waiting for the early-morning train to Denmark. The two guards looked at our papers and decided we were okay. But the guards thoroughly grilled the Romanian gentlemen who also waited there.

Once we arrived in Denmark, my Danish exchange sister, Linda, and her family spoiled us. Linda and I had developed a strong relationship when she joined my family as my American Field Service exchange sister in California during high school. I missed seeing her, and we hadn't been in touch as much after she started her own family. We laughed and caught up, talking long into the night. Reconnecting with Linda filled me with joy.

My exchange brother, Steen, a professional photographer, took exquisite black-and-white photos of us, which captured the feeling of adventure and wonder that had filled us at the start of the trip. Steen had become a highly-sought-after photographer, traveling all over the world. We were quite honored to pose for his lens and treasured his photos as documentation of our trip.

Linda's husband, Per, had started his practice as a physician. "Carla, did you know that I did part of my medical training in India?" he asked.

"Really? I didn't know that," I said.

"Well, I'm concerned that you didn't receive a hepatitis shot," Per said. "It's my medical opinion that you need this before you go to India. I can give you both your second shot for cholera also."

"Thank you so much, Per. I'm not looking forward to more needles, but I'd rather be protected." I grimaced and rubbed my arm in anticipation of the pain.

Per laughed. "That's not the injection site."

Dermot groaned. "Oh, no!"

"The hepatitis vaccine requires two doses. If we start tomorrow, I'll have time to give you the second one before you leave to catch your flight."

As promised, we received our vaccinations. For the final one, we lowered our pants discreetly in the airport parking lot in Copenhagen. My eyes welled up as we said goodbye, but Linda and Per said they would visit us in Los Angeles when we returned from our odyssey.

CARLA FOUNTAIN

We spent a few days in London to regroup and pick up our malaria pills, which we needed to take diligently for the next few months of travel in Africa, India, and Southeast Asia. We received the old-fashioned chloroquine tablets from the clinic we visited in London. We didn't know it at the time, but we were fortunate not to have bought our pills in California before we left. The United States had introduced a new, once-a-week pill developed for Gulf War soldiers. Many people ended up with severe side effects from the new drug: anxiety, dizziness, mouth sores, and psychiatric reactions. Because of the debilitating side effects, they stopped taking the prophylactic and left themselves vulnerable to malaria.

Malaria frightened us—and for good reason. Dermot had contracted malaria on a bicycle trip in Belize years before we met and relapsed a few months after we started dating. In 1984, the ailment wasn't common in Los Angeles, so several weeks passed without a proper diagnosis as he grew weaker, thinner, and more ill. His fever climbed to 104 degrees while he shook, shivered, convulsed, and soaked through multiple sheets and blankets. His fever lowered for a short time, but the cycle started all over again. His doctor first misdiagnosed it as the flu, but Dermot's illness worsened. We were all frightened. I took him to Harbor-UCLA Medical Center, where they kept him overnight. Thankfully, he was correctly diagnosed. It turned out that the illness he had thought was dengue fever many years prior in Belize had really been malaria. Malaria lies dormant in the liver, and a person can have a relapse later if the immune system weakens. No treatment at that time could completely eradicate malaria from the body. Dermot needed to take care and not become run down, leaving himself vulnerable to a recurrence.

PART 3

• Africa—No One Sacrificed a Goat in Our Honor

September 14 to November 15, 1991

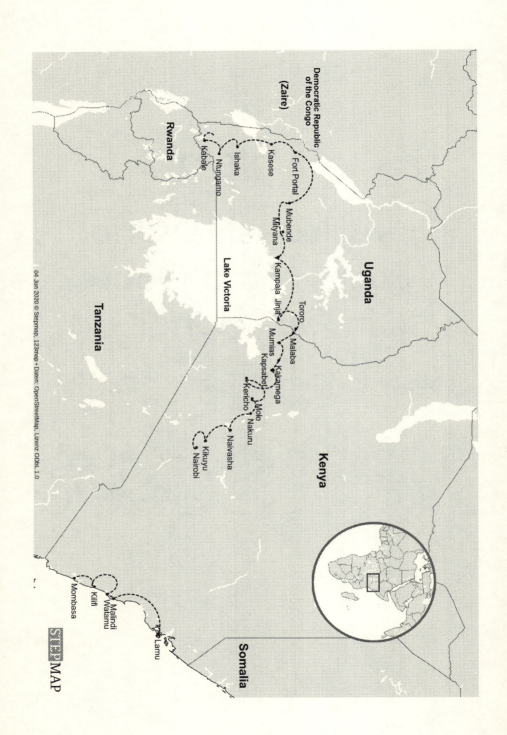

6

Kenya—Following the Pan-African Highway

Before our trip, I met with a documentary filmmaker who had been a Peace Corps volunteer in Kenya for two years. She was helpful and even gave me several names and phone numbers of her friends at the University of Nairobi. But when I told her I was a vegetarian, she frowned and said I should be aware that people in Kenya weren't going to understand that. Deep in the countryside where we would be bicycling, villagers might invite us in for a meal and kill, and cook a goat in our honor. It would be rude to refuse a meal. I discussed this with Dermot, and we decided to prepare our systems so we could graciously accept any meal our hosts offered. When a person is a vegetarian, as I was for a long time, the body stops producing the enzymes it needs to digest meat. Dermot and I slowly reintroduced chicken and fish into our diets a few months before we left. I also added small amounts of dairy. We wanted to be ready for any grilled goat served to us.

We landed at Jomo Kenyatta International Airport in Nairobi in the morning and rolled our bikes out to pump up the tires. We fortified

CARLA FOUNTAIN

ourselves with a sweet roll and tea with milk at the airport, clipped on our panniers, and biked ten miles into the city. Traffic was light on the two-lane road in the early-morning hours. We cycled past zebras and giraffes grazing in the plains. The view of those wild animals in their natural habitat felt like the authentic beginning of our adventure.

We had both lived in Europe before and had friends and family there. The continent was cozy and familiar. The European portion of our trip was a visit to reconnect with people and share familiar lands with each other. Dermot showed me his English and Scottish heritage and what he had experienced on previous trips in England, Scotland, and Holland. I connected him with my years of living in France and Spain and my extended family in Denmark. But from now on, we would face the new and unknown together at the same time.

We picked up a used copy of *Africa on a Shoestring* in a bookshop in London, and we found a small and useful pamphlet, *Bicycling in Africa: The Places in Between*. The author, David Mozer, was a former Peace Corps volunteer. *Bicycling in Africa* explained bucket baths, basic supplies we would need, and customs we should know about.

We found our way to a hotel after a search through the budget traveler's section in our guidebook. Most people came to Kenya for organized safari trips to the game parks. But we didn't want to do what most people did. We planned to recover from jet lag, try to contact the local Kenyans our filmmaker acquaintance knew, and bicycle west along the Pan-African Highway.

We showered and rested in the clean, quiet room and woke at three o'clock to eat and see the city. Every local we met that day stressed that we must never go out after dark in Nairobi because we would surely be robbed. That news made us nervous. The hotel manager recommended a nearby restaurant, where we devoured a tasty Swahili meal of vegetable curry with rice along with passion fruit juice. Feeling fortified, we walked the streets and found Nairobi to be smaller and more manageable than we had anticipated. We relaxed and enjoyed our walk. On our way home, we took a shortcut down an alley. We started to attract attention from a few men lurking in the shadows but found our way back on the right street and arrived safely at the hotel.

Dermot and I explored the city the next day. Our first stop was the mosque. We wanted to learn more about the building and Islam, but the guard politely told us non-Muslims were not allowed there and asked us to leave. So we visited the Nairobi National Museum to learn more about Kenyan culture and history. The Kenyans we interacted with were low-key without any hard sell or aggression. The city possessed a gentle vibe, and we wandered around with ease.

At the local cinema that night, we saw *Purgatory*, an engaging story about two female Peace Corps volunteers who were framed, wrongly accused, and locked up in an oppressive women's prison in an undisclosed African country. The film's description said, "Arrested 7,000 miles from home! Sentenced for a crime she didn't commit!" We munched on popcorn and drank fresh pineapple juice from the concession stand as we watched this cautionary tale at the beginning of our two months on the continent. Darkness met us when we left the cinema, so we hurried to the hotel. The back of our necks prickled with uneasiness as we navigated the unlit streets, but we didn't encounter any trouble. I breathed a sigh of relief when we reached the restaurant by our hotel. After that, we decided not to go out again at night.

I wore my hair in braids at that time for the ease it offered while traveling and bicycling. I could forget about my hairstyle for two to three months—just wash and go. No combing, styling, or visits to a beauty shop were required. I also liked the look. Nairobi was a perfect place to get my hair braided. In the United States, I would have spent a day by myself to undo the braids so I could go to a hair salon and spend another entire day to have the stylist braid my hair again. The process took only three hours in Nairobi. I was thrilled! At the hair salon near our hotel, three women worked together and quickly undid my braids using single-edged razors to cut the excess extensions. They unpicked the braids with a touch so light I thought fairies were working on me.

CARLA FOUNTAIN

Growing up in the States in the '60s, I was used to hairdressers complaining about my "bad" hair, meaning it was too curly or nappy and too hard to comb. They usually brought me to tears as they yanked and pulled and then expressed surprise, commenting that I was "tender headed." Having my hair done had never been a pleasant experience for me. But in Nairobi, I was in heaven. After unbraiding my hair, Miriam combed it out with a soft touch. She washed and dried all my curls. When she started braiding, her helpers, Mercy and Grace, came to finish the job. I was purring—their gentle touch was so pleasant.

Miriam spoke in a musical voice as soft as her hands, but her words came with a warning. "Since you have just arrived in Nairobi, you should know there are certain areas where you need to be careful."

I relaxed under her gentle touch. "We've had good experiences here so far," I said. I arched an eyebrow in question.

"This road is fine," Mercy said. Her hands continued with the braiding. "But if you go one street down, it is dangerous."

"No! You must not go past that street," Miriam said.

Shouts rang out on the street. Mercy and Grace rushed outside to investigate. They returned, agitated.

"A thief pushed down a Japanese tourist and grabbed his fanny pack!" Grace cried out.

"The thief ran off with his valuables!" Mercy said.

"Sunday is the worst day for robberies in Nairobi. We don't have many police patrolling the streets on Sundays, and not many people are around. You have to be careful," Miriam said. "The thieves even snatch wigs off women's heads and then sell them for a pittance—maybe one hundred shillings for a seven-hundred-shilling wig."

"The nickname for Nairobi is 'Nairobbery,'" a customer said.

46

I left the salon with a smile on my face but heeding the cautionary tales they had told. Shaking my head back and forth, I marveled at the lightness of the braids. When I'd had my hair braided in the United States, my head hung heavy with the weight of extra hair. Miriam created a breezy and natural style for me in Nairobi.

Even though we hadn't planned to go on an organized safari, we decided to sign up for a short safari to the Maasai Mara, one of the oldest wildlife conservation and wilderness areas in Kenya, after being approached five times by tour operators. They wore us down. We thought it would also be a good way to get the feel of the country before setting out alone on our bike trip. We chose a budget company and brought along our own sleeping bags. It felt strange to be thrust into a group of other tourists, but we soon enjoyed talking to the others and sharing stories and travel tips. In fact, our decision to go to Uganda later was the result of a conversation with an English woman we had met on safari. She had traveled to see the gorillas in Zaire, and she said the best part of that trip was going through Uganda and meeting the Ugandan people. She told us she would do the trip again just to go through Uganda. Her opinion stayed with us and influenced our decisions later.

The organized safari was a good way to finish acclimating, see African wildlife up close in the Rift Valley, and learn more about Uganda. Our little group included the two of us, our Kenyan guide and driver, a Dutch couple, a German couple, and a young woman from London. We all hit it off fine. About thirty people stayed at the base camp. Typically, Dermot and I liked traveling on our own because we could be more open to meeting local people. When you travel alone or with one other person, you are more approachable and open to the new sights, sounds, and people. In a large group, my attention focused on the people in the group; I became part of a unit that was impenetrable. But a group was the only way to go on a safari. We traveled on our own soon afterward.

CARLA FOUNTAIN

The Rift Valley enchanted me. We were miles from civilization, and open savannah stretched as far as we could see. The black night sky filled with stars that remained invisible in the city. Snuffling and lapping animal noises sounded outside our tent, thrilling and spooking us at the same time. I gave thanks for the tall, brave Maasai warrior who sat guard by the campfire all night with his spear. But I was so scared by the noises that, when I had to go to the bathroom in the middle of the night, I woke Dermot and begged him to go with me to the latrines.

The day started at dawn with a quick breakfast. The group climbed into our minivan, which had a pop-up top for viewing. We rode around the vast game park in search of animals. The drivers communicated via walkie-talkies to tell each other the best areas for animal viewing. The days filled up with a visual feast of wild creatures. Hordes of wildebeest thundered across the plains and through the rivers in their annual migration. We managed to spot a few shy rhinos and even a cheetah. Our guide told us we were fortunate to see a cheetah. Most groups he took out didn't see the rare animal. We encountered a handsome pride of lions lazing about, content and sated after a kill and feast. We saw numerous herds of zebra and giraffe not only on safari but also throughout our trip around Kenya. The elephants were my favorite animal to see up close. Their babies delighted us as they frisked and played.

On our last day, we stopped at a small Maasai village. The tall and dignified chief, with a *shuka* (a red plaid cloth) draped around his shoulders, came out to welcome us. The game park we visited during our safari, the Maasai Mara, was named in honor of the Maasai and stood on their ancestral lands. The Maasai live a semi-nomadic, pastoral lifestyle and raise cattle, goats, and sheep. Cattle determine a person's wealth, and all the Maasai's dietary needs are met with the meat, blood, and milk from the cattle. The chief showed us around the small village, a cluster of circular stick huts inside a barrier made of acacia branches. Women adorned in brightly colored fabric and intricately beaded jewelry plastered the stick frame huts with a mixture of mud and cow dung for waterproofing. Traditionally,

48

BICYCLE ODYSSEY

women made the huts, and the men made the barriers around the compound. The cattle stayed inside the barrier at night for protection from lions.

The designs and colors in the Maasai dress and beaded jewelry are striking but also symbolic. Red symbolizes the Maasai culture, and they believe the color scares away lions. Red also represents bravery and strength. Blue is for the sky and the rain, white for cow's milk, green for plants, orange and yellow for hospitality and friendship, and black for the people and their struggles. Both men and women stretched their earlobes and adorned them with beaded earrings. Stretched earlobes are a symbol of wisdom and respect—the older you are, the longer the earlobe.

When we returned to Nairobi, we both fell ill. We spent a day recuperating in bed, getting up only for frequent trips to the bathroom. We drank tea, ate toast, and took in lots of fluids. The advice in *Bicycling in Africa* told us that the best course of action was to hydrate and rest rather than to take a pill to suppress the symptoms. We supported the body's natural cleansing action and healed in a day or two. At one point, my back itched. When I scratched it, I came away with a tick that had been attached to me. I was appalled. If Rocky Mountain spotted fever and Lyme disease existed in the States, I wondered what disease ticks might carry in Kenya. But to this day, nothing has ever come from that tick bite.

We left Nairobi by bicycle, choking on dust and exhaust for the first five miles. With a lack of emission control, trucks belched thick, noxious clouds of diesel smoke. We stopped at an animal orphanage for a cool drink and a look at the animals. But after our short travel break, my energy flagged. I struggled to continue. The traffic fumes, combined with my recent illness, drained me. When we reached the suburbs, traffic moved slower, and our ride became more peaceful and safer. We stopped again at the Karen Blixen Museum. Although the author of *Out of Africa* intrigued me, my weak body demanded that I wait outside.

49

CARLA FOUNTAIN

Before leaving Denmark, I decided to get new prescription glacier glasses for eye protection when we biked. Dust, sun, and gravel were big concerns on the roads, especially as we approached the equator and traveled in more rural areas. The glacier glasses protected the sides of the eyes from light and flying objects. To shield himself from the sun, Dermot wore long-sleeved shirts. Flaps of cloth hung from a hat under his helmet to protect his neck and the sides of his face. As a redhead with fair skin, he was especially concerned about the equatorial sun for the rest of the trip.

Before we left on our voyage, I had purchased a bike dress designed by an enterprising American woman bicyclist. I thought the dress would be a good idea for a modest cover-up and would make me more presentable on the road and in villages. But it proved to be too short for the more conservative Kenyans, and my bike pants were too formfitting. After I overheard disapproving remarks, I covered up with a wraparound *kanga* (a sarong) when we stopped for meals or shopped in the marketplace. In Kampala, I purchased a custom-made outfit of loose-fitting long pants and a tunic top made from a stunning African print. The light cotton breathed well. The breeze blew through the fabric and cooled me as we cycled. I also blended in much better with the modest East African attire.

Every day, we slathered sun protection on our faces. Every night, we coated ourselves with insect repellant chock full of deet because the best malaria prevention is to *not* get bitten by a mosquito. We brought water-purifying tablets with us. In the mornings, we each filled two bottles with water from the tap and added a tablet. By midmorning, we were drinking warm, chlorine-laden water. It tasted like we were drinking from a swimming pool. It wasn't great but strangely comforting because we knew we wouldn't become sick from the water.

As we traveled farther away from the city and the other tourists, we became more of a curiosity. Shouts of *"Mzungu, mzungu, mzungu!"* (White person!) greeted us as we rode by houses or people walking on the side of the road. I found this vexing. I am not White. I am African American, and I had wanted to visit sub-Saharan Africa for the better part of my life. Unrealistically, I thought people would recognize my African heritage and be more welcoming. If I conversed with people at the market, and they said *"Mzungu,"* I responded with "No. I am not a *mzungu!"* But then they looked puzzled. When I explained that I was African American as well as part Irish and Native American, people seemed even more puzzled.

On the Maasai Mara safari, our guide asked whether I was from Thailand. Finally, one of the men said, "Oh, you are like the Swahili people on the coast." On the Swahili coast, there is a big mix of people from India, the Arabian Peninsula, and Africa. When Dermot and I later traveled there, I understood what he meant.

I heard similar accounts by other African Americans and African Europeans. One young man who had an African mother and a German father summed it up perfectly when he said, "In Europe, I am Black. In Africa, I am White." *Black* and *White* were more cultural terms. For me in America and Europe, I am Black. But in Africa, I was perceived as White. It took a while for me to come to grips with that and not feel disappointed about it.

But for the most part, locals greeted me by calling out, *"Jambo Mama!"* (Hello Madame!). We passed a multitude of people bustling on the roads. Women balanced large loads of firewood or other goods on their heads. They walked erect with sure strides for miles on the side of the road. Men on bicycles transported loads of colorful, plastic buckets or produce.

CARLA FOUNTAIN

We always looked forward to our meals and tea stops. A typical meal we could get on the road in Kenya was either fish or a stew of chicken or beef served on a base of rice or *ugali*. *Ugali*, a staple in Kenya, is cornmeal or millet flour cooked to a thick porridge consistency, similar to polenta. We weren't eating a lot of meat yet, so we ate the stew without the chicken and asked them to ladle copious helpings of sauce on our *ugali*. But we weren't consuming enough food or protein, since we couldn't find a source of legumes, except for occasional peanuts. The heat, combined with the miles of biking every day, caused us to drastically drop pounds.

We kept all our valuables—passports, money, Travelers Cheques, and plane tickets—in fanny packs around our waists under our voluminous clothes. Consequently, even though we became thinner by the week, I looked about four months pregnant for most of the trip. No one ever robbed us, and we didn't lose any valuables. "If it is not on our body, we can lose it" became our motto. Anything irreplaceable needed to be touching us. This method worked well for us.

But there was the time when Dermot left his fanny pack in a bathroom stall at a guesthouse in Thailand. In the middle of our dinner at a restaurant, it dawned on him that his fanny pack wasn't around his waist. He had become so comfortable without the pack on that he had relaxed and forgotten about it. We were fortunate that an honest and helpful person staying at the same guesthouse found it in the communal restroom stall and tracked us down.

We joined the organized safari earlier because people couldn't enter the game parks unaccompanied—we needed to be in an official group. At

BICYCLE ODYSSEY

that point in our trip, we didn't know about Hell's Gate Park, the one game park we could go into on our own, even by bicycle. We could also camp inside unaccompanied. We later stumbled on the park by accident. As we biked into Hell's Gate National Park, we passed zebras and giraffes grazing in the fields. No one else visited the park that day. We checked in with the solitary ranger sitting at his station at the entrance.

"Jambo." I greeted him in Swahili.

The young man, dressed in a smart khaki uniform, put down his fly whisk and stood. *"Jambo. Habari gani?"* (Hello. What's the news?)

"Nzuri" (I am well), I replied. I pride myself on at least always initiating a greeting in the language native to the country I travel in. "Are we allowed to bike here in the park?"

"Oh, yes!" He smiled. "You can even camp out here. Did you bring a tent?"

"No. We have a campsite at Fisherman's Camp, so we just came here for the day," Dermot said.

"That's too bad. This area is full of wildlife. Last night I saw a lion take down an antelope from where I stand right here. There is a lot to see in this park. I suggest that you bicycle in farther and hike through the gorge."

"Asante sana!" (Thank you very much!), we replied.

We didn't see any other visitors at Hell's Gate National Park that day. The only sounds we heard on our hike through the gorge were the rustling of plants in the breeze and the hum of insects. We followed the narrow stream at the bottom of the twisting gorge. Layers of multi-colored rock rose up the steep sides. We wished we could have spent the night at Hell's Gate. But we headed out after a few hours to reach our campsite before dark.

53

CARLA FOUNTAIN

Our lakeside campground, Fisherman's Camp, overlooked a manicured lawn by the shores of Lake Naivasha. We pitched our tent and cooked fresh fish from the lake. That night we found out how the lawn was maintained: large hippos came out of the lake to walk around and graze. The park rangers patrolled the area with sharply pointed metal poles under their arms.

"Will we be safe in our tent?" I asked a ranger. "I'm worried that the hippos might trample us in the dark!"

"Don't worry. The hippos are very sensitive. You will be fine," the ranger said.

Later that night, we felt the earth vibrate as the hippos walked around our tent. I was terrified when, once again, I had to go to the bathroom in the middle of the night.

I whispered to Dermot, "I have to go to the bathroom."

"Now?"

"Yes! And I'm scared! I can hear the hippos right outside our tent. I need you to come with me and hold the flashlight."

"I don't know, babe. It could be dangerous to go out there."

"I can't wait until morning, Derm!"

We inched the zipper open and peeked out. The huge, black hulks of hippo bodies stood too close for comfort, with their red eyes reflecting back at us. We could hear them quietly munching the grass, and we gave them a wide berth. The next day we took a boat out on the lake and glided by the same hippos who had walked around our tent the night before. We could see only their eyes and ears, which flicked back and forth as they watched us. That ranked high among the best camping on the trip—gorgeous surroundings and an abundance of fresh fish to cook up for our meals. We were

54

the only ones camping; most people stayed in rental cabins. And few people fished at the lake.

I didn't find out until many years after our trip that the hippo is considered one of the most dangerous and deadly land mammals in the world. They are aggressive and unpredictable, and they kill an estimated five hundred people a year in Africa. Their massive weight—an average of three thousand pounds for females and as much as nine thousand pounds for males—can crush a human to death. Had we known that at the time, we would have been even more terrified.

From Nakuru on, the cycling was wonderful. Once we left the tourist trail, the people we met welcomed us with genuine friendliness and excitement. Almost everyone greeted us as we cycled by on the back roads. Our basic Swahili didn't progress much, but we excelled at the greetings. Cycling northwest of Nakuru to Molo was a long, smooth ride of green hills interspersed with pine forests, dairy cows, and fields of corn and pyrethrum daisies. From Molo, we dropped down in elevation to Kericho, into undulating fields of perfectly manicured tea bushes. Workers spread out through the mounds, picking tea leaves. Kenya is the world's third-largest producer and exporter of tea. We stopped for a tea break and a snack at the grand, colonial Tea Hotel. In the tea fields, a strong worker could pick 155 pounds a day, earning the equivalent of three dollars. That wasn't much, but better than the wage the sugarcane workers received.

The next day while bicycling from Kericho to Kapsabet, we dropped into a steamy valley and rode through a sugarcane area. We stopped near Muhoroni in a village of mud huts with thatched roofs. The people in that area were mostly Luo, the fourth-largest ethnic group in Kenya. Two companies owned all the sugarcane fields. People said it was a much harder job to cut cane than to pick tea leaves. After the workers burned the cane fields, they cut the stalks with their *pangas* (machetes).

We bought soda, fruit, and *mandazi* (a fried bread similar to a doughnut but not as sweet) from friendly women vendors by the side of the road. After this short rest, we continued cycling past the bustle of the cane harvest for about fifteen miles.

We climbed into the Nandi Hills. By one thirty, we had already traveled forty miles, but there was no sign of the town of Nandi Hills, where we had planned a lunch stop. We knew we were crazy to be out at midday bicycling and crossing the equator, so we pulled over to rest and eat our snacks in a shady spot by the side of the road. Derm read while I studied Swahili. Even though English was one of the official languages of Kenya, in those out-of-the-way areas, we found few people who spoke English. I quickly fell asleep, though, tired from our strenuous bicycling in the hills during the intense heat of the day.

We set off again at three o'clock, and the afternoon grew cooler. But the hills were extremely steep, and we struggled. Our water bottles were empty, and we still saw no sign of Nandi Hills. Finally, after about forty-five miles, we reached a small settlement. We hadn't arrived in Nandi Hills, but we found a one-room store.

The store owner, James, stepped into the doorway when he heard us putting down our bicycles. "*Jambo*! Welcome! You must be very hot and thirsty."

We entered the cool shade of his store. "*Jambo*. Thank you. We are parched and tired. What do you have that is cold to drink?" I asked.

James walked over to his cooler and pulled out two icy bottles. "I have this bitter lemon soda. Will that do?"

"Ah, yes, thank you!" We drank in a comfortable silence, relishing the cool effervescence.

James pulled out a plate of fresh, homemade *mandazi*. "If you are hungry, I also have food."

I took a bite and tasted a hint of cardamom in his delicious *mandazi*. "Your English is perfect," I said. "I wish I could manage to learn more Swahili. Out in the countryside, we don't always meet people who speak much English."

James uncapped two more bottles of soda for us. "In this area, the main language is Nandi. The people are Nandi, and we speak Nandi at home and among ourselves. When children go to school here, all the instruction is done in Swahili. Children learn to read and write in Swahili, never in Nandi. After that they learn English. Before independence from the British, children learned to read and write in Nandi first, then in Swahili. Even though English is one of the official languages of Kenya, only 25 percent of the population speak it well."

Thirst quenched and belly full, I pushed back my plate. "Thank you for clarifying that. I work in education in the United States. Right now, there is a big difference of opinion about how best to teach children whose native language is not English."

Dermot finished the last crumbs of *mandazi* and reached for a banana. "We've been reading in the newspapers about the movement for multiparty democracy the past few days. What do you think of it? Why is the government opposed to that?"

"I think the government is against multiparty democracy because the officials feel it is too soon," James answered. "Kenya has forty different tribes. The government is afraid it would deteriorate into a tribal party system. They want to keep the government system to only one party to help unite the people."

Dermot wiped his brow. "Thank you for your frankness. It has been hard to talk about politics with people. We read that there will be a multiparty demonstration soon in Nairobi. But when we asked a few people about it, they changed the subject and talked about the weather."

CARLA FOUNTAIN

A plump woman in her fifties entered the shop, said, *"Jambo"* with a smile, and sat down next to us. She leaned toward me with warm, friendly eyes and spoke to me in Nandi or Swahili—I didn't know which.

James translated her questions and my answers. "Where are you from?" she asked.

I looked into her brown eyes. "I am from America."

She nodded. "What crops do you grow? What is the land like?"

"I live in California, and we grow oranges, lemons, and grapefruit. The land is not as green as here. It is very dry where I live."

She nodded again and smiled. "Do you have many cows? How many exactly? How much milk do they give?"

My grandmother grew up on a farm in Virginia, so I was happy that I could share bovine experiences with her. "My grandmother owned two cows when my mother was a child. They gave good milk. But when they ate onions, the milk tasted like onions. My mother didn't like the milk then."

The woman laughed at this. She'd probably had the same experience with her cows.

"My grandmother grew tobacco on her farm. That is an important crop in Virginia," I added. "What about you? Do you have cows? How is their milk production?"

"Well, the abundance of milk depends on the grass and how green it is."

"Ah, that makes sense," I said.

We all stood to leave. The woman took my hand. "It is so good that Blacks and Whites can sit together in the same room and talk.

I remember before independence when that wasn't the case." She squeezed my hand and smiled. "I wish I could give you a carton of milk to take back to America so that Americans could taste how good the milk from my cows is."

That was such a beautiful encounter. It didn't matter what race she thought I was. We had made a sweet connection that filled both of us with joy. We didn't take our cameras out; that would have broken the magic. Rather, the experience remains etched in my memory, and the Nandi Hills is one of my favorite places in Kenya.

I found out later that the British struggled to colonize that area. The Nandi fought fiercely and held them off with spears and sticks, resisting their attempts at domination for eleven years. That period is known as the Nandi Resistance. That is why there is no railway track through the area. The British gave up and laid the tracks elsewhere.

We had a connection to look up in Eldoret. One of my mother's childhood friends, Percia, had retired from her career as a physical therapist in the United States and now volunteered with the Church of Kenya. She helped teach people how to rehabilitate severely handicapped children. She worked with parents in their homes, fitted children with prosthetics, and supported community caregivers. I appreciated meeting a family connection. Even though we had never seen each other before, Percia was warm and kind. She took us under her wing for the day, showed us around, treated us to lunch, and told us about her work and what she had learned in Kenya.

After our visit with Percia, we headed off down the Pan-African Highway, where we ran into other Americans who had decided to volunteer after their retirement. One couple came over with the Peace Corps and volunteered in a village farther west. They enjoyed their post and related well to the Kenyans with whom they worked. We often think about the Peace Corps as volunteer work for young college graduates, but these retired volunteers possessed a lifetime of experience to share.

A potentially confrontational demonstration was supposed to take place in Nairobi on October 5. Members of the Forum for the Restoration of Democracy, the multiparty democracy advocates, wanted to hold a peaceful demonstration. President Moi denied their permit, declaring that they wanted to cause dissension and violence. Since the newspapers were in English, we could keep abreast of current news in Kenya, and we followed the developments. We enjoyed talking to people we met about current events and situations. Because we liked to be informed, we were aware of the planned demonstration and made sure to stay out of Nairobi that day.

On the day of the scheduled demonstration, we were deep in the Kakamega Forest, a tropical rain forest near the border of Uganda. Without newspapers or television in the forest, we didn't know what had happened until much later. Most tourists we met were blissfully unaware that there was any trouble brewing. The year before, twenty-one people had been killed in a pro-democracy demonstration in Nairobi.

The Kakamega Forest is Kenya's last remnant of the ancient rain forest that once spanned across Central Africa. We stayed in a wooden hut built on stilts. Our hut even came equipped with a Western-style toilet. But after weeks of squat toilets and outhouses, it seemed strange to have such a modern convenience in our hut in the middle of the Kenyan forest. We met the other travelers who had also rented huts, including a young US Peace Corps volunteer based in the Tuareg area in Niger and a friendly Australian making his way down to South Africa for a windsurfing competition.

BICYCLE ODYSSEY

Joseph, a knowledgeable local guide, took us on a forest tour. He pointed out the different varieties of orchids, trees, birds, and butterflies as we walked along the shady paths. The tall trees and vines created a cooling canopy over our heads as we meandered. We saw plenty of insects, especially ants and beetles. Other wildlife was abundant but elusive. But we did catch a glimpse of a monkey we had startled.

We had the opportunity to visit a high school class during our stay in the Kakamega District. These ambitious students and their teacher were eager to talk with us and be interviewed. We sat outside together on the lawn. The young men were dressed in crisp, white shirts and dark pants. The young women wore dark skirts with white blouses.

I held the microphone while Dermot taped. "If you had the power to change anything in the world, what would you do?"

Catherine gazed intently into the camera. "If I had the power, I would invite people from the United States to come stay with us and see what life is like here."

Another girl chimed in, "I would continue my education to university level. I'd be educated and be one of the people who could keep on improving our country."

John added, "I'd take my people to foreign countries to learn more about them and how they live. I'd like to be a teacher. I'd help my fellow people to learn so we might develop our country in the best way."

They stood and sang a cappella with lovely harmonies for us as a parting gift.

On Sunday I wanted to go to the local church. Joseph invited us to go with him to a service. The congregation gathered in a large pavilion with a hard-packed dirt floor. We sat on wooden benches for the ceremony. The melodious singing, with the acoustic accompaniment of guitar and drums, moved me. After the service, Joseph asked if Derm

CARLA FOUNTAIN

and I would like to have dinner at his house and meet his family. We were happy to accept his invitation.

Joseph opened the door for us. "Welcome! Please come in and meet my children. My wife will be home shortly."

We smiled at the children and said hello. Joseph's tall, elegant wife walked into their home a few minutes later.

"Friends, this is my lovely wife, Sarah."

"I have just come back from the market where I sell handicrafts," she said. "Look at this pretty umbrella I bought to protect me from the hot sun." She opened and twirled an enormous, multicolored umbrella. "Business was good today!"

We admired her purchase and sat down. "It's so kind of you to have us in your home. It's a real treat to have dinner with you. Thank you, Sarah," I said.

She nodded and smiled.

"Joseph gave us a great tour of the forest," I said. "I love the area."

Joseph ushered the children around the table to eat with us. "I enjoy my work. It is good to be out in nature instead of pushing papers in an office all day. People from all over the world come to visit the Kakamega Forest. I like meeting and talking with them."

Sarah ladled food onto our plates. "I hope you like *ugali*. It is our Kenyan staple. And I made chicken stew."

After the delicious meal, with full bellies and content hearts, we made our way back to our hut to rest and prepare for an early start. The next day we planned to cross the border into Uganda.

7

Uganda—Into the Unknown

Back in Nairobi after our safari, we had applied for Ugandan visas on the suggestion of a fellow traveler. In our initial planning, we had given ourselves two months to travel within Africa. There were lots of possibilities. We could go down all the way to South Africa, but we were unwilling to visit the country until they abolished apartheid. Other travelers told us South African hospitality was wonderful, especially in the countryside. I wasn't sure about the reception a mixed-race couple would have there. American Blacks were granted honorary "White" status in South Africa in those days. But, off the beaten track where bicyclists like to roam, that could be a different story. Uganda beckoned. We would follow the Pan-African Highway west and see what happened.

Uganda took its name from the Buganda kingdom. The official language was English. Years after our trip, Swahili became the second official language. There are about forty different languages spoken in Uganda, including Luganda, which is the most widely spoken native language.

While bicycling through Uganda, we came across numerous reminders of the recent wars. Idi Amin's reign of terror was fresh in our memories. He was president of Uganda from 1971 to 1979; many called him the "Butcher of Uganda" and considered him one of the most brutal leaders in world history. Between three hundred thousand and five hundred thousand people were killed during his rule. He gave the South Asian population of eighty thousand a short time to leave the country or be put into concentration camps, and he seized their assets. The new president, Museveni, invited Asians who had been forced to leave during Idi Amin's reign to return to the country in 1990. The government even returned a portion of their assets. Throughout our trip, we saw businesses owned by Asians that had reopened. A positive and hopeful spirit abounded. We learned much history as we bicycled through this stunning, verdant country.

Few tourists had visited Uganda since the early 1970s because of the political turmoil. Tourism was starting up again slowly, so we saw very few other travelers on our trip. This made for many pleasant encounters with Ugandans, who were welcoming and eager to talk to us.

At the time we entered the country, a large project was in progress to rebuild the roads. For much of our ride, we cycled on freshly asphalted roads built by either Chinese or Yugoslavian aid workers. We also cycled on long stretches of hard-packed dirt roads. The earth was a rich red, a gorgeous contrast to the sharp blue of the sky.

We bicycled for eighty miles from Tororo to Jinja, near the source of the White Nile by the enormous Lake Victoria. The date was October 9, Independence Day in Uganda. Memory is a strange thing. Dermot and I both have vivid memories the other oddly enough has no recollection of. Years after our journey, we met for coffee and talked about our epic bicycle trip. We remembered stopping for a snack break off to the side of the road in a shady spot before we reached Jinja. As we sat and ate, Dermot noticed several ragged and hungry-looking men approaching us. They stood around us without saying a word and looked at us with interest.

BICYCLE ODYSSEY

Derm sprang into action. "I'm going to give these men some crackers." He started passing out food to the silent men. "Get on your bike," he said in a low voice.

"What?"

"Get on your bike and start to pedal. I'll catch up."

He soon caught up to me, and we raced away. Dermot was convinced that those men were going to attack us. To his credit, he must have handled that incident so smoothly that I have no recollection of feeling unsafe. At the time I thought, *How generous of Dermot to share our snack! Those men looked hungry.* I don't even have a record of it in the journal I kept on our trip, which I wrote in almost every night no matter how tired I was. There are other incidents etched in my mind when I feared for our safety and even our lives. But that would be later on another continent.

Safe at our hotel, we showered, changed, and left for dinner at dusk, ravenous as usual after a day of cycling. As we walked to find a restaurant, we heard high-pitched chirping noises echo in the air. I looked up and saw hundreds of enormous fruit bats flying out of the trees near us. I shivered at the eerie sight, reminiscent of a scene out of a Dracula movie.

We could hear music as we approached the Mango Bar and Restaurant. "Wow! The joint is jumping!" I said.

Dermot shrugged and frowned. "It's pretty dark in there. I'd like to be able to see my food."

"Come on! It's fun and festive. This is the liveliest place we've been in."

I persuaded him to stay. The waitress seated us at a table with other people and served us two large Tusker beers. The light beers came in full pint bottles. An Indian man and several Ugandan women

65

CARLA FOUNTAIN

in colorful dresses sat at the table with us. One woman cradled a six-month-old baby in her arms. Everyone was out to celebrate Uganda's Independence Day. The music was hopping, and spirits were high.

Mr. Gaj, the middle-aged Indian gentleman at our table, perked up when he saw us. "Hello! Welcome! Are you enjoying your dinner? Please, I want to buy you another round of beer. Join us in celebrating."

It would have cut the conversation if we refused. The light beer worked in our favor, so we could safely drink more. "Thank you!" I said.

We moved our chairs closer to hear him above the music. "Have you lived in Jinja long?" Dermot asked.

Mr. Gaj toasted us with a clink of glasses and took a sip. "I first came to Uganda in 1962 after independence. But I had to leave when Idi Amin expelled all the Asians living in Uganda. After Amin fell, I returned in 1982 for a visit. Then in 1987 I decided to settle in Uganda again. I came back because I owned land in Uganda."

Dermot finished the last of his chicken stew. "Uganda is beautiful. We're bicycling through the country."

"Oh, yes!" Mr. Gaj's eyes lit up. "This country was God's gift to the world. Uganda and also Vietnam. The fertile soil, the beauty of the land—everything grows bigger, better, and sweeter here. Pineapples, coffee, tea, bananas, and sugar."

"Do you grow crops on your land?" I asked.

"Yes, but mainly I am a sugar technologist. Here is my card. I would like to invite you to come visit the factory tomorrow. You will see the whole process."

Early the next morning, the bats settled into their trees for the day with lots of bedtime chirps. Thunder rumbled and lightning streaked

66

BICYCLE ODYSSEY

across the sky. Rain fell. The weather dictated that we stay in Jinja that day rather than bike out. October and November are the months for the "short rains." Short? It poured for five hours, starting at three o'clock in the morning. We had planned our trip around the seasons. People had told us the short rains in Uganda wouldn't be a problem.

We decided to take Mr. Gaj up on his invitation to visit him at the sugarcane factory. The rain still pounded as we finished breakfast, so we couldn't bike anywhere until it let up. We took a *matatu* (an independent taxi van) to a quarter mile from the factory grounds. As we walked toward the factory and asked directions, we met a friendly man, Mr. Quincy, who showed us the way. When he found out we were teachers, he asked us to visit the primary school where he was the headmaster after we finished our tour of the factory.

The factory grounds stretched out on manicured lawns. We toured the huge factory and learned how sugarcane was processed from start to finish. Four Indian brothers owned the factory. They generously provided schools, a clinic, and housing for the workers.

The primary school delighted us. Mr. Quincy was overjoyed to have American visitors share with his pupils. He pressed Dermot to give an impromptu lecture on harvesting machines and on America in general. Dermot did a great job for a city boy caught on the spot and improvised well. Later, I videotaped other classes singing their favorite songs for us in front of the school grounds.

The cute, enthusiastic children lined up in their tidy, dark-blue uniforms with white collars and performed with gusto. The class was a mixed group of mostly African and a few Indian children. Afterward, we walked over to the secondary school where we met the headmaster, Mr. Kevin. He invited us to sit, and we talked in his office about the differences in curriculum between Uganda and the United States. He later took us to tea at the sugar factory's private club.

We enjoyed a marvelous day, and we connected with people. Both of the headmasters encouraged us to come back and teach in Uganda.

67

We planned to visit the Ministry of Education in Kampala and look into how that could be done.

We returned to Jinja with Mr. Quincy by hitching a ride on three different pickup trucks. At one point, he stopped a driver so he could buy a Nile perch. The enormous fish, about three feet long, cost only ten cents. One man bicycled past us with a four-foot Nile perch strapped to his rear rack.

Back in town on Clive Street, we found stalls with an array of colorful materials and rows of tailors waiting by their old-fashioned, foot-pedal-controlled sewing machines. Dermot picked out material for a long-sleeved cotton shirt; I chose material for loose pants and a long-sleeved shirt to protect me from the sun.

While the tailor sewed, we hired *boda bodas* to take us to the source of the Nile. A *boda boda* is a regular one-speed bike with a cushioned seat on the back rack. A person sat on the back while the bicyclist pedaled to the destination. They told us the name came from "border, border" because the bicycles were used in the past to get people across the border to Kenya more easily, maybe even clandestinely and with less paperwork. After getting over my initial fear, I relaxed and enjoyed the ride. Derm was so comfortable that he shot video as he rode down the streets on the back of his *boda boda*. We passed through the exclusive suburbs of Jinja where Idi Amin had lived at one time. A few of the neighborhoods had been damaged in the war, but overall the area was pleasant and peaceful.

Our drivers took us to the commemorative plaque for British explorer John Speke, who had found the source of the Nile and was the first European to reach Lake Victoria in 1858. We looked out over the Nile and the expanse of the lake. By the time Speke arrived at Lake Victoria, he was partially blind and couldn't see the full expanse of the lake, one of the African Great Lakes and the world's second-largest lake. He was ill from his arduous, thousand-mile journey and the various tropical diseases he had contracted along the way.

We planned to stay in Kampala for a few days. At our first stop, the Tourist Hotel, our room looked over the market. The hotel was clean and comfortable for an economy class and was eight dollars a night. But a nightclub across the street boomed loud music until two in the morning. At four o'clock, the Muslim call to prayer came over a loudspeaker. At six o'clock, the market crowd arrived with loud noises and vehicles. Even though we slept poorly the first night, we stayed at the same hotel another night, thinking we would go out and dance at the club. "If you can't beat them, join them!" rang true for us. The house band that night was the Central Volcano Band. We enjoyed their music. The lead singer, a tall and scrawny guitar player, possessed a great deal of stamina.

We danced to "Music Makes Me Feel Happy" the next night at the club and appreciated hearing a familiar reggae beat. The people at the club dressed smartly; the men wore slacks and white shirts—a few of them even sported ties—and the women wore Western-style party dresses. The crowd on the dance floor was subdued. We definitely didn't have the wardrobe for a night out, but I dressed up the best I could with my long skirt and hid my fanny pack by tying my *kanga* around my waist. Dermot wore his button-down shirt and slacks.

We left before the last song. Back at our hotel, the music pounded into our room, followed by the calls to prayer and the bustling market activity. That was it! We needed to change hotels, or we would be frazzled wrecks when we left Kampala in two days to resume bicycling.

We checked into our first "luxury" hotel of the trip, The Speke Hotel, for twenty-five dollars a night. The Speke Hotel was across the street from a Sheraton. For two quiet nights, we indulged with soft sheets on a comfortable bed in a spacious room. The Sheraton's rooms cost over one hundred dollars a night, and in 1991, that was far out of our budget. But we could enjoy tea there, read the paper, and watch CNN. Foreign aid workers, missionaries, and government employees filled the hotel and the lobby.

Music may have kept us awake at night at our first hotel, but it was a welcome sound throughout our trip. At that time, the Afrigo Band ranked as one of the top Ugandan bands. Their hit "Born in Africa" became the soundtrack to our travels in Uganda that month. We heard that song at rest stops and restaurants throughout our month there. Today, you can find them on YouTube for a taste of their wonderful music.

Kampala was still getting back on its feet after the war. The city bustled with construction projects. Large, impressive national buildings and huge offices graced the center. We spent all day trying to get a map of the country. When we did find one, we paid nine dollars—more than a night in our first hotel. The Office of Tourism had almost no information and seemed happy to see us leave. Things have changed since then. Uganda has built up its tourism industry in recent years and is earnestly promoting itself.

We visited the Royal Palace and Makerere University, one of the oldest and most prestigious English language universities in Africa. The lovely campus sits high on one of the many hills around Kampala. Many post-independence African leaders and prominent writers studied there.

Tired and thirsty from biking the hills, we took a tea break back in the city center.

BICYCLE ODYSSEY

A man sitting at the next table introduced himself. "I heard your accents. You must be from the United States."

"Yes. You're right!" Dermot answered.

"I'm Don."

Dermot finished off the introductions. "It's nice to meet you."

Don stretched out his hand to give a solid handshake to both Dermot and me.

"We haven't met many Americans traveling in Kenya and Uganda yet," Dermot said. "We've been bicycling west since Nairobi."

"Do you live here?" I asked.

"Yes, but I'm from California. I've been living in Uganda for thirteen years. My wife is Ugandan. She's in Kenya now for a golf tournament near Kericho."

Dermot poured us more tea. "We biked through there. We loved traveling around the tea cultivation area. What do you do here, Don?"

Don paused for a sip of tea. "I work on different media projects."

His vague answer left us curious. I contemplated how we could work abroad one day.

Later that evening, we attended the National Theatre and saw the play *Thirty Years of Bananas* by Alex Mukulu. The play centered on the thirty years of craziness after independence from British rule in Uganda in 1962. The first half was mostly in English, and we understood and learned quite a lot. But after the intermission, most of the dialogue was in Luganda, and we got lost. We enjoyed the costumes, music, singing, and dancing. The play caused us to want to read more about Ugandan history. The audience loved the show. In

71

2006, *Thirty Years of Bananas* had a revival with updates to mark fifty-plus years of independence. The satire was considered as important then as when it played in 1991.

The night before we left Kampala, we sat outside at a restaurant. I inhaled the aroma of grilled meat. "That shish kebab smells so good."

"Are you crazy? You always say red meat repulses you."

"I know. But it smells irresistible tonight. I just crave it."

Dermot shook his head. "That's so strange. You haven't eaten red meat in five years."

"I'm ordering a beef shish kebab. Do you want one?"

"No, I'll just stick to chicken stew."

The lack of necessary nutrients must have run me down. We hadn't been able to eat legumes in a while. We had ladled sauce without meat over our starch of rice, *ugali*, or *matoke* (the mashed plantain staple of Uganda). That steak shish kebab was satisfying going down, but I suffered for days after eating it. My system wasn't used to red meat, and my stomach ached the whole night. The pain continued the next day, and I couldn't eat breakfast or lunch. I figured that I had introduced too much meat at once into my system. I needed to eat very small quantities of beef on a regular basis to activate those digestive enzymes again.

The day we left for Mityana, forty miles away, we had an easy exit from Kampala without crazy traffic. After four miles, we began to climb the undulating, green Ugandan hills on a quiet road. As usual, people near the city were reserved and merely watched us, choosing not to return our greetings for the most part. We thought that once

BICYCLE ODYSSEY

we reached the countryside, things would be different, like it had been between Tororo and Jinja. We rode on, but the people didn't get friendlier. They shot us wary glances. I thought the area had probably seen a lot of action during the war, and that was why people were guarded. We came upon an old, burned-out tank on the side of the road. The military vehicle was new enough to be from Idi Amin's era and old enough to be rusted and covered with vines. We better understood the reticence of the people.

My body weakened. My muscles hurt after being inactive for three days and my insides churned trying to digest the meat. We stopped in a little town for a stack of one-cent banana pancakes. We spread peanut butter, which we had bought in Kampala, on them. About ten miles later, we stopped again for a pineapple break at a roadside fruit stand. Since the enzymes in pineapple aid digestion, I hoped it would help me feel better and help move the meat out of my system. Needless to say, I didn't eat red meat for a long time after that.

While we ate the freshly sliced pineapple, a large car pulled up, and a well-dressed man stepped out.

The man walked over to us and smiled. "Hello! What is your business here?"

"We are bicycling through Uganda. We started in Nairobi," I answered.

"That's quite a journey," he said.

Derm wiped pineapple juice from his hands. "Are you the mayor of the area?"

The man laughed. "I'm a bit higher than that. I am a minister in the government. I'm on my way to Kampala now. I stopped to buy pineapple to bring with me. Here's my card. Give me a call if you return to Kampala. If you like, I will try to get you an introduction to President Museveni."

CARLA FOUNTAIN

I choked on my last bite of pineapple. "Thank you," I said. His offer intimidated me.

Unfortunately, we never did call him when we returned to Kampala. We didn't have clothes to meet the president. How silly of us! Who knows what would have happened had we followed up on the invitation? As of 2020, nearly three decades later, Museveni is still the president of Uganda.

After the minister left, another man walked up to buy pineapple and stayed to talk with us. We discussed Uganda's future and past, his job, AIDS, religion, and the United States.

David was eager to connect with us. "I am a primary school teacher."

"We are teachers too," I said.

"David, we read about the AIDS crisis in Africa. How is it affecting Uganda?" Dermot asked.

He sighed. "It is terrible. There is an area in the south with whole villages of abandoned houses. In other villages, only the elderly and orphaned children remain. The adults have all died from AIDS or 'slims,' as we also call it."

"What hopes do you have for Uganda?" I asked.

David's eyes lit up. "Uganda is special because of its climate and the people. Some Ugandans are revolutionary and very hardworking. You can grow your own food here. There is a saying in Uganda that if you stick anything in the ground, it will grow. The land is rich."

"What does Uganda need in order to prosper?" I asked.

"We don't need ready-made goods. The best way people can help us is to give us knowledge."

BICYCLE ODYSSEY

Dermot gave him our contact information. "We've enjoyed talking to you, David. Here's our address in the United States. We should be back home in July of next year. Please write to us. We'd like to come back to Uganda one day."

David smiled. "I will, if I am alive then."

Later, after we left him, I thought about his last words. I wondered if he *would* be alive the next year. We never did hear from him.

We slept at the New Highway Hotel in Mityana and left at eight thirty the next morning. Derm woke up with a sore throat. We thought about taking a bus, but we biked out. The terrain was fairly dry with no forest. Numerous cows grazed in the fields. We noticed how the cows changed from region to region on our trip. In this area of Uganda, the cows had three-foot-long horns spread far apart, similar to a Texas longhorn. At one point, we almost ran into a bull crossing the road when he stopped to look us in the eye. We braked furiously to keep our distance.

We traveled up and down hills with few flat areas in between. About thirty miles into the ride, we tucked into a traditional Ugandan lunch of *matoke* and chicken stew. We found *matoke* bland but comforting with its smooth consistency and texture similar to mashed potatoes.

We pushed on after lunch. About thirteen miles later, we saw our eighth police check since biking into Uganda from the border with Kenya. All the police checks had gone well, and we usually ended up laughing and sharing photos with the men. We carried a small show-and-tell book with our family photos and photos of home. At the last checkpoint, the police even asked us to take their pictures. When we reached the next checkpoint, the head policeman glared at us sternly. Even though I slowed down to stop in front of him, he held out his hand and yelled.

75

CARLA FOUNTAIN

"Stop!" he commanded. "Show us your papers!" He scowled as he glanced from me to my passport. "Take off your glasses so I can see that it is really you."

I did as I was told.

"Where are you traveling to?"

"Fort Portal," I answered.

The policeman mocked and laughed at us. "Ha! You won't be able to bike to Fort Portal! It will take you two days."

Two other policemen marched over to us and pointed to the side of the road. "Pull over there so we can check your bags."

We obliged. As Derm was turning around to explain what he had in his bags, he noticed a beautiful chameleon on top of his pannier. I scrambled for the camera so Derm could take a photo of the chameleon.

Our activity infuriated the head policeman. "Did you put that chameleon there? Do you have a permit to take photographs? Put that away!"

I yanked the camera from Derm and stuffed it back into my handlebar bag. A government official's truck drove up, and the policeman stopped hassling us and told us to move on. I thought about the minister who had given us his card. I would have dropped his name if the hostility had escalated. Relieved to be dismissed, we dashed away.

We spent the night in Mubende, and in the morning, we discovered that the tarmac road ended three miles out of town. Ahead of us, we could see only graded dirt, which the rainy day had turned into soft mud. We decided to take a *matatu* (a minibus) from the bus stop back in town. The *matatu* pulled up, already fully loaded. The men in charge of loading the baggage took our bicycles. Derm climbed onto the roof of the bus to direct them, and the men hoisted the bicycles up to him.

76

BICYCLE ODYSSEY

Derm attached the bikes to the rack with his lock. The men threw our panniers up, tied them under the tarp, and we raced off down the road. At first, we had no seats, and Derm swooned with a fever. He asked the ticket guy if he could pay fifty cents for a seat. The man laughed and discussed it with his friend in Luganda. Derm told the man he was unwell. Out of sympathy, the man stood and gave Derm his seat. I stood next to a feisty, petite woman who breastfed her tiny baby, wrapped snuggly to her body in a *kanga*. She yelled and pushed at people who moved too close to her.

The rain poured as lightning flashed and thunder boomed during our entire *matatu* ride. At times, the road became a stream of mud. Great splashes of reddish-brown water shot up as we zoomed down the one-lane road. Our bikes rode on the top of the bus and seemed to survive unharmed. Later, we found out that Derm's handlebars had deep gouges from the friction of rubbing against another object during the bus trip. We were fortunate that nothing was damaged.

We checked into the Wooden Hotel in Fort Portal. After a shower, we headed down to eat. In the dining room, we met a Kenyan man. We learned that he was on a motorcycle journey around Kenya, Uganda, and Tanzania to raise money for child immunization. He had stopped for lunch at our hotel and was headed to Kampala.

Derm returned to our room to take a nap, while I set out to explore the town. The sky cleared, unveiling the forested slopes of the Rwenzori Mountains, which stretched up into the clouds. *Rwenzori* means "rainmaker" or "rain mountains" in the local Bakonjo language. The range is known as Mountains of the Moon because of its white snowcaps. I stayed out for two hours, walking all over town and enjoying the view and the freshness. I found supplies in a small shop for the next day's hike: avocados, chocolate, and tasty peanut-sesame candies called "simsim." The walk lifted my spirits so much that when I returned to the hotel, I pulled Derm outside on the pretense that the fresh air would help him feel better. We ended up walking two miles to the Mountains of the Moon Hotel for a hearty dinner. Even if we couldn't afford to stay at the higher-end hotels, we could enjoy their food and ambiance.

Back at our hotel, we met up with a group of tourists from Britain, who had hired a truck to visit the hot springs and the Pygmy village near Bundibugyo. Since the hotel owner had told us the road was a dirt one and the worst road in Uganda, we decided to go in a vehicle. The next morning we met up with the others and split the cost of the van and guide with them.

We all squeezed together in the van. The back door and other rough metal parts of the vehicle rubbed against me for the two-hour drive to the hot springs. I shifted in my seat often so I wouldn't scrape my skin. A cut or blister could take a long time to heal in the tropics, and the risk of infection was high.

At first sight, the spot was a letdown. Waste from past picnickers filled the swampy area with broken eggshells, peelings, and bones. Steam and bubbles rose all around. As we walked on, we found a more interesting area behind a large clump of reeds. A natural fountain gushed boiling water over a raised bed of mineral deposits, radiating intense heat. A thick, steamy fog swirled around us.

We drove on farther to the Pygmy village. A diminutive man greeted us and introduced himself as the teacher sent by the government to help educate the Pygmy group. He made sure to point out that, even though he was short in stature, he wasn't a Pygmy.

Our arrival interrupted the teacher's outdoor lesson under a tree. "Welcome. Please sign the visitor's book. I want to warn you that the chief is often drunk. Don't be offended if he insults you or yells at you. He becomes ill tempered when he drinks."

BICYCLE ODYSSEY

The teacher helped us reach an agreement with the chief of the village about how much to pay for our visit. They both walked us around while the teacher talked. "I have been working with this Pygmy group for seven years. When I first met them deeper in the forest, I had to persuade the villagers to move near the road."

Derm walked close beside me as we stepped past a small family, who sat beneath the shade of their hut.

"They still hunt monkeys for food," the teacher said. He grimaced. "I can't eat them. The monkey's face looks too human. They buy food with the money they receive from tourists. They also buy alcohol." He laughed. "I am trying to work on that."

Each dwelling stood separated by a short path in the forest. Leaf roofs covered the wooden-framed huts. We stopped in front of a dwelling, where a mother cuddled and nursed her baby.

"There are sixty Pygmies living here. The chief has two wives and twelve children. This is one of his wives," the teacher said.

The villagers brought out wooden bongs and clay opium pipes to sell. They lined up for pictures. The situation was awkward and absurd—all of us snapping photos and twenty Pygmies posing. Several Pygmies hammed it up and struck fierce warrior poses for the cameras. Derm shot footage of the group of tourists taking photos. The unease in our little group was palpable. I could tell everyone else was also uncomfortable and wished we hadn't visited the village in this way.

Depressed and sad, we all shuffled aboard the van. I don't know what we had expected. Dermot and I usually traveled on our own and naturally met people along the way when we stopped to rest or eat a meal. I regretted taking the trip to the village. The experience reinforced why we traveled on our own, not in a group, and why we stayed off the beaten path.

In my research later, I found that this small group of Pygmies was the Basua. They had suffered greatly over the years. Anthropologists have described this group as marginalized and disinherited. The government had moved the Basua out of the Semliki Forest, where they had lived until it became a national park in the early 1990s. It is estimated that there are less than one hundred in their community now. They are no longer allowed to hunt in the forest and live mainly by selling palm oil to locals and handicrafts to tourists.

Since visiting this village in the 1990s, anthropologist Stan Frankland of the University of St Andrews in Scotland has been working with and advocating for the community. Rebel troops near the area ended the tourism for a while and brought violence, rape, and disease to the small group. The troops left, but now the Pygmies face the problems of HIV, malnutrition, and untreated malaria. In recent years, nongovernmental organizations helped with health education and security for the small group so they wouldn't disappear. A larger subset of Pygmies, the Batwa, live near the Bwindi Impenetrable National Park to the southwest.

The sadness of that day reminded me of old highways in the American Southwest. In the 1980s, when I had driven from Los Angeles to Santa Fe, I saw signs saying, "See Real Live Indians Next Exit!" I drove that highway with an African friend of mine from Senegal. When we passed several of those signs, he became quiet and sad. He said they reminded him of how Europeans had treated Africans in the days of colonialism when he was young.

The bike ride from Fort Portal to Kasese showed us the most magnificent scenery at that point of our trip—verdant and undulating. That luscious vegetation required water, though. A downpour forced us to pull over and wait about ten miles from town. It rained for fifteen to twenty minutes, once or twice a day, during the short rainy season. The cloudbursts came on without notice, and the sheets of driving rain cut off visibility. We couldn't walk or ride a bicycle, so we sought shelter.

A lovely camaraderie existed in Uganda when it rained. An unwritten rule extended hospitality to all who passed by when the showers hit. When the sky opened up, people welcomed us onto porches, under awnings, in front of houses, or in the doorways of establishments. We stood and waited quietly under the shelter for twenty minutes to half an hour. A few times about ten of us huddled together on a stranger's porch. Even trucks and cars (not many drove on the roads) stopped for those short, fierce downpours. We stared out into the gray sheets of rain and watched the water run down the side of the road in muddy rivulets. We shared a brief bond in those moments, a fellowship of humans thrown into a difficult situation together. We drifted into a reverie, a quiet meditation amplified by the sound of the rainfall. When the showers eased up, we all moved on with a polite "Thank you" and "Goodbye."

Uganda possesses spectacular natural beauty. Fertile, red earth abounds. Every day we delighted in the lush, green hills we rode through. The daily rainfall was a small price to pay to bicycle through such gorgeous nature.

We left Kasese late, around noon, thinking we would bike only the twenty-five miles to Queen Elizabeth National Park that day. We were in Uganda's Rift Valley, and we passed herds of antelope grazing in the lush fields. But after twenty-five miles, at the turnoff for the park, we saw that we had another fifteen miles ahead of us on a rough dirt road. We waffled for several minutes, then decided to skip the park and the thirty-mile detour it would cause and push on to Kabale. This area was near Zaire (what is now the Democratic Republic of the Congo). We stopped for lunch at a small roadside café, where truck drivers gathered.

CARLA FOUNTAIN

We struck up a conversation with John, one of the drivers, while we ate together.

John sipped a cup of hot milk tea. "We are waiting here to cross the border to Zaire, but we need to get a large convoy together for safety."

"Why is that, John?" Dermot asked.

"Across the border, bandits often force trucks off the road and rob them of their goods."

My eyes grew wide. "Oh, my!"

"The road conditions are very bad—muddy roads full of potholes."

"We thought about going to Zaire, but we didn't get visas," Dermot said.

John shook his head. "You would be wise not to go. It wouldn't be safe for you on your bicycles."

We pushed on past Lake George and Lake Edward, climbing slowly out of the Rift Valley. It grew late with no hotels in sight. We asked people on the road where we could find a place to stay, and they directed us to Father Michael's parish in the next town. We climbed on through the vibrant hills for about two more miles and approached a church and a house overlooking the hills and the Rift Valley. In the valley, we saw deep craters filled with lush banana trees and blue lakes. White clouds dotted the azure sky. The sight was refreshing, gorgeous, and pure—a hidden Shangri-la.

We knocked on the door of the parish and met Father Michael, an affable and gracious man in his thirties. He greeted us with a smile.

"How may I help you?" he asked.

"Hello. My name is Dermot. This is my wife, Carla."

BICYCLE ODYSSEY

"Hello."

"We are sorry to bother you," I said. "But we are bicycling, and we won't be able to make it to the next town before dark. Would it be possible to camp at your parish?"

"We have a tent," Dermot added.

"Of course! But please, I invite you to stay in my guest cottage." Father Michael pointed to a nearby structure.

He walked us over to the cottage and opened the door. "Make yourself at home," he said.

Dermot and I chatted for a while as we watched the sun set over the view of the hills and the Rift Valley before we washed up and changed. Since we weren't sure whether we were going to be invited to dinner, we stalled for time and ate peanut butter and crackers as an appetizer. Shortly after seven o'clock, we gave up hope and fired up our camp stove to boil water. We decided to make soup with the packets in our emergency rations stash. As the water came to a boil, Father Michael knocked on our door.

"Aren't you coming for dinner?" he asked.

We happily accepted and walked over for a meal of chicken with *matoke* served in a banana leaf bowl with a delicious groundnut (peanut) sauce on the side.

Dermot helped himself to more *matoke*. "We've heard a lot about the AIDS crisis in Uganda."

Father Michael frowned. "It is extremely bad. Every week, I bury someone in my parish. It saddens me to see the number of children who have lost their parents."

The conversation was sobering.

83

In the morning, Father Michael invited us for breakfast. When we left, we gave him a donation for the parish. His generosity and hospitality touched us and helped us in a time of need.

We bicycled hills for nearly twenty-five miles to an intersection with a dirt road at Ishaka. The unpaved path offered a scenic route to Ntungamo. We decided to have lunch and stay the night in Ishaka to be fresh for our off-road experience.

Traveling the dirt road to Ntungamo was splendid right from the beginning. The peaceful road held vistas of densely forested, green hills and valleys offset by deep, blue skies and white clouds. Heavenly.

About ten miles from our destination, our journey turned sour. We passed a group of adolescent boys leaving school and exchanged the usual rounds of "Hello! How are you?" They ran after us and alongside us. More boys joined the group. Unseen hands pushed me uphill, which was okay at first. But too many boys joined in to push my bike, and I almost lost my balance. I yelled for them to stop, and they did. The long dirt road uphill slowed us down, so the pack of boys kept pace with us. One of them pushed me more forcefully, and I nearly crashed into Derm.

I lost my temper. I stopped and yelled at the boys tearfully. "If you push like that, I might fall, and then I will get very angry. Please stay back."

They looked horror struck by my outburst. I started riding again. Derm pedaled fast and was several meters ahead of me.

The boys continued to run after us, mocking me and repeating what I had said. "I asked you to stay back! Stay back!"

BICYCLE ODYSSEY

Panicked, I yelled, "Derm, wait up!" When the road turned downhill, I pedaled hard, and we lost them. I sighed with relief, but my limbs trembled, and my eyes filled with tears.

With frayed nerves, we continued to bike under a passing rain shower. We arrived in Ntungamo covered in mud as the rain stopped. I may have been hypersensitive, but self-consciousness seized me as everyone stared at us and murmured, "*Wazungu, wazungu, wazungu*" (the plural of *mzungu* for "White people"). After that scary experience with the boys, my stomach cramped with acid from tension.

The first two hotels we found were dilapidated, so we continued our search and found a lodge on the other side of town. They gave us a tidy room with a single bed, clean sheets, and a kerosene lamp for less than two dollars. The management didn't speak English, but we found our way to a private cubicle in a corner of the courtyard, where we helped each other take bucket baths. Our "Bicycling Africa" pamphlet had prepared us for a situation like this. We scooped water from a bucket with a cup, poured it over our bodies, soaped up, and rinsed off from head to toe. A bucket bath was an efficient and surprisingly satisfying way to wash, and the method helped to conserve water. We enjoyed our first open-air bathing experience. We continued to use this system on many occasions throughout the rest of Uganda and in India and Thailand.

We rested while I tried to calm my nervous stomach. After several hours, we had recuperated enough to go out for food. Fortunately, we sat at a table with two affable, local men who engaged us in lively conversation for the next hour. Exchanging friendly words with them helped wash away the bad taste of the afternoon. The day had been one of extremes—from the heavenly vistas to a mob of rowdy boys, finally to end with a nice dinner, new acquaintances, and pleasant conversation. We learned a few things during dinner: Minimum wage was about forty cents a day. Teachers made about ten dollars a month. A condom cost five cents (about one-eighth of a day's pay). Even with the threat of AIDS, many people didn't use condoms because they weren't affordable.

CARLA FOUNTAIN

We set out for the long ride to Kabale. Heavy rain gave us a well-needed break in between two mountain passes. We waited out the rain for over an hour at a house where the owners invited us to sit out the downpour. A crowd of kids, a few young adults, and another local cyclist waited under the awnings. Derm fixed his flat tire while I wrote in my journal.

> October 26, 1991
> I am enjoying traveling in Uganda so much. Even in the rain! The first words out of people's mouths here are "Welcome!" When we walk into a shop or a house, they say, "You are welcome!" with such sincerity that it warms my heart. I am so thankful we listened to the English woman in Kenya and continued bicycling west through Uganda.

When the showers lightened, we set off down the road for food. The establishment offered one choice: *matoke* with beef stew. We ate the *matoke* and a small serving of gravy from the stew. I avoided the red meat. We washed the meal down with hot milk tea, enjoying the warmth.

All proceeded well for the next two miles until we spied a huge crowd of adolescents leaving school. Derm sized up the situation. "Why don't you move over to my right. The children are swarming on the left side of the road and into the middle. I'll block them."

"Thanks. It was no fun getting jostled and pushed yesterday. And you zoomed off ahead! I got panicky. What if I had fallen?" I shot him an accusing look.

Dermot's face softened. "I'm sorry. I didn't realize you had gotten so far behind. But I'm here beside you now." He increased his speed. "Let's go! Try and keep up."

We ended up cycling on the right side of the road. An oncoming cyclist rang his bell and screamed at us to get over. We nearly collided

BICYCLE ODYSSEY

head-on with him! (Ugandans and Kenyans drive on the left, a remnant from the British colonial days.) The pavement made it easy to sprint past, so the teenagers didn't bother us too much. I escaped with only a slap on the bottom from a girl who extended her hand.

"Give me help! Give me money! Give me my money!" she called out to us.

As usual on this journey, an uplifting encounter followed any negative experience. Five miles later, the faint sound of band music came from a school up ahead. We wondered about the music when an older man with a huge smile waved at us from across the street.

"Stop and rest so I can greet you and wish you well," he called to us.

He shook our hands and beamed. "I am the schoolmaster here. Welcome to Uganda and to my lovely district. I wish you well and a safe journey."

He was an angel sent to us to boost our spirits and keep us from giving up.

A woman in colorful dress came up to me, grabbed my hand, and swung me into a dance. "Come dance and celebrate with us!" She grinned as we danced on the side of the road.

Others joined in, and a few people clapped. We moved in a happy rhythm. I became caught up in the joyous energy of the crowd.

Children played on the street and smiled at us with friendly interest. Ugandan children made ingenious toys for themselves out of necessity. They fabricated toy trucks, cars, and even ride-worthy one-speed bicycles. They engineered many of the toys with movable parts. One boy had crafted a large, toy helicopter, which he pulled along with a stick, making the propellers spin. He decorated it by writing "Uganda Red Cross" on the side.

We pedaled on, feeling better. Encounters like the one with the schoolmaster and the children in his village brightened our days. Riding into Kabale after the last hill, I let out a whoop of joy as we zoomed down into town.

In the morning, a chilly fog blanketed Kabale, the highest town in Uganda, so we decided to stay there for a day. When the mists cleared, we cycled out to see Lake Bunyoni. The weather turned sunny and hot as we cycled one mile to the turnoff and then three miles on a dirt road up the steep mountain. On our way up, we met a local man walking home from work. Sam lived by the lake and worked in town. He walked four hours each way. Sam left his home at six o'clock in the morning and arrived to work at ten o'clock. He left work at two o'clock in the afternoon and arrived home at six.

He waited for us when Dermot stopped and leaned on his bicycle. Sam expressed concern when he saw Derm bent over, trembling. We walked with him to the top of the steep hill overlooking the lake and gazed at the rich, terraced farmland stretching all around us. A few animals grazed in the fields. Women in *kangas* hoed crops of potatoes and beans. No one else was traveling on the road but the three of us.

I shaded my eyes against the sun. "I see a roadside stand up ahead. Let's stop for a soda. That will help settle your stomach, Derm."

Dermot's face brightened. "That's a good idea. Sam, please have a soda with us. It's our treat."

"Sam, tell us about your village and family," I said.

Sam took a sip of soda. "I have a wife and two sons. I wouldn't mind marrying another wife." He turned to look at Dermot. "How many wives do you have?"

BICYCLE ODYSSEY

"Just one."

"I've heard that Americans only have one wife. I'm surprised that they are content with just one," Sam said.

Dermot nodded while I stifled a chuckle.

"I was born in this area, and all my family lives here. I have several acres of land and grow potatoes, beans, corn, and sweet potatoes. I also raise goats, chickens, and cows."

"You are a busy man!" I said.

"Would you like to come home with me and meet my family? You would be most welcome."

His home was still a two-hour walk, and we would have had to spend the night there since it would be dark by then, so we declined. We managed to catch a ride back to our hotel in Kabale with an off-duty taxi, and we whizzed down the mountain. We must have climbed over two thousand feet that day. We traveled down so fast with the taxi that I noticed the effects of altitude sickness afterward.

That night we dined at the Highland Hotel. As we waited for our meal, a soft *boom, boom, boom* like thunder resonated in the distance. I turned to a young staff member, who was bringing our dishes of *matoke* and groundnut sauce. "Is another storm coming?"

He placed the steaming plates of food in front of us. "No, that is from the military at the border with Rwanda. We are not far away. They often have border skirmishes."

Feeling ready for a night of rest after our meal, we biked back in the dark to our hotel, which charged three dollars for a double room. Kabale had almost no electricity at that time, and the Skyblue Hotel was lit with candles and kerosene lamps. The ambiance relaxed our mood, but we couldn't charge our batteries for the video camera. The

89

CARLA FOUNTAIN

Skyblue was clean and pleasant—a high-caliber, budget hotel. The staff members were young, enthusiastic, and helpful. They gave us a bucket of hot water to take to the bathroom. We stood in the concrete cubicle in our flip-flops and took our bucket baths by candlelight. Washing with hot water soothed us to our core. For the past five weeks, we had bathed with water that was either room temperature or cold.

The other foreigners we ran into in Kabale used the town only as a way station on their safari to Zaire to see the gorillas. They paid for a visa and visited the gorillas over the border with a tour group. A gorilla encounter intrigued us, but we didn't want to go on another group tour, and the high fee was out of our budget. We also hadn't procured our visas for Zaire earlier because of the unstable political situation at the time. Officials in Zaire were contemplating imposing martial law. American, British, French, and Belgian citizens had been advised to leave the country. The travelers we met who had journeyed to encounter the gorillas said they hadn't experienced any problems. Most of the political upheaval was in the capital, Kinshasa, which was hundreds of miles away.

Instead, we set off on our own exploratory bike ride to the Bwindi Impenetrable Forest without gear, taking only a few snacks and our cameras. We took Kisoro road, which everyone warned us was twenty-five miles uphill. They told us we would have to push our bikes and that we would never make it. We cycled over rolling hills and through valleys with terraced farms. There was one long, steep summit but nothing drastic. Often other people's perceptions of the road ahead were very different from what we encountered.

We met up with other cyclists—local men on one-speed bikes—who marveled at our ability to cycle in low gear up the hill while they needed to walk their bikes. Many of them transported loads of bananas or household goods for sale. We chatted and biked with them for a mile. One of the men had also left from Kabale and was going to the Echuya Forest, a vast expanse of bamboo near Kisoro. We were uncertain which forest to explore. The cyclists directed us to the ranger station ahead, and we stopped there to ask for advice.

The Ugandan ranger in charge greeted us. "Welcome!"

Derm wiped his brow. "Hello! Thank you. We are trying to decide whether to go to the Echuya Forest or the Impenetrable Forest. What do you suggest?"

The ranger's face lit up. "Both forests are interesting, but the Bwindi Impenetrable Forest has more plant and animal species. There are gorillas, mountain elephants, and over four hundred species of plants." He gestured toward a poorly maintained, dirt road. "It's only five miles that way."

"Gorillas!" I said.

"Yes. Right now, we are working to condition them to humans. In a few years, supervised groups will be able to visit them."

His information tipped our decision toward the Bwindi Impenetrable Forest. Our extra efforts to reach the forest boundary were well rewarded.

No other humans walked through the dense forest that day. Bushes and trees grew so thickly alongside our road that we couldn't even see signs of a path leading into the forest. We walked about two miles on the dirt road to better savor the sounds, smells, and sights of nature. Insects buzzed around us in the heavy, humid air. Vines draped across the trees and into the thick undergrowth. The forest stretched farther than we could see, going over the mountains and on into Zaire and Rwanda. We walked quietly, hoping to catch a glimpse of wildlife.

A deep-throated sound resonated from the trees. I stopped and grabbed Dermot's arm. "Shhh. Did you hear that?"

CARLA FOUNTAIN

Dermot peered into the thick forest beside us. "Was that a gorilla?" His voice was hushed.

"Either a gorilla or another large animal." I shivered with fear and excitement.

I took a step forward, but Dermot pulled me back to him. "Let's listen for a moment longer," he said.

We never saw the source of the sound, so we couldn't say for sure, but we like to think we heard a great ape.

Gathering clouds formed a thick, gray wall above us. The wind blew, swirling leaves in the air. A flash of lightning lit up the darkening sky.

I paused. "Wait, Derm. Let's count the seconds before we hear thunder and calculate how far away the storm is."

"One, two, three, four, five—"

BOOM!

"It's five miles away," I said.

"Let's continue a few minutes more. I want to see if we can find out what animal made that noise," Derm said.

The first drops of rain fell—time to turn around. We put on our rain gear, covered the camera equipment, and headed back for Kabale at four o'clock. Although the rain didn't pour down in torrents, it did rain enough to turn the rough dirt road into a quagmire. Red mud covered our bikes and our bodies. Our tires locked up with the thick coating of earth. We skidded and slipped the last half hour to the graded road. The worst of the storm was over, and we continued on in semidarkness. Since we reached the town after nightfall, we were fortunate not to encounter any traffic. We nearly missed hitting several cows and goats that crossed the road in front of us, hidden in the darkness.

Back at the hotel, we rinsed off our bikes with pitchers of water. There was no running water that night, so we did the best we could. We luxuriated in our hot bucket baths. A warm meal of spaghetti with tomato sauce finished off a wonderful day. Dermot had received a bottle of vodka as a gift the day before, so we drank shots with cola after dinner. We reflected on our day's ride and decided it had been one of our best riding experiences in Uganda. The terrain had been splendid from Fort Portal to Kasese with rolling hills, green fertile valleys, and terraced fields. We wished we could have stayed in the forest and explored deeper in. We could have gone onto the next ranger station four miles farther up the road. We would have liked to see the Echuya Forest as well. I decided that I wanted to return one day and spend more time in the area.

In spite of the wonderful day we experienced, we slept poorly that night. We didn't have an alarm clock and needed to rise early, so I woke throughout the night to check the time. At five o'clock, I slid out of bed to go to the toilet and accidentally slammed the door shut. The noise woke the resident rooster, who started crowing every five minutes after that. We had hoped he would wake us at dawn so we could catch the six o'clock bus, but instead we rose before the sun (and the rooster!). We straggled out to the bus, bleary eyed and unwashed after a final effort at hosing more mud off our bikes, since the water was on again. There wasn't much water pressure, though, so the brakes and chains remained caked with mud.

Dermot supervised the hoisting of the bikes up to the bus's top rack while I dealt with the rest of the luggage and found seats. We settled in for the six-hour ride to Kampala, which turned into eight hours. For breakfast at the next two stops, we bought soda, warm *mandazi*, bananas, oranges, and *chapatis* (Indian flatbread) from various vendors. We devoured tasty samosas filled with rice and peas later for lunch. A variety of food vendors always occupied the bus stop areas.

CARLA FOUNTAIN

We arrived in Kampala late and took a *matatu* (minibus) to Tororo to make up for lost time. After removing the wheels, we stuffed the bikes into the back of the *matatu*. We paid twenty dollars for the three extra seats the bikes took up as well as our two seats.

The staff at the Rock Classic Hotel in Tororo remembered us from before and welcomed us back warmly when we checked in. We headed to our room, bathed, and ate a gourmet meal of Chicken Maryland— battered chicken fried with banana and pineapple. The hotel was the best one in the area. The staff told us that even President Museveni had stayed there. Everyone wished us well as we left the next morning.

With an early start to our advantage, we rode to Malaba near the Kenyan border. Even though the bus rides, the teenagers, and the shouts of *wazungu* had frazzled me, sadness filled me as we prepared to leave Uganda. Before we crossed the border, we stopped at the bank in Malaba and ran into people we had met at the sugar factory. We appreciated seeing them before our departure. I chatted with the bank guards, while Derm changed our remaining Ugandan shillings back into US dollars.

A detailed and drawn-out customs and immigration process at the border with Uganda and Kenya took two hours. But our stop there proceeded without a hitch, and everyone was cordial. We struck up a friendly conversation with a Ugandan man who was also waiting to cross the border. He drove a truck and transported fish from Jinja to Mombasa for shipment to Switzerland. He asked us about our country. Dermot and I shared our pictures of home with him. He showed us a picture of his wife and family; his wife was of Indian origin. They had met in Somalia and had two children. They were the first interracial couple we had met in Uganda and it was refreshing to see.

On the overnight train to Nairobi, we enjoyed a first-class sleeping car and access to the dining car for dinner. The uniformed staff served our meal on starched linen. The porters reminded me of the Pullman porters from long ago in the United States with their sharp uniforms

BICYCLE ODYSSEY

and polite manners. At our destination, we gasped when we saw that our bikes had been packed with furniture piled on top of them and sticking through the spokes. Thankfully, they survived the train ride unscathed.

In Nairobi, we picked up our mail from the American Express office and verified our plane tickets for India. For variety in cuisine, we treated ourselves to lunch at a Japanese restaurant. As much as we loved out-of-the-way villages in the countryside, we enjoyed having more choices in food and being able to take care of necessary business in the city.

We also managed to connect with a local documentary filmmaker at his office. He told us about his work in East Africa and said we had been wise to avoid the capital because of the demonstrations. A few years earlier, he had lost his hand from an explosion while on assignment in a conflict area. We looked on, wide eyed, as he showed us how his prosthetic worked and enabled him to operate a camera. My stomach flipped over when I thought of how our lives can turn in an instant. Hours later, we dashed off to catch the five o'clock train to Mombasa.

8

The Swahili Coast

Mombasa, once a slave port, displayed strong Indian and Arabic influences. The city—steamy, hot, and laid back—intrigued us with its mix of cultures. The Swahili coast was mostly Muslim, and the city boasted at least fifty mosques. Many women wore a head covering with a long tunic over their other garments. A few even wore a full veil covering their faces. I noticed intricate *mehendi* (henna) patterns on women's hands. I loved the clothing styles on the coast. In addition to Western apparel, men also wore a *kikoi* (a woven cloth wrapped around their waists, which reached to the ground) and a colorful top. They often wore a plain white or intricately hand-embroidered *kofia* (cap). People migrated to Mombasa from Saudi Arabia, Yemen, India, Pakistan, and Persia; and the various cultures were evident. The mix of people varied more than we saw anywhere else in Kenya or Uganda. I also saw many people who looked like me. We found an assortment of shops with a multitude of spices, fabrics, and foods. The different tastes delighted us. We enjoyed Indian, Swahili, and Arabic foods. We ate biryani (a spicy Indian rice dish with nuts, chicken, and dried fruit), samosas, and curries. For dessert, we drank chai and ate *halwa* (a sweet concoction made with tapioca starch, ghee, nutmeg, cardamom, toasted nuts, and rose water).

The colorful textiles in the shops caught our eyes. We spent an hour in a fabric shop, where I ordered a loose blouse, plus culottes in a colorful tie-dye fabric, to be sewn up for the next day. It would be a modest way to stay cool as I bicycled. I also had a tie-dye caftan made for after-cycling wear. Derm bought a traditional family tree sculpture carved in black wood, which we planned to send home to my parents for Christmas.

Dermot and I avidly read the packet of mail we had retrieved from the Nairobi American Express office the day before. Intuitively, I saved my parents' letters for last, fearing bad news. I tensed up as I read. We had arranged for a management company to collect the rent from our tenants and send it on to pay our mortgage. My stomach tightened with anxiety when I found out this transaction hadn't happened; our house was going into default after three months of nonpayment. I planned to call my parents the next day to see what had happened and to find a lawyer so I could give my father power of attorney.

We also discovered that our uncle, who was supposed to collect our mail and help take care of our affairs, hadn't done so. Dermot feared he was very depressed. My parents found out about the default on the mortgage only by chance. I felt helpless being so far away and knowing that our affairs were in danger because a task as simple as forwarding the mail hadn't happened. If I gave my father power of attorney, he could arrange for our mail to be sent to his house. He could save our bills and deal with any bank accounts if needed. Even though we'd made arrangements beforehand, our affairs had become tangled and complicated. The next day, I called my parents to tell them about our plan, and Dermot and I found a lawyer in the business district to draw up a power of attorney.

Back at the hotel, we unloaded our bags to make a lighter load for the rest of the trip. We filled a large box to send home with clothes, batiks, books, and a present for my parents. We left several of our personal items for the hotel workers as gifts. Other cyclists had told us it would be too difficult to camp in India and the rest of Asia, so we sent back our tent and sleeping bags. It would be more private, easier, and inexpensive to get a hotel room when we stopped for the night.

The day was a whirlwind of activity. My emotions rode a roller coaster. After dinner, I sighed and sank onto a chair in the hotel room to write.

> October 29, 1991
> As we prepare to move on, different emotions rush through me. I'm excited to explore new areas: the Swahili coast and, soon, India. At the same time, I'm filled with unease and worry about our affairs back home. I hope my parents will be able to help straighten things out.

I loved the Swahili coast. I could have stayed there for months, and I wanted to learn Swahili. The population on the Swahili coast was much more mixed. People didn't look at the color of our skin to make a snap judgment about whether we were African. I noticed that no one shouted out, "*Mzungu*." I looked forward to seeing what the rest of the coast had in store for us as we ventured north.

We biked from Kilifi to Watamu along a flat road, but we left late, as often happened, and the day became quite hot. When the heat and fatigue hit us, we came upon a coconut stand and replenished ourselves with fresh coconut juice. The vendor cut the top off a green coconut and gave us a straw to drink the juice. After we finished drinking, he cut the nut in half. We took the small piece he had cut from the first opening to use as a scoop for the tender pulp. For the rest of the trip, we continued to travel in climates that grew coconuts, and we drank and ate them two or three times a day. I'm sure that drinking and eating coconuts so often kept us healthy and balanced our electrolytes on the trip.

BICYCLE ODYSSEY

The Gedi Ruins—a fascinating maze of crumbled mosque walls, mossy stones, and centuries-old dwellings overtaken by the jungle—gave us a small glimpse into the past. At every turn, we found yet another image we wanted to capture with our cameras. As we wandered alone around the quiet ruins, we encountered a family of monkeys. A female monkey, breastfeeding her baby, sat placidly in a tree near us while we watched. When a larger monkey bounded through, they all scampered away. I tried to imagine what it would have been like to live there when Gedi was at its peak and bustled with people. Dermot and I strolled separately through remnants of houses and arched entrances of mosques. Before we left, we sat for a while in silence, each of us lost in our own reveries.

People told us that the coral reefs at Watamu Marine National Park offered the best snorkeling on the coast. We decided to take a boat to the reef to see for ourselves. At the high-end Ocean Sports Hotel, we booked a snorkeling trip or "goggling trip," as they called it. The sea teemed with colorful fish. In spite of having a few issues with my mask and swallowing water because I wasn't used to swimming for such a long time, the colors and sizes of the fish dazzled me. My eyes danced with the turquoise, vivid lime green, bright orange, and various neon colors that swam around me. Afterward, we enjoyed proper tea and scones with delicious crab sandwiches. The hotel was a British resort, filled mostly with British tourists. We stayed at a reasonably priced hotel down the road, but for us it held four-star quality. The ambiance and decoration were excellent for the same price as many of the more run-down, budget hotels.

In the evening, a group of young Maasai warriors stood around town in all their finery, adorned with beadwork. Rumor had it that they hung out to have their pictures taken and to pick up on European women tourists. Or it could have been the other way around.

We headed north when we left town the next day and met another touring cyclist who was traveling south. The breezy, cheerful woman rode up to us, and we stopped to talk.

CARLA FOUNTAIN

I took off my helmet, giving my head a chance to cool down. "Hello! We heard about a woman cycling around Kenya on her own when we were in a village farther back. They said she was from Belgium. That must be you."

The petite woman smiled. "Yes! I'm Marie. I started the first part of my trip alone. Now I've met up with a woman from Arizona, and we're traveling together down the coast. Sandy is behind me. I plan to bicycle down to South Africa."

I envied her. Marie had ventured out alone with such confidence. "How has your journey been so far?" I asked.

Marie took a drink of water and pushed back her hair. "My trip has been great! People in Uganda and Kenya have been welcoming."

"Yes, our trip in East Africa has also been wonderful. We plan to spend the night in Malindi and fly to Lamu tomorrow."

"You will love Lamu!" Marie checked her watch. "I need to get going. I want to arrive in Watamu before noon. Have a good journey!" She waved goodbye and glided off down the road.

Five minutes later, a tall and muscular American woman joined us.

"You must be Sandy! We met Marie a few minutes ago. It's so good to meet other bicyclists touring Africa," I said.

Sandy slumped over her handlebars and wiped the sweat from her brow. "I met Marie last week on the road. We decided to team up to cycle to Tanzania."

"How long have you been bicycling in Kenya?"

She took a long swallow of water and poured a splash on her neck. "I've been on the road for six months. I had planned to be away for a year and a half, but now I'm ready to fly back home."

BICYCLE ODYSSEY

Dermot offered her a handful of simsim. "Why is that? What's wrong?"

"Thank you. This heat saps my energy." She ate two of the candies. "The worst part is the loneliness. I had started cycling alone. I'm finding it difficult to meet people here in Kenya. I wish I had a partner to do the trip with. I am so glad I met Marie. I don't think I will go all the way to South Africa with her, though."

Those were gutsy women. As we departed ways, I reflected on whether I would have done this bicycling trip in Africa alone. Although I had already taken solo cycling trips in the United States and knew I could cycle through Canada and Europe by myself, I might have been too intimidated to complete the rest of this world trip on my own.

9

Lamu Island—Our Dark Night of the Soul

Lamu Island lies off the northeast coast of Kenya near the southern border of Somalia. Buses on the coastal road from Malindi to Lamu suffered frequent attacks by armed Somali bandits. It wouldn't have been safe to bicycle. From Malindi, we took a short flight in a six-seater plane to get near the island and then took a ferry the rest of the way. We planned on staying for almost two weeks to rest and discover this corner of Kenya. Lamu exuded a warm and gentle vibe. Lamu Old Town twisted in a maze of narrow streets, where donkeys wandered among the people. Most men wore a *kikoi*. The women wore a long piece of black cloth as a shawl and head covering. Because of Lamu's history of trade with Arabia, the town's population included a wide mix of people in a rainbow of hues from light to dark. I blended in well there—so much so that when I greeted people, they answered back in Swahili.

We stayed at an attractive, well-maintained hotel called Tini in Lamu Old Town. Elaborate mosaic tiles covered the floors, and lovely arches graced the windows and balconies. The hotel had a completely different aesthetic from those we had stayed in before in Kenya. Our room provided two double beds, a ceiling fan, and mosquito nets that hung above the beds from a circle. The nets spread out and draped over

BICYCLE ODYSSEY

the sides of the beds. It looked romantic. We had the penthouse suite, with windows on three walls for a refreshing cross breeze. From our huge terrace, we could look out over the town and see the harbor. We sat out there at night and gazed at the constellations shining brilliantly in the dark sky. Our first night there, we saw a shooting star with a burning tail—the largest and brightest I'd ever seen.

Lamu bustled with woodworkers. Many buildings had massive, magnificently carved wooden doors. We never tired of admiring the different entrances and architectural designs as we walked around town. The narrow, sandy lanes weren't conducive to bike riding, so we explored the town on foot. Walking or riding a donkey was the only way to get around the island. No one used cars.

At that time, Lamu was 90 percent Muslim and had twenty-six mosques for a population of about fifteen thousand. At four o'clock every morning, the *adhan* (call to prayer) woke us over a loudspeaker. We grew accustomed to the rhythm of this, except for one morning when the *muezzin* called out slightly off-key, which jarred us awake. As we walked through town in the evenings, men filled the mosques and performed their prayer rituals. Women prayed at home.

Besides carrying people and loads, many donkeys wandered through town on their own. After visiting Lamu on a vacation, Dr. Elisabeth Svendsen of The Donkey Sanctuary in England founded another sanctuary in Lamu in 1987 to care for sick and wounded donkeys. The organization started a regular deworming program for donkeys on the island.

I met a local girl in town, Fatima, who offered to henna my hands with a pattern and to braid my hair. I needed my hair braided again, but I didn't want to sit for a long time, so I asked her for a simple cornrow style, which was quick to execute. We sat at her house in the courtyard, while her mother prepared the family meal. Her mother grated coconut using a contraption with a large blade that stuck straight up. Holding half the coconut by the shell, she quickly and easily grated the coconut

103

meat out. Fatima mixed henna with water and lemon juice to make her *mehendi* paste. She drew an intricate design on my palms and a scroll of leaves on both sides of my feet. I sat in the sun to let the paste set for an hour while we talked.

Derm and I became restless in Lamu during the first few days. Our legs twitched from not bicycling. We found it difficult to be in one place for so long. With our usual routine, we moved and used our muscles every day or at least every other day. We wondered whether we really wanted to stay on the island for two weeks. Eventually we relaxed and sank into a slower rhythm. We forced ourselves to greet the day early so we could enjoy Lamu before the noon heat descended. We sipped strong coffee and ate little sautéed potato pieces at Café Jambo. Then, video and still cameras in hand, we walked around town. We explored Lamu's twisting, narrow streets and alleys. I loved the intriguing mystery of shadowed streets and stone houses with black-veiled and robed women strolling by. Men, dressed in *kikoi* and *kofia*, lounged in doorsteps. The lilting sounds of Swahili music floated in the air. I inhaled the rich smell of spices wafting out from a shop door and the scent of burning sandalwood from another. Antique brass urns glinted in rays of sun. Donkeys ambled in a line, carrying loads through town. Without cars the air was peaceful, clean, and quiet. Back at the harbor, *dhows* (sailing vessels common on the East African, Arabic, and Indian coasts with long, narrow sails on one or two masts) glided by silently.

We tried to visit a school, but the district educational officer said that would be impossible without official permission from the Ministry of Education in Nairobi. Perplexed, we left the office. We had visited several schools in Kenya and Uganda, and the teachers and headmasters had been delighted to have us.

For consolation we drowned our disappointment in two fruit smoothies at our favorite café. As luck would have it, Derm met a

BICYCLE ODYSSEY

fisherman eager to be interviewed on camera, and we asked him several questions. Ali, a short and plump, good-natured man with a wide smile, made us feel better as we talked to him.

"You can call me 'Ali Hippie.' Everyone in town knows me by that name. I have that nickname because when I was younger and worked as a waiter, I liked to talk to travelers who came to Lamu. I played music with them."

"Ali, what makes you happy?" Dermot asked.

"I love my life. Music and friends make me happy. If I see people and talk with them, it makes me happy. I love living here on Lamu Island. It's a small place without many problems. Lamu is a piece of heaven."

"What makes you sad?"

"If I don't have people over to my house, I feel sad."

"Ali, if you could change the world, what would you do?"

"I don't want to change anything. I would like things to be just like this. My father told me, 'You've got to be satisfied with one shilling because if you have a million, you won't be satisfied.' The world is perfect the way it is."

Later in the week, Ali Hippie invited us to his house for a typical Lamu meal. He invited a few other travelers as well, and we ate with his family in the dining room Lamu style—on the floor in a circle. After dinner, he played the harmonium, his son beat out a rhythm on a drum, and his daughter played another percussion instrument while he and his family sang for us. They sang the Kenyan classic and encouraged us to sing along with them: *"Jambo! Jambo Bwana!"* (Hello! Hello, Sir!). The lively song always ended with everyone joining in at the end with *"Hakuna Matata!"* (No problems!).

We ate an abundance of delicious, fresh food in Lamu. Every morning as we strolled the dock on the way to the beach, we saw the fishermen bringing in the catch. In the afternoon at lunch, we savored fresh fish cooked in various sauces: coconut, curry, and tamarind (a sweet and tart tropical fruit). We also dined on crab sandwiches, pancakes, and simsim candy. Every meal was a feast topped off with pineapple, tamarind, or coconut juice. We stocked up on nutrients and replenished after our long, intense journey. In the morning, we swam in the water at the beach—a half hour's walk from town—and made our way back to wash and rest during the hottest part of the day. One morning when we came back from the beach late, Ali Hippie chided us for walking around in the sun in the intense heat. He worried that we would become ill. A few times we took a small water taxi out to the beach. The captain used a *dhow*. The sloped, triangular sail glided us along, and we caught a refreshing breeze.

Another day we rode donkeys to the other end of Lamu Island to the village of Matondoni. After a few minutes, I hopped off my donkey. "This donkey's back is not comfortable. I'm going to walk the rest of the way."

"Me, too. I'm sure they'll appreciate it," Derm said.

We inhaled the scent of freshly cut wood as we passed boatbuilders, who made wooden *dhows* by hand in that village. The rhythmic sounds of their tools as they sawed, hammered, and planed the planks echoed in the air.

Many travelers took *dhow* trips to nearby islands. We thought about embarking on a three-day sailing trip but decided against it. We were enjoying our time on Lamu.

BICYCLE ODYSSEY

One morning, near the end of our stay, we ran into Ali Hippie as we walked around.

Ali Hippie looked at us with sad eyes. "I am so sorry, my friends. I have terrible news. One of yours has died."

"What happened, Ali Hippie?" I asked.

"A young, American woman, only twenty-five years old, went on a three-day *dhow* trip. She had stopped taking her malaria pills for about four days because she didn't like the side effects. She became ill with cerebral malaria."

"Oh no," I said. I glanced over at Dermot; his face looked pale.

"When malaria goes to the brain, it can kill you very quickly. She died this morning in convulsions before the doctor could reach her." Ali's voice broke.

The news stunned and saddened us. We didn't know her, but we grieved for her.

Sad news and death filled the air. A man from Lamu, a twenty-five-year-old, died of AIDS that day as well. And as we walked to the beach the next day, we saw two policemen carrying a body bag on a stretcher. A man had stabbed his son to death. We grieved for them all. We felt vulnerable, and especially far from home.

Two weeks to relax in Lamu without the pressures of dealing with life on the road gave us many opportunities for reflection. I found myself wondering about how our lives would be when we returned to the States. What direction did I want my life and career to take? My head swam with stories, doubts, desires, and worries about the future.

One evening near the end of our stay, we sat talking in our room. "This time on Lamu has been so wonderful up until now." I sighed.

CARLA FOUNTAIN

Dermot sat slumped on the bed. "It shook me up to hear about the American woman who died. That could so easily happen to me. I'll always have this damn parasite in my liver just waiting to come out if I get rundown."

"I've been wondering if we should go home now. Just cut the trip short. But we've done so much to get here."

"I worry about our house. But I think your dad will be able to sort things out. We should have just had him take care of things in the first place instead of our uncle." His hazel eyes met mine.

"That's frustrating. When we do go home, I want to take some time for myself. I've been thinking about exploring a different career and ..." I hesitated and broke from his gaze, stalling for time.

"What? What is it?"

"I don't know ... Sometimes I feel like we should take some time apart ... I'm sorry. I feel like I need some time alone to sort things out."

"Sort what out? That's so lame! I'm not always happy either, you know." His eyes blazed.

"Oh." My eyes filled with tears.

"I don't think time apart is the solution though."

I walked away and went to sit out alone on the terrace. If we knew what the problem was, we could have talked about it. But we both just had feelings we couldn't put into words. I watched as the sky darkened over the town.

After a while, Dermot stepped out on the terrace. "Look! Another shooting star!"

BICYCLE ODYSSEY

I stood up to take in the sight, and we gazed out over the night sky. He pulled me into a tight embrace, and we both cried.

"We'll be okay, babe," Dermot said, giving me a squeeze.

"Yes. We've come too far to abandon this." I sniffled the last of my tears and wiped my nose. "Let's just try to be patient with each other."

Dermot drew in a ragged breath and held me tighter. "Agreed."

When we met up again fifteen years after the trip, with fourteen years of divorce behind us, Dermot alluded to that night on the coast of Kenya. More centered now, I am certain I wouldn't have been so reactive to those feelings that dark night in Lamu. But back then, we both were emotional and reactive.

With our spiral into sadness, we saw that Lamu had another side as well. Down a side street, dust and the smell of donkey excrement filled the air. Black rivers of sewage water spilled through another street and into a far section of the harbor, which was littered with trash. I wondered about the cleanliness of our swimming beach when I came down with a sore throat twice after swimming. We stumbled upon carcasses of cats as well as a dead donkey with vultures circling overhead. We wanted to flee from Lamu as much as we had earlier wanted to become lost forever in its mysteries.

I found myself vacillating between those two feelings about Lamu at the end of our stay there. Lamu's main economy came from tourism, so everyone's livelihood depended on our business and patronage. People tried to charm us and cater to us to get our business. I began to wonder whether I could really trust anyone's sincerity.

But Lamu hadn't changed. The island remained a piece of heaven, as Ali Hippie had described it. The inhabitants were still welcoming and kind. Our inner state had colored our vision, causing us to see darkness.

CARLA FOUNTAIN

Subdued, we flew back to Malindi and took a bus to Nairobi to prepare for the next country on our itinerary. No one had sacrificed a goat in our honor on this two-month bicycle adventure along the Pan-African Highway and beyond. But we had gathered treasured encounters and wonderful experiences and faced challenges we conquered. We were stronger, more seasoned, and determined to carry on for the next leg of our journey.

PART 4
• India—Down the Rabbit Hole

November 16, 1991 to
January 19, 1992

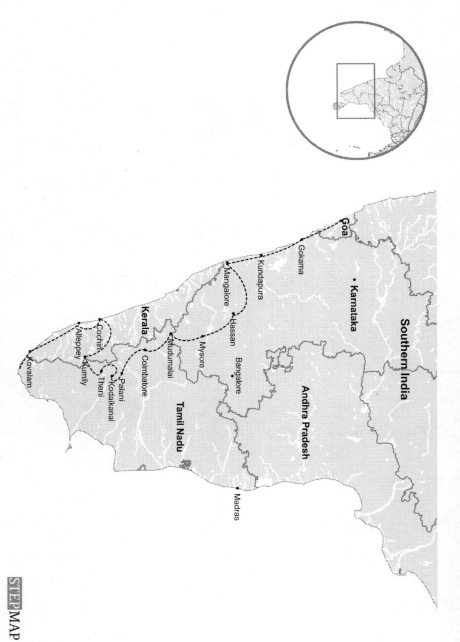

10

Bombay and Goa

We arrived at the international airport in Bombay (Mumbai), tired and on edge after an all-night flight with little sleep. As we circled in for a landing in the early-morning light, Bombay spread out for miles and miles before us, full of high-rises, large buildings, and highways. Moments before we hit the runway, the view filled with shanty towns. The makeshift huts, crafted out of planks of wood covered with tin roofs, jammed together amid heaps of trash.

We wheeled our bikes out of the baggage claim area. Earlier, we had considered staying in Bombay for a few days, but the sight of the immense city daunted us. We thought it better to stick to our original plan and travel to the state of Goa as quickly as possible. Once there, we would start our cycling trip of the subcontinent. We wanted to skip the huge city of Bombay and begin our bicycle journey in a more manageable area. We found out we had to change terminals for our domestic flight. We pumped up our tires, snapped on our lightened load of one pannier each, and cycled out onto the streets in search of Bombay's domestic terminal.

When we had started out, we didn't know India was known for having some of the world's deadliest roads. But shortly into our trip of bicycling the subcontinent, we would have concurred. Trucks, motorbikes, and cars zoomed around us, honking nonstop. We passed

CARLA FOUNTAIN

paving work and construction sites. Women squatted next to piles of rocks, breaking them into smaller chunks. Their bright-colored saris in pinks, yellows, and greens contrasted sharply with their arduous labor.

We asked three different people for directions to the domestic airport and received three different answers.

"It is ten miles away. Go straight," an older man answered.

"You must go five miles. Then turn left," another man said.

"It's twenty minutes from here. First go straight, then left," a third man told us.

We biked straight, turned left, and joined honking buses, three-wheeled taxis, and mobs of pedestrians on the road.

A helpful man gave us new directions. "Go there and then that way."

We bumped into more road construction, which blocked off our lane. Joining other local cyclists, we braved the oncoming traffic. But after several three-wheeled taxis swerved toward me and forced me off the road, we decided to walk the road construction out.

We followed new instructions: "Shortcut. Very good. Ten minutes away."

Those directions led us into a slum with narrow streets. The smell of excrement filled the air. We had to be careful not to run over piles of human waste on the side of the road. Amid all the squalor and dirt, a woman fluttered by in a pink and mauve sari. She was a butterfly floating over a dung heap. Her beauty transcended the filth and chaos.

Farther on, three children squatted, bare bottomed, with their backs to the road, adding piles to the trash. Afterward, they helped each other clean up with water. A fat, muddy pig with swollen teats rooted in the

BICYCLE ODYSSEY

garbage. Men scrubbed down oxen. Another woman in a dazzling, green sari walked by.

We could see that the road construction progressed slowly. Men broke up the old road with pickaxes or power tools, while women scooped up the broken asphalt in trays, which they carried on their heads over to a pile away from the road. The tedious, hard work kept many people occupied and employed.

When we reached the domestic airport, it felt like we had cycled in a huge circle. Six hours after landing in Bombay, we boarded our flight to Goa. We arrived after nightfall. Because we couldn't bike to the city of Vasco da Gama in the inky darkness, we took a taxi and replenished with meals at two different restaurants. We ate chicken kebabs in the first and vegetables and rice in the second. We strolled through the bazaar and ordered a nightcap of whiskey and soda in a cozy bar. The sweet scents of incense and flowers filled the night air on our way back to the hotel.

I paused to admire the lights and color of the bazaar. "This is wonderful, Derm! I'm so glad we decided to fly to Goa to start our trip in India."

"No one told us that we would have to bicycle ten miles to change terminals. That was a crazy ride. It feels good to relax now in the calm." Dermot sighed.

Music played from the shops and accompanied us back to our hotel. Exhausted from the past twenty-four hours of travel, we fell into a happy slumber as soon as our heads touched the pillows. The dark, stormy night on Lamu was behind us. Our bond was even stronger now.

When we applied for our Indian tourist visas in Los Angeles, we met an Indian man in the line with us who influenced our itinerary for India. At that time, a representative from the Consulate General of India traveled to Los Angeles from San Francisco for periodic visa applications. We stood in line with about thirty people, mostly Indian,

CARLA FOUNTAIN

who were delighted to hear about our cycling plans through their country of origin. One man said he thought the state of Karnataka would be the best place for cycling. Many in the line agreed. India is a massive country, and we were delighted to obtain a suggestion for an area to hone in on.

With that starting point, we crafted a flexible route that began in Goa, headed through Karnataka and Tamil Nadu, and continued south to the tip of Kerala. We planned to fly back north and stop in Madras (Chennai) and Calcutta (Kolkata) before leaving for Kathmandu, Nepal. Once again our openness and receptivity to advice from a chance encounter shaped our travel plans. Our adaptability opened the way to meet people and discover places we wouldn't have otherwise. Those detours made up the highlights and gems of our journey.

After our first night in India, we woke up and took in the vast Arabian Sea. The Portuguese arrived in Goa in 1510 and occupied the area for almost five centuries. They left a strong legacy, which we observed in the churches, architecture, cuisine, and language. We bicycled down the coast to the southern portion of Goa and found a little cottage at a hotel in Benaulim a few yards from the beachfront. Over the span of several days, we rested, swam in the warm Arabian Sea, and explored Velha Goa—the old town—and churches. Goa gave us an easy, soft landing on the subcontinent. We walked for miles on clean beaches, cycled the quiet back roads past elegant mansions from the colonial era, and ate lots of fresh seafood, vegetables, and fruit.

Resting on the beach became difficult, though. Vendors from Rajasthan walked the shoreline, selling colorful tie-dye silk scarves and other attire. Dermot bought me a scarf I admired as it fluttered in the wind—a peace offering. I was touched by his gift. I would have hugged and kissed him, but public displays of affection were frowned on in India. My loving smile conveyed my emotions.

A roaming ear cleaner with shiny metal tools approached and offered to clean out our ears. To my horror, Dermot agreed. The ear

BICYCLE ODYSSEY

cleaner beamed as he produced several large pebbles, which he claimed had been clogging Derm's ear canal. Thankfully, Derm survived unscathed.

Our cottage was at the other end of Goa, far away from the well-known "Hippie Beach." Among European travelers, Goa had a reputation as a hippie hangout with music, drugs, and parties. But there weren't many tourists where we spent our time. In the mornings, when we walked the beach, the fishermen worked together to haul in their nets. They pulled rhythmically and sang as their muscles strained with the heavy loads of fish. Some of the fish looked strange; others were long and thin like snakes. After I set eyes on the unfamiliar and scary shapes of the sea creatures, I hesitated to venture far out into the water the next time I swam in the ocean.

We often ate dinner at the same restaurant, Pedro's, by our cottage, where Sejun, a young man from Nepal, waited tables. Sejun had journeyed to Goa with another traveler and had decided to stay and work for a while. One evening, we ran into an American couple, whom we had met at the airport. We learned that they had retired early to embark on a two-and-a-half-year world trip.

Benaulim was a relaxing and good introduction to India. Many Indian tourists and foreigners visited the area, which made for a nice change from Africa. We hadn't met African tourists on our travels in Kenya and Uganda.

After four days in Benaulim, we were ready to set out to see the "real India." We left our idyllic cottage by the beach and cycled south for thirty miles. We ended up making a few loops on the back roads and going around in circles because of the lack of signage. Posters covered the signs on the road so we couldn't read them. We managed to find Palolem, a tranquil beach town with a small, crescent-shaped bay, which our hotel looked out over. This was a popular tourist area for Indian families. A few families played at the calm water's edge. The women always stayed fully covered with a sari or a *salwar kameez* (a long-sleeved tunic and loose trousers), even when they waded or splashed in the water.

At dinner, we tasted our first *dosas*. The cook spread a thin layer of batter on a circular hot plate. He toasted the batter, filled it with spicy potatoes and vegetables, and rolled it up into a tube. *Dosas* could be up to two feet long! The waiter served them with a spicy dipping sauce. I never tired of eating the crisp and delicious *dosas*. They remain one of my favorite foods to this day.

We strolled along the beach after dinner and admired the colors in the sunset. As we approached the shoreline, we noticed several men squatting on the sand. Walking closer, we realized they weren't there to enjoy the view but to use the water's edge to relieve themselves. We discreetly backed away.

A recent *Los Angeles Times* article stated that more than five hundred million Indians lack access to toilets. There is a movie, *Toilet: A Love Story* (*Ek Prem Katha*), released in 2017, that addresses the problem of open sanitation in India. The satirical comedy was well received by viewers worldwide and won nominations for Best Film, Best Director, and Best Actor in India's Filmfare Awards. *The Times of India* gave the movie four out of five stars.

We bicycled south out of Goa to the state of Karnataka. Goa had been peaceful with narrow roads shaded by coconut palms and light traffic. Even so, when cars, motorbikes, trucks, and buses passed, they honked repeatedly. We called the phenomenon of the ubiquitous tooting "I honk, therefore I am." We saw no real hotels in the next town of Karwar, but we found other foreign tourists and asked them about accommodations. They directed us to an old, Portuguese guesthouse, complete with sitting room, outhouse, and bathing room. We spent two days and three nights taking in the sunsets, exploring the beach at

BICYCLE ODYSSEY

low tide, and swimming at high tide in the morning. We gobbled up banana pancakes for breakfast and prawns with garlic sauce for dinner. We met our first "hippies" there, an Austrian-German couple who had traveled to India every year for the past ten years. They worked for six months in Europe to earn money and spent the rest of the year in India and Thailand. They shared stories about their travels in India and gave us helpful pointers. When the Austrian man told us he had cut his foot on broken shells at the beach, I gave him a pair of socks to protect his wound from infection.

We spent a pleasant day cycling from Karwar to Gokarna. We finally managed to rise before dawn and hit the streets by six o'clock. Because we left in the cool morning, we covered forty miles before eleven o'clock on a smooth road, which rolled up and down the coastline. Dry vegetation covered the ground, but we had minimal traffic, wider roads, and fewer potholes in Karnataka. Trucks no longer forced us off the road when they passed. There was room for the vehicles and for us.

Obtaining information on the road conditions left us perplexed, frustrated, or amused, depending on our mood. A typical inquiry resulted in a variety of responses.

"Is the road to Gokarna flat?" Derm asked a man on the road.

"No, no," he answered as his head wobbled in a circular, figure-eight motion—a uniquely Indian gesture that to our eyes looked somewhere between a yes and a no. "Not flat. Level."

"Flat?"

"No. Level."

When we met another person and asked the same question, the response was, "Pretty flat but hilly."

"Is the next town far?" Derm asked.

119

"Not very far but many miles."

A great advantage to traveling in India was the wide use of English. There are so many different languages in India—twenty-two official ones—that many people use English to communicate with each other. English-language Indian newspapers kept us abreast of the politics and events in the country while we traveled, which proved useful later in the trip when we ran into political unrest on the roads.

An article in *The Times of India* said the government bemoaned the fact that so many foreigners changed money on the black market, thus depriving the government of foreign currency. One afternoon we arrived at the government bank at two o'clock, and the clerk told us to return at three o'clock to change our money. When we returned at three o'clock on the dot, another clerk said we couldn't change money because it was too late. He instructed us to come back in the morning and gave no apologies for the misinformation. Changing money legitimately was difficult. The same situation happened to us in Uganda. We often changed money on the black market because the few banks we could find closed early.

11

Karnataka—A Week of Festivals

At one of our coconut water breaks, we met a lone French traveler carrying a small backpack. Jean, lean and tan from months on the road, traveled by bus.

We stood together under the shade of a tree and enjoyed refreshing sips of coconut water. Jean glowed with enthusiasm. "I've just come from the most wonderful place. It's not on the main road. I highly suggest you go there. In fact, right now they are having a festival."

We perked up. "Please tell us about it!" I said.

"It's a town called Gokarna. I know it's not the way you are going, but it's worth it. You won't regret it. Take the next side road to the right."

Jean didn't give us more details. But we trusted his enthusiasm and the look on his face as he spoke to us.

Gokarna was barely on our map; there wasn't a single mention of it in our guidebook. And we hadn't heard of the town before our trip. But we headed there, traveling about fifteen miles off the main road. Tips like this—random, chance encounters with people eager to share and talk about their experiences—directed us toward the highlights of our

CARLA FOUNTAIN

journey throughout the whole year. When we followed our intuition while talking to people, we always had rewarding experiences.

Gokarna offered much more than we expected. We found a room at an elegant government hotel situated high on a hill overlooking the sea. The hotel, surrounded by immense grounds, was so quiet that we felt as if we were the only ones staying there. Our airy room held a double bed and a twin bed, both draped with canopies of mosquito netting. The room included a spacious bathroom. We showered, drank chai, and then biked a mile into town to eat and exchange money.

While waiting for Derm outside the bank, I watched a parade of pilgrims dressed in *lungis* (a cloth tied around the waist like a sarong) enter and exit the building. Gokarna is a holy city with numerous temples. People told us the town was the birthplace of an important guru. Many of the pilgrims walking by me had shaved heads, except for a small tuft of hair on the top or back called a *shikha* or *choti*. The *shikha* symbolizes personal sacrifice to God and is also a sign of cleanliness. They believe it allows God to pull one to heaven or at least out of the material world of *maya*, illusion.

While in town, we met a man who told us about a family who took in boarders. We decided to meet them and look into our options. The Pai family rented rooms for one dollar a night, but the rooms were small areas divided by plywood with a blanket on the floor. Our room at the government hotel for two dollars a night overlooked the sea and had a patio, a fan, a private bathroom, and beds with mosquito netting. We decided not to move. We chose instead to take meals with the Pai family so we could get to know local people.

The young mother, Isha, welcomed us warmly into her house. She enjoyed talking with us while she prepared our meals. She rolled out dough for fresh *chapatis* and told us stories about her family. Her playful little boys—Ved, who was three; and Arjun, who was eight—constantly wanted us to take their picture.

BICYCLE ODYSSEY

After a tasty lunch, we set out for the town center to see the festival. We arrived in Gokarna during Karthika Masam, an important, month-long festival. A different temple celebrated each night. We talked to several people regarding the festival and asked when it would take place.

One person said, "Tonight at eight thirty."

Another said, "Next week."

A few others said, "In two days."

But as we walked through town, we witnessed people setting up for a festival. Men focused on building a long, wooden passageway. An arbor covered with mango leaves graced each end. Others filled oil lamps and set them along the sides to light the passageway later.

That afternoon we met Rishi, an engaging nineteen-year-old with a huge smile. Rishi approached us when he caught sight of our photo equipment. He introduced himself and told us he was interested in photography and video.

"But," Rishi said, "I am studying to be a priest. My father is a priest, and we are Brahmin. I am in my first year of Sanskrit school. We study about the mantras and Hinduism."

I offered him one of our cameras to examine. Rishi turned it over in his hands for a few moments. He looked up at us and continued, "The state Sanskrit college of Karnataka is here in Gokarna, and there are two hundred and fifty students like me. Our studies usually last five years." Rishi handed back the camera. "Hey! You should come to Ganesha Temple tonight for the festival."

"Yes," I replied. "We would love to!"

"Ganesha is very important. He is the god of wisdom and study, and he removes obstacles. We pray to Ganesha for our exams. And Ganesha is the son of Shiva. You know Shiva?"

CARLA FOUNTAIN

Dermot and I nodded.

"Parvati is Ganesha's mother. You know Parvati?" he asked.

We hesitated and nodded, less sure. We later discovered several books and articles on Hinduism that helped us better understand the various deities. The stories we read were fascinating.

"Gokarna is an important historic town," Rishi continued. "It is even mentioned in the *Ramayana*."

Rishi delighted in our interest in his life, and he allowed us to videotape him and take his picture. We hesitated to use our camera equipment around locals because people didn't always welcome photographers in Kenya and Uganda. But people encouraged us to take their photos throughout our stay in Gokarna.

Outside the temple, men lit the candles in the passageway. A trio with a drum and two wind instruments led the procession, followed by banner carriers. The statue of Ganesha rested on embroidered silk cushions on a palanquin (a canopied couch) carried by several men holding it aloft with poles. An attendant with a large umbrella brought up the rear. They stopped about six yards short of the passageway. *Bang! Bang!* Loud bursts of exploding firecrackers filled the air. Rockets flared, and sparklers burst on the ground. The display lasted for an ear-deafening thirty minutes. We turned off the camera microphone so the high decibels wouldn't damage it.

The procession continued to the middle of the passageway, where another round of firecrackers blasted for twenty minutes. Rishi took us into the temple ahead of the others so we could record with our Hi8 camera before the temple became overcrowded. He even held the microphone for us. Respectful of customs, we took our shoes off before entering the small temple. The priest performed a Hindu prayer ritual called *puja* to honor Ganesha. On the right in an alcove reigned a large, ornate, silver-plated Ganesha with a red ruby in his forehead. Ganesha has the body of a man and the head of an elephant. Offerings of broken

124

BICYCLE ODYSSEY

coconuts and bowls of vermillion powder, small coins, flowers, and leaves were set in front of Ganesha. Directly opposite the alcove with Ganesha was a dark alcove that held Shiva's *lingam*, a small statue in the shape of an egg representing the deity.

Parallel rows of bells hung suspended on beams above the main room between the two alcoves. The devotees reached up to ring the bells. The sound of the bell is used to bring a devotee's attention to the present moment. As Ganesha entered, the devotees chanted loudly while ringing the bells. Two rows of people lined up and faced Ganesha's alcove. The men carried Ganesha in, and the priest brought out an oil lamp on a tray to start the *aarti* (ceremony of light) ritual. He carried it to the alcove to infuse the flames with Ganesha's love, energy, and blessings and then took the lamp around to everyone in attendance. The devotees passed their hands over the flame to receive the blessings. The priest walked through the temple again with a tray of red pigment. He put a tilak (dot) in the middle of everyone's forehead. He also brought out a tray of toasted rice and gave everyone a handful to eat.

The ceremony ended, and we left the temple at about eleven o'clock at night. Rishi took us to his friend's house to get our bikes, and we walked to our hotel through the deserted streets of the sleeping town. By the time we climbed our hill, midnight had come and gone. We fell into bed elated and exhausted from all we had experienced that day.

At seven o'clock in the morning, Rishi knocked on our door. He invited us to visit his temple for their festival preparations. His temple was a large one for Saraswati, the goddess of knowledge, music, arts, and science. Rishi took us inside and showed us the altar with Saraswati. Flower garlands draped around the gem-encrusted gold statue, which was surrounded by more flowers, coins, and bowls of red powder. Canopies covered both the temple courtyard and a cooking area off to the side. People arrived and prepared for the feast. Women swept the hard-packed dirt area, men and women cooked food in huge pots over fires, and others dug pits to deposit the waste after the festivities.

125

CARLA FOUNTAIN

At nine o'clock, we arrived for breakfast with the Pai family. Vir, the father, was home for festival week. He was dressed for the heat in a blue-and-green plaid *lungi* and a short-sleeved, white cotton shirt. He sat with us.

"I hope you are enjoying Gokarna and our festivals," he said.

"Yes, yes," we said with a nod.

"Do you know that I have a large coconut plantation south of here near Mangalore? My oldest son attends a boarding school near there, which is run by Sai Baba. Do you know Sai Baba?"

We didn't know him, but we would learn more about Sai Baba during our trip. We later read a book about an American girl's experience in his ashram. Sai Baba, an important guru from Puttaparthi in the state of Andhra Pradesh, had about five million Indian devotees at that time.

Vir's youngest son, Ved, ran past us naked, giggling as he escaped after his bath. "Hello! Hello!" He was excited to see us again.

Isha laughed and caught him in her arms. Ved squealed as she took him to get dressed so she could prepare our breakfast. Once he was dressed for school in his blue shorts and shirt, Ved posed for us. "Take photo! Take photo!" he said.

We obliged, and he was delighted. But when his mother said he needed to leave for school, he cried. "No! I want to stay here!"

I took more photos of him and his mother, and he calmed down, sniffling back tears. He slung his bright yellow satchel on his back and marched off to school, holding hands with his older brother, Arjun.

We tucked into our breakfast of chai and delicious, piping-hot *idli*—steamed, round cakes made from a batter of ground rice and lentils and served with coconut sauce and a savory chutney.

BICYCLE ODYSSEY

After our meal, Rishi stopped by and walked us through town on the way to our hotel. We passed youngsters, who were creating flowers and elaborate geometric designs with colored powders in front of the entryways to their dwellings.

I paused to take photographs. "These are so beautiful!" I said.

Rishi smiled. "This is my cousin's house. These designs are called *rangoli*. We draw them at festival time. It is good when Ganesha or another god passes over the *rangoli* in the procession. The designs encourage them to enter the house."

Back at our hotel, we rested for a few hours before walking down the hill for the luncheon feast at Saraswati Temple.

Rishi paused his *puja* ceremony when he noticed us standing in the doorway of the temple. He popped out to tell us he would be done in a minute. We studied the engaging temple from outside until Rishi joined us a moment later. The clean-swept courtyard was considered part of the temple during the festival, so we removed our shoes before setting foot on the stony, packed dirt. We sat around the courtyard and talked with the men and children. The women arrived later and sat apart to one side.

At around two o'clock in the afternoon, attendants served the meal. About fifty of us sat in several long lines with a large banana leaf placed on the ground in front of each person. Servers entered the courtyard with more than nine different food items—rice, pickles, dal (spiced lentils, mung beans, or split peas), sweets, beans, potatoes, and other spicy dishes—which they placed on our banana leaves. A tall man wearing a golden orange *lungi* sang a blessing. Derm and I ate with our right hands, without utensils, like everyone else. (Eating with the left hand was considered unclean and rude.) We tried not to spill all over ourselves, since we weren't accustomed to eating that way.

We were dying of thirst but unsure whether we wanted to drink the water and risk dysentery. We broke off a piece of a water-purifying tablet to put in our cups. Ten minutes later, we drank.

We finished our meal and split up to wash our hands and faces, men to one side and women to another. Inside the temple, the priest accepted donations and gave blessings. Derm donated a generous amount, and we received our blessings, a red tilak on our foreheads, and flowers behind our ears. Women tended a fire in the temple, where people took pinches of ash to place above the red tilak on their foreheads.

Rishi prepared the palanquin for Saraswati, while people left the temple and courtyard after the feast. The deity rested on silk cushions under a tasseled canopy. That night, temple devotees would parade her through the town. The procession for Kali would be held the next night. During our stay, we participated in five nights of processions for Ganesha, Saraswati, Kali, Rama, and Vishnu. The evenings all followed a similar pattern. The sounds, colors, and fragrances saturated our senses as we were held in a warm embrace of friendly and welcoming people.

We loved having our meals with the Pai family every day. We ate with them and occasionally watched television together. Rishi joined us one of the days, and we all watched a Hindi language-learning show. In the skit, a woman in a village filled her earthen pot with water at a well. I learned the word for water (*pani*) and how to write it in Hindi.

After taking a sip of his chai, Rishi explained, "Many people in India do not speak Hindi. This is a tribal woman learning Hindi. Here in Karnataka, we speak Kannada. But this area is also home to many tribal people."

Much later, I found out that the *Indian Journal of Medical Research* (May 2011 issue) reported over fifty tribes living in the state of Karnataka. We sighted tribal women throughout the town. They balanced large loads of firewood, bundles of straw, and other goods on their heads as they gracefully walked by.

In my post-travel studies, I also learned about a specific tribe scattered throughout Maharashtra, Gujarat, Karnataka, and the city of Hyderabad. The Siddi are an ethnic group of East African origin. Africans entered India centuries ago as merchants, indentured servants, and mercenaries. Others were brought in as slaves by the Portuguese. Escaped slaves established communities in forested areas. In the hierarchical caste system, they were below the untouchables, and most lived in extreme poverty on the fringes of society. The Siddi have been in Karnataka for over four hundred years.

Later in the week, we explored the quiet beaches outside of town. A small group of foreigners had rented one-room beach shacks near the water. A little café served tea, coffee, and snacks. We ordered coffee and sat at the café to relax. I was disappointed that we didn't connect with them—almost as if we were on a different wavelength. The four other travelers at the café smoked *ganja* with their early-morning coffee. Many tourists visited the area for rest and relaxation, which could also mean copious amounts of *ganja*. Before our setting out, Derm and I made a pact with each other that we wouldn't smoke *ganja* or try anything stronger than alcohol on the trip. Besides our personal reasons, the horror stories we had heard about foreigners jailed for years abroad after being caught with illegal drugs scared us.

We visited an idyllic beach about two miles from town. After climbing a hill to Rama Temple, we took stairs to the crest of the hill and walked down the other side to reach Kudle Beach. Tourists could rent inexpensive mud huts on the clean beach. Over the hill to the south from Kudle Beach, we found the more remote Om Beach with three bays—one rocky and two sandy. A few foreign tourists had set up makeshift shelters with palm fronds and plastic sheets. Most foreigners stayed at the beach; we observed very few in town. We dipped into the water and enjoyed the warm Arabian Sea. I didn't venture out too far. As I floated in the water and gazed up toward the sky, a soothing calmness washed over me.

On our way back to town, we stopped by Rama Temple again. Three priests with long, white beards and elaborate tilak designs on their foreheads made preparations for the festival. They invited us inside their temple. The priests wanted to show us around and encouraged us to videotape and take photographs.

We stepped out of the temple to leave, and each of them sang a blessing for us. "*Om namah Shivaya. Om namah Shivaya*" (Adoration to Lord Shiva).

The last priest sang with a lovely smile. When finished, he motioned for us to wait while he ran back inside the temple. He reappeared with red powder and flowers. The priest placed a tilak on our foreheads and put a small cluster of flowers behind our ears.

Their heartfelt welcome and generosity touched us.

Of all the festivals, the Kali festival dazzled me the most. Kali is the goddess of time, creation, destruction, and power. She is a destroyer of evil forces. She is also considered the kindest and most loving of all the Hindu goddesses. She is regarded as mother of the whole universe and is seen as a great protector.

As we walked through town to find the procession, everyone welcomed us and encouraged us to videotape. The experience warmed our hearts. The goddess Kali rode through town on her palanquin while torchbearers led the way and followed behind her. Several men and boys held racks of torches to form a passageway. They stayed in front and lit the way for the goddess. Others, playing drums and horns, paraded in front of Kali. Two priests tended the flame by the goddess. The procession stopped in front of each house or business in town that wanted a blessing, and a member of the household stepped out, bearing a tray with an offering and a small, unlit oil lamp. A priest presented the tray to Kali for a blessing, lit the wick, and handed the lamp back to the devotee to take into his house or establishment.

The evening grew wild at times. Two groups of men and drummers played music most of the night while one man sang and danced. Every now and then, the tempo increased, and the dancer accelerated into a frenzy of movement. One group held court in front of Rama Temple; the other celebrated in the street on the way to Kali Temple. *Boom—boom!* Brilliant fireworks exploded! *Sizzle—hiss*! Sparklers, spinners, and flares lit up the darkness.

The vibration of the drums resonated through my body. The crowd pressed around me in a comforting embrace. We moved slowly down the street together like one living organism. The twirling sparklers illuminated children's enraptured faces as they rode on their fathers' shoulders. In the midst of the pressing crowd, I felt safe, completely at ease and accepted. We stayed with the festival crowd long into the night. I drank it all in, fully immersed in the experience. The moment was glorious, and my heart filled with gratitude to be there.

We promised Rishi that he could try out our bicycles, so we arranged to meet for a ride. Derm rode an old one-speed bike that Rishi borrowed from a friend, and Rishi rode Derm's bike. Rishi led us down country roads to the harbor by the village of Tadadi. He showed us a Danish fishing project and introduced us to the man in charge. The project included a fish processing plant. The large harbor provided the villagers with a rich source of fish and mollusks. On the return trip to town, Dermot handed Rishi our video camera to shoot footage of us riding our bikes since we had no visuals of the two of us together. He asked him not to touch the zoom. When we watched the video later, we saw that Rishi had taken delight in zooming in and out.

On our last night at the hotel, we stepped into our room, exhausted from the sensory overload and excitement of the festival. I glanced at the walls and the ceiling, and noticed a few black moldy blotches about two feet in diameter. "Derm, was that mold on the wall before?"

Dermot looked closer. "That's not mold. The spots are moving!"

I shrieked in terror. "Oh, no! They're swarms of ants!"

"The room's been closed up all day, and it's sweltering in here. Maybe the ants came out from inside the walls because of the heat."

The ants swarmed around the double bed more, so we squeezed into the tiny single bed. My skin crawled. "I can't sleep! Every time I close my eyes, I see ants—masses of ants—swarming and dropping down from the ceiling." I couldn't fall asleep until late into the night. From then on, when I thought about that hotel, which had enchanted us the first night, I could see only the black swarm of bugs.

The generosity and friendliness of Rishi and the Pai family gave us a privileged entry into the life of Gokarna. When we visited, we experienced a magical week. Locals treated us like welcome guests of the town. The week in Gokarna is one I will cherish forever. Throughout the rest of our trip, we thought back and wondered why we didn't stay there for the remainder of our time allotted in India. But we had just begun our journey in the massive country, and we anticipated many more positive discoveries and encounters. Gokarna gave us what we hoped for on our trip—a connection with local people who warmly

BICYCLE ODYSSEY

shared their culture and lives with us. Sometimes when what you seek materializes too quickly, you don't realize what a rarity it is. Our adventure in Gokarna transpired from a chance encounter on the road and because we opened ourselves up to listen, accept guidance from a well-meaning stranger, and deviate from our set route.

When we returned to the States, I made copies of the photos of all the people we had met in Gokarna. I mailed a package to Rishi to distribute them but never heard back from him. I wonder whether the package ever made it to India. The workings of international mail are such that it might have disappeared without even reaching him. I hope the photos arrived and that he and the Pai family received our thanks and appreciation. Our encounter with them was one of my treasured highlights of our year on the road.

12

The Karnataka Coast and Inland to Mysore

We biked out of Gokarna in the early-morning coolness and rode about fifty miles to Murdeshwar. We arrived at the city in time for lunch and then found an alluring hotel with a terrace overlooking the ocean. The building was tiled inside and out. The hotel owner ran a tile factory and had taken over the renovation of the temple as well. Devotees journeyed from all over to visit the eye-catching temple, which sat on a small peninsula. Derm and I walked out to the tip to take in the surf crashing on the rocks and the sun setting over the Indian Ocean. Fishermen paddled out in their canoes amid the tiny rock islands for the evening catch.

Our bodies craved protein. Derm and I realized we hadn't consumed enough legumes for the past six days. The dal we ate for lunch had been watery, lacking the protein we needed. We searched for a restaurant that served chicken or fish to remedy the situation. At the back of town, we found a small fish joint that served tasty, panfried fish. The catch in the area seemed to be on the small side, mostly sardines and mackerel. I had yet to see a fisherman bring in anything larger than twelve inches—no huge tuna, marlin, or kingfish like in Lamu.

BICYCLE ODYSSEY

After sunset, we strolled into town to buy a coconut in the market. At the stand, two local couples in their early twenties picked out coconuts to eat. The men smiled and greeted us, but the veiled women huddled together with their backs to us as they ate their coconuts. The couples mounted their shiny new motorbikes, with the women perched sidesaddle on the back, and zoomed off.

The next day we had lunch in a restaurant on stilts over the beach with the waves crashing around us at high tide.

Dermot pushed away his half-eaten plate after dinner. "I don't know what's wrong. I'm not that hungry tonight. I feel a little under the weather."

I patted his hand across the table, my eyes filled with concern. "Let's stay another night so you can rest and get better. Plus, this town is lovely. I feel like we're staying at an exclusive resort."

"I know. It's hard to believe that we're only paying one hundred rupees or about four dollars a night."

"Let's walk on the beach on our way back to the hotel. We can cool off with a dip in the water. Maybe that will make you feel better."

Our beach walk after lunch quickly turned unpleasant as we swerved around cow dung and other dubious stains on the sand. Unfortunately, the fishermen used the beach for personal hygiene. We decided to skip an afternoon swim. Thankfully, Per, our physician friend in Copenhagen, had given us the hepatitis shots before we left Denmark.

But we had no more proguanil, the malaria medicine we took in Africa. We were supposed to take the pills for one month after leaving Africa, but we had run out after two weeks. The pharmacy in Murdeshwar didn't carry the medicine, and the pharmacist didn't think we would find it in the next big city, Mangalore (Mangaluru), either. Travelers require different antimalarial medications for specific areas. Apparently, the medicine most effective in Kenya wasn't used or

135

needed in this part of India. We thought we would probably be okay, but we did worry because we had been in the same town, Lamu, as the American who had died of cerebral malaria during our stay. We continued taking the chloroquine we'd needed for India once a week and hoped for the best.

We said our goodbyes to Murdeshwar and reached Mangalore after two grueling days of biking over a hundred miles. Our ride was extended by three hours because traffic conditions forced us to take a detour on a smaller road over hilly terrain. On the main road, the crazy drivers grated on our nerves, and vehicles nearly collided with each other on several occasions. In one instance, two trucks honked to pass a bus, while three other trucks and buses rushed at them head-on. Miraculously, nobody crashed in front of us.

The trucks we saw in India displayed SOUND OK HORN signs. We wanted to make a different sign—NO HORN, OK? Throughout our journey on the subcontinent, truck drivers would honk several times as they passed by us.

We arrived safely in Mangalore with sore knees and sunbaked skin. After stashing our bikes in our hotel, we took a ride in an auto rickshaw (a small three-wheeled taxi with a motorcycle engine) around town. The short trip was exciting yet scary as the driver dodged in and out of traffic to avoid other vehicles, animals, and people. Our rickshaw experienced several near collisions. We satisfied our craving to see a movie with a film from America called *Bird on a Wire*. I enjoyed the experience, even though I had to tuck my legs under me on the seat to avoid the fleas jumping from the floor to bite my ankles. I noticed that I was the only woman in the theater. Young men between seventeen and twenty-five years old made up the entire audience. On the street at night and on the buses, we also saw only men.

We enjoyed a cycle-free day to rest in the city before we loaded the bicycles onto a bus to Hassan, with plans to bike to Belur and visit several historic temples. The bus climbed for three and a half hours to the Western Ghats before cruising for one hour on the plateau. We reached coffee country, with clean, crisp air in the high altitude. At that point, we experienced the intense ogling at foreigners we had heard so much about. Before the bus trip out of Mangalore, people had been easygoing. Our interactions with people were polite and friendly. But when we disembarked in Hassan, masses of people surrounded us.

A few of them yelled, "Cycle! Cycle!" Their shouts drew even more people.

One man, thinking our bikes were motorized, reached down and squeezed my water bottle in its holder on the bike and said, "Petrol!"

We commenced our usual routine, stacking our items together for me to watch over while Derm supervised the task of removing our bikes from the top of the bus. The driver sent a young boy to assist Derm. The boy was too small for the job, so an adult from the crowd stepped forward and offered to help catch the bikes. Derm passed each to him from the roof.

Derm wheeled the bikes to me. About one hundred people gathered around us and stared intently. I focused on making sure our things stayed with us and that our items were secured to the bikes. People commented on the bikes. Four men squeezed the tires. We escaped the crowd and took off in search of a hotel.

We spent a day touring the two large temple compounds at Belur and Halebid (Halebidu). But we made the mistake of taking the bus instead of biking. We would have savored the experience much more on our bicycles. That was always the case anytime we took another form of transportation. Minimal traffic circulated through that quiet agricultural area on the plateau. The bicycling would have been splendid.

A bus was necessary for our journey to Shravanabelagola, an important Jain pilgrimage site. The town boasts ancient monuments and buildings, rising majestically above the plains. The largest monolithic statue in the world stands there—a fifty-seven-foot-high statue of Gommateshwara carved from a single block of granite. Gommateshwara (also known as Bahubali) translates as "the one with strong arms" in English. Legend says Bahubali, a Jain prince, meditated motionlessly in a standing position for one year while plants grew around his legs. After that year in meditation, he obtained enlightenment and *moksha* (freedom from rebirth).

We encountered few foreign tourists during the three days we toured the temples. Our guide gave us an introduction to Jainism, an ancient religion of India, whose main premise is *ahimsa* (nonviolence), considered one's highest religious duty. Devout Jains take five main vows: *ahimsa* (nonviolence), *satya* (truth), *asteya* (not stealing), *brahmacharya* (chastity), and *aparigraha* (nonattachment). There are between four and five million followers of Jainism.

Without the bicycles in tow, people didn't pay much attention to us. Until that point, we hadn't realized that all the attention we received was due to our method of transportation and our strange attire. People weren't used to seeing cyclists with helmets, glacier glasses, gloves, and panniers. Going about our business without the usual fanfare brought a welcome calmness to our day.

After our dark night of the soul in Lamu, Gokarna inundated us with a sensory bombardment and left me no time to ruminate on our marital problems. But in the quieter hills of Karnataka, I had more time to reflect. I found myself agitated and disturbed, unable to sleep. When

BICYCLE ODYSSEY

I contemplated what I wanted or needed, uncertainty swept over me. Two disturbing dreams unnerved me. I dreamed I had traveled to France and come upon the gravesite of a dear friend. The newly engraved tombstone stood over freshly turned earth. Grief filled my heart, and tears spilled from my eyes.

In another dream, I stood in a kitchen. While I was talking on the phone, two ghouls appeared at the window. When they floated in after me, I screamed and ran. Suddenly, I was airborne. I flew out of the house and tried to fly faster, with the ghouls hot on my trail. I awoke in terror and climbed into bed with Derm.

Most of our hotel rooms included twin beds. I rather enjoyed having my own space. I rested and slept better. But the nightmares spooked me so much that I needed comfort. I wasn't sure what those dreams meant, but they stood out as important.

The next day, as I sat by myself in a quiet corner of the hotel with my journal and a chai, I reflected on the trip and our marriage.

> December 3, 1991
> I feel fortunate to be on this bicycle journey with Dermot, and we travel well together. But I struggle again with thoughts about what is going on with our relationship as a married couple. I love Dermot, but sometimes I feel smothered and overwhelmed by his huge personality. I think it would be good to spend some time apart when we complete our odyssey. I need space to hear my own thoughts and make my own independent decisions.

Our hotel hosted a man who sold an assortment of pearls from Hyderabad. Needing to boost my spirits, I bought a string of the small cultured pearls. The real ones were out of my price range. I fingered the smooth pearls, which warmed in my hand, and put them on to help me feel more feminine and attractive. But when I looked in the mirror later, a dumpy (thanks to the darn money belt), puffy-eyed, tired, and

139

CARLA FOUNTAIN

sad-looking person gazed back at me. The high altitude and weather change had brought on congestion and headaches. Yet I knew I couldn't blame all my problems on the elevation and weather.

We allowed ourselves another day to acclimate before we biked to Mysore (Mysuru), because our bodies drooped with fatigue and our morale sank low. We weren't eating well enough to sustain our level of activity. The lack of adequate nutrition affected our emotional state, although we didn't realize it at the time.

Throughout our odyssey, Dermot and I discussed the possibility of ending the trip early during periods when exhaustion overcame us. But on days when we buzzed with exhilaration, we contemplated extending the trip by teaching in Taiwan to earn more money before returning to Los Angeles. We heard from another traveler that we could earn forty dollars an hour as an English teacher in Taiwan. The opportunity would be an interesting way to work since we would also learn about another country and culture. With the money earned, we could travel to Japan and bike the countryside.

Thoughts whirled around in my head that night as I waited for sleep to overcome me. Sweet, nostalgic music poured in through the window from downstairs, and my thoughts drifted up with the notes, swirling into space, traveling and exploring what different turns my life could take. Trying not to disturb a slumbering Dermot, I sat up in bed and wrote by the beam of my flashlight.

> December 5, 1991
>
> I want to make changes in my relationship with Dermot, but I am afraid to step off the path I'm on—afraid of the risk and of losing what I have. I shouldn't be afraid! How ironic. I risk my life almost every day in traffic on this incredible trip. I venture out into the unknown, and yet why don't I take more risks in the direction of my life? Why can't I be content with what I have? I always strive for more. My life doesn't seem to hold

enough time and space for all I want to accomplish and experience.

We biked to Mysore from Hassan through gently rolling hills with no motorized traffic. Villagers worked in the fields, cutting and winnowing grain. They made temporary shelters out of wood and fronds, and used them for a reprieve from the heat during the harvest. We rode past oxcarts stacked high with grain or straw. They rolled along on huge wooden wheels, a rhythmic *thump, thump* filling our ears. It was as if we had journeyed back in time hundreds of years. The terrain was a cyclist's dream, the undulating slopes broken up with long stretches of flat land. The brisk, clean air freshened our skin. The sun bathed everything in a golden light. A perfect day!

At our chai stop by the side of the road, an elderly man approached us. He was clad in saffron-colored cotton robes and a turban; ropes of *rudraksha malas* (prayer beads) graced his neck. He had embraced the pilgrim's path and let go of his worldly belongings to travel with his begging bowl and staff. His dark-brown forehead was painted with white horizontal lines and a red tilak in the middle. When I placed an offering of rupees into his alms bowl, he shared a radiant smile with us and chanted, "*Om namah shivaya*" (Adoration to Lord Shiva). His peaceful soul shone out to us in the amber light.

That evening I fell ill with the worst cold I had ever experienced. The congestion descended into my lungs as we rested in our hotel in Krishnarajanagara. As midnight approached, my symptoms worsened. I struggled to breathe. With every breath, I wheezed and heard a rattle in my lungs. I coughed up phlegm all night. I feared that I suffered from bronchitis or the beginnings of pneumonia. Panic seized me, but I calmed myself and concentrated on inhaling enough air into my lungs

CARLA FOUNTAIN

through the night in between coughing fits. Many days later, I realized that all the chaff in the air from the harvest had irritated my air passages.

We made the fifty-mile journey to Mysore (Mysuru) the next morning. As we approached the city, the pleasing pastoral fields faded behind us, and the heavy traffic met us with full force. My weakened lungs functioned far below their normal capacity. We lugged our weary bodies to a more upscale hotel than those we usually stayed in. The soothing, hot water in our showers eased our sore muscles. (Most places we stayed in provided room temperature or cold water to bathe with.) We showered, rested, and enjoyed a hearty meal at a restaurant across the street.

The next day we visited the Maharaja's Palace. Its grand arches and pink marble domes, surrounded by well-manicured grounds and gardens, reminded me of the fairy tales from my childhood. We treated ourselves to high tea in Lalitha Mahal Palace Hotel, built by the Maharaja Krishnaraja Wadiyar IV to house his important guests. Musicians played the sitar and a tabla (a pair of small hand drums). That was one of the few times during our two and a half months in India when we heard the classical Indian music we had listened to in the States. The majority of the time, we heard the popular Bollywood tunes drifting out of tea shops or on the radio. The hit that year was "*Ilu Ilu*," which played on a loop everywhere. We heard the catchy tune several times a day, and the refrain still rings in my head years later. While we enjoyed our tea and sweets, Derm and I talked about how fun it would be to return to Mysore one day when we acquired the means and stay in Lalitha Mahal Palace Hotel.

Later in the afternoon, we watched *Born of Fire*, a movie about a musician in Turkey in search of a master flutist with supernatural powers. Again, I was the only woman in the theater. With my muscles rested after the calming high tea and the relaxing theater time, I held hope that my body would be back to normal by the next day.

At a nearby hotel, we met a few American yoga students, who were in Mysore to study with a master teacher. We wanted to take

BICYCLE ODYSSEY

yoga classes because we could use a counterbalance to all the cycling we did. One of the students, a young man named Chris, invited us to his hotel room to have tea. He told us about his studies and his time in Mysore.

As Chris washed the cups before serving us tea, he looked over his shoulder and warned us, "You need to be very careful here. I got hepatitis. Man, is it ever debilitating! And it takes a long time to recuperate. I'm still weak."

I gave Dermot a nervous glance. I hoped Chris had done a thorough job of washing our cups.

Chris sat on a chair with the effort of a much older man. "I've been here a year studying yoga with a master. I wanted to stay longer, but this illness wore me down. It's time for me to head back to the States."

Tenzin, a young Tibetan monk in his twenties, joined us for tea. Tenzin grinned and told us about himself. "I am visiting from a Tibetan refugee camp not too far away. Chris is coming to visit me before he goes back to the States. You should come visit too."

"That sounds wonderful, Tenzin," we replied. "How far is it from here?"

"Only one hundred and sixty miles away."

"We'll think about it. Thank you!"

We invited both men to come with us for lunch. Chris needed to rest, but Tenzin joined us. Over a meal of *dosas*, Tenzin shared more about his life.

"I am Tibetan, but I was actually born in India. We Tibetans have a lot of problems with the Chinese. We want our freedom."

Tenzin handed me a sticker. "Here, I have a gift for you."

"Thank you, Tenzin."

The message on the sticker—"Free Tibet"—echoed Tenzin's commitment to spreading the word about Tibet. He explained more about the struggles of his people. We could sense that, even though his life held hardships, he was a kind and generous human. Although we enjoyed this new friendship, we knew we probably wouldn't go to the refugee camp, because the long distance was out of our way. And we didn't want to travel there by bus, especially when we heard the next bus left in four days.

Tenzin invited us to a going-away party for Chris. A yoga friend hosted the small potluck gathering on the roof of the hotel, where all the students of the yoga master stayed. The yoga students kept to themselves at the party. As the evening progressed, many of the students spontaneously moved into advanced postures and inversions, then discussed them.

I took a swallow of soda and looked out over the city lights. "Derm, did you notice that there aren't any Indians here at the party?"

"Yes. It seems strange to be in India at a yoga gathering with only Europeans and Americans."

"I thought it would be good for us to study yoga here, but this practice looks acrobatic and competitive."

Derm gazed in awe at two men executing complicated arm balance poses. "Maybe we'll have an opportunity later on in the trip. We sure need yoga with all the cycling we do."

"In the meantime, we can try to do more yoga at night in our hotel room," I said.

BICYCLE ODYSSEY

Coming out of the movies one night in Mysore, we spotted two African men. When our gazes crossed, we said hello and conversed. Since we'd recently traveled in East Africa, we felt a bond with them. We invited the men to join us for chai. They were from Tanzania. We enjoyed talking with them about Kenya, the future of East Africa, and cultural differences. One cultural difference stood out from the others. These well-educated and well-traveled young men were adamant that the man should be the boss in the house and that the woman should follow his orders, even if both were educated and earned an equal salary.

Adam seemed the easygoing type, at least more so than his friend. "I could see that, if I lived in the West, I would come to accept helping out with chores at home. My wife would have a more equal footing," he said.

I nodded in agreement.

Adam continued, "My brother went to England to study, and he married an Englishwoman. When my mother visited and saw him washing the dishes after a meal, she became very upset and lectured my brother. She told him, 'You are crazy!' and asked, 'Why are you doing this woman's work?'"

I couldn't help but stare at him, wide eyed. I glanced at Derm, who grinned and nodded. *Did a deep part of him agree with Adam's mother?*

Robert said, "My mother would have done the same thing. But I could never accept to be in a nontraditional marriage. A woman should do the housework and keep up the home. That is not a man's job. The man's job is to work and pay for all the household expenses."

Both men felt that a woman's position in India was even more restricted than in East Africa. I hadn't interacted with Indian women on our trip, except in Gokarna. Few women bustled in the streets and shops. Men dominated the crowds and tea stands. Women seemed to keep a hidden existence. In California a friend had given us the contact information for two Indian doctors to look up in Bangalore (Bengaluru). I looked forward to meeting more people from diverse walks of life and talking with them.

145

13

Civil Unrest and into Tamil Nadu

After enjoying Mysore for a few days, we looked for a bus to Chamundi Hills for a day trip. While searching for bus signs, we noticed at least one thousand, if not more, young men in the distance. Their shouts and chants filled the air as they streamed down the road. Frightened, we took off the other way and found a side street to reach the bus stop. Later that evening, we read in the paper that the national government wanted the state of Karnataka to release a portion of its water held in reservoirs from the Kaveri River to the neighboring state of Tamil Nadu. Karnataka didn't want to increase the amount of water it shared. The water dispute between the two states raged for over a hundred years. As Karnataka's agriculture developed and used more water from the Kaveri River, Tamil Nadu received less.

The protesters in Mysore, Bangalore, and other cities in Karnataka forced shops to close. They stoned the shops as well as buses, blocked the train lines, and burned effigies of the prime minister in the streets.

When we returned from our hilltop temple excursion, the city was very quiet. Almost all the shops and food establishments were shuttered and closed. The state had declared a four-day *bandh* (a general strike). Buses and trains weren't allowed to operate, and most shops were to remain closed. The few shops that stayed open closed their shutters halfway, ready to lock up tight at a moment's notice. On our way to

BICYCLE ODYSSEY

find dinner, ten mounted police with large batons, helmets, and riot shields passed us. It set a frightening tone, but we didn't see any violence.

The next morning, as we clipped the panniers on our bicycles, I glanced up at Derm. "You know, today is Friday the thirteenth. But I think we'll be lucky. The strike will hold up all the traffic, so we can bike out of the city easily."

Dermot grinned. "I'm looking forward to a nice countryside ride without cars, trucks, or buses. Those darn trucks and their honking. They drive me crazy!"

The managers of the hotel wished us a good journey as we left. Our ride progressed well for about ten miles. We didn't encounter any motorized traffic, only other cyclists, cows, oxen-drawn carts, or people. We caught sight of five children on the road ahead, wielding sticks like baseball bats. They didn't try to hit us, so we kept going. One mile farther down the road at Kadakola, we met several cyclists and travelers on motorbikes coming from the other direction.

They shook their heads as they passed us. One of them said, "You can't get through! Go back! They are throwing stones and blocking the road because of the strike!"

Another man told us he thought they would let us through since we were on bikes. A third man told us we could take a detour that would only be twenty miles out of our way. Derm and I decided to go straight on and see whether they would let us through. About fifty yards before the crowd, we dismounted and walked slowly and calmly toward the mob. They approached us, waving sticks above their heads. "Go back! Strike!"

About sixty people, mostly boys and teenagers with a few adult males, surrounded us. They yelled and jeered with an edgy excitement. We talked to the ringleader and asked if we could continue through. We explained that we wanted to travel to Bandipur, twenty miles up the road. He instructed us to wait ten minutes while he considered our

147

CARLA FOUNTAIN

request. We leaned our bikes against one of three trucks the crowd had forced off the road. We put our backs to our bikes and turned to face the pressing mob. The ringleader held a flexible stick about a yard and a half long, which he snapped like a whip around the throng to keep them in check. He nearly hit us. The agitated crowd yelled, their frustration fueled by those around them. Derm asked whether the roadblock was because of the Tamil Nadu water issues. No one understood that much English, but when they heard him mention the name of the state, they yelled louder and beat the air with their fists.

Before the ringleader gave us an answer, we decided to return to Mysore. Even if we had passed through the screaming mob in front of Kadakola, we might not be so lucky in the next town. We risked becoming stuck in the middle of nowhere. We turned and sped away, but soon more agitators spilled into the road in front of us. They shouted and approached to block us from traveling farther. When a police van drew near with officers wielding batons, the crowd scattered, which enabled us to pass through. We were almost home free, with only two more miles to our hotel, when Derm yelled back at me, "Turn around! There's another mob ahead!"

Masses of protesters swarmed in the road, blocking our path. I caught sight of flames grabbing at the blue sky. The young men chanted and pumped their fists in the air while an effigy of the prime minister was set ablaze. We cut down a side street, veering off course. When we thought we had dodged the mob, we swung back to the main street but encountered yet another mass of protesters marching in our direction. We turned down more side streets and arrived safely at our hotel, only to find that the gates were locked.

The hotel opened for us and still had our room. It was comforting to be back in a safe haven during the political storm. We downed two beers and consumed a sumptuous meal at the restaurant across the street from our hotel. But we jumped from nerves whenever we heard a loud cheer or yell from the nearby cricket game.

BICYCLE ODYSSEY

The next day we read in the paper that an estimated five thousand demonstrators had marched in the streets of Mysore. Ten people had been wounded in Bangalore, one person had died from a gunshot wound, and mobs had burned two movie theaters. Miraculously, the next morning things were almost back to normal. About half of the stores in town reopened for business.

We ate breakfast, strolled downtown, and shopped. I purchased a dressy silk *salwar kameez* (a tunic with matching loose trousers) in a rich brown and gold as well as one for everyday wear in a peach-colored cotton. Derm bought a silk dress shirt and a cotton long-sleeved shirt for biking. For a soothing indulgence, I pampered myself with a facial in a beauty shop for less than two dollars. The aesthetician steamed and massaged my face and shoulders with ointments, gave me an ice-water rub, and applied a mask. The facial lasted almost two hours. Heavenly! I resolved to treat myself more often to help boost my morale.

We met Brian, a Canadian cyclist, at our hotel. After learning that he was traveling around India on a mountain bike, we invited him to join us for dinner at the restaurant across from our hotel. The three of us devoured the chicken *tikka masala* (chunks of roasted, marinated chicken in a spicy, creamy tomato-based sauce) and *palak paneer* (puréed spinach cooked in a rich sauce with soft Indian cheese and seasoned with ginger, garlic, and other spices). We scooped up the delicious sauces with warm naan (Indian flatbread).

After helping himself to seconds, Brian said, "I thought traveling by bicycle would be the way to get to know the 'real India' this time. But I don't think it has helped. This is my fourth trip to India. I met more people when I traveled on buses and trains and could strike up conversations with Indians while moving from city to city."

I tore off more naan and scooped up the last of my *palak paneer*. "We haven't traveled by train in India yet. I think a person has to travel alone like you do or at most with one other person in order to connect with

149

people in the country you are in. If you travel in a group, people are less likely to approach you. It's like you're inside a bubble."

"I agree," Brian replied.

"I heard the roads will be clear tomorrow," Derm said as he pushed his empty plate aside. "It should be safe for us to travel now."

I looked at Brian. "When are you planning to head out of Mysore?"

"Tomorrow seems like a good day to me. How about you two?"

"We were planning to leave tomorrow at dawn in order to avoid any possible roadblocks—that is, if there are any remaining protesters," I replied.

"You could join us, if you wanted," Derm said to Brian as we stood to return to our hotel.

"That sounds great. I'm going as far as Mettupalayam."

"The government has delayed the decision on the water issue for a couple more days, and we want to leave the state before then. I hope that the people in the neighboring state of Tamil Nadu don't retaliate with a strike of their own, if the decision is unfavorable to them," I said.

We managed to rise early and leave Mysore at dawn. We had no issues with the trip departure. The countryside stayed peaceful and quiet with little traffic. You wouldn't have known that two days earlier hundreds of screaming people had thrown stones, waved sticks, and threatened us on the road.

We tucked into breakfast in Kadakola, the town we had been forced back from two days before. We continued on a rolling plateau to

BICYCLE ODYSSEY

Gundlupet, where we ate lunch. Once nourished, we started on the ascent to Bandipur. There weren't any available hotel rooms there, so we continued on to Mudumalai. That day's ride was splendid—minimal traffic, wild forest all around, clean air, and wonderful views. Having a third person with us for a while was a welcome addition. Brian brought a fresh perspective to things.

Being together with Dermot twenty-four hours a day could be a strain. While Dermot and Brian spent time talking, I considered how it might be beneficial for me to have time away from my husband, even for a day or a couple of days. But how? Where? Maybe participating in separate activities once when we settled in a place where we planned to spend several days would offer the needed break from our fully intertwined lives. We clung to each other since the surroundings, culture, and experiences were all so new and, sometimes like the last couple of days in Mysore, frightening and uncertain. We were safer and more secure together, yet I also felt the need for time apart from Dermot.

After an extra day in Mudumalai, we left for Ooty. We debated whether to take the shortcut, which was twenty-two miles with thirty-six hairpin turns, or the road through Gudalur, which was twice as long but not as steep. Several people advised us not to take the shortcut. Clouds filled the sky and threatened to rain when we left, so we decided to go to Gudalur. Once there, we planned to determine what the weather was like before we chose between traveling on to Ooty or jetting down the mountain to the beach.

The skies cleared after our lunch at Gudalur, so we climbed up and up and up. The gorgeous mountain ride provided spectacular vistas of peaks plus fragrant sections of forested bamboo, eucalyptus, sandalwood, rosewood, and tea plantations. The vegetation changed every five to ten miles, bringing with it a different mood and fragrance. We pedaled in low gear to climb the hills, but it was one of our most pleasurable days. I loved moving at a slower pace so I could drink in the beauty around me. I could slip into a steady groove, even in the steepest

151

CARLA FOUNTAIN

terrain, as long as I used the right gear on my bicycle. I enjoyed the meditative state I entered going up the steep hills surrounded by forest.

When we were about nineteen miles from Ooty, we met Bruce. He was bicycling in the opposite direction on a one-speed Indian bicycle. We stopped to talk to him.

Dermot offered him a piece of candy. "How far are you bicycling, Bruce?"

He gave us a broad smile. His whole body radiated happiness. "I've been cycling since Madras. I've come about three hundred and fifty miles so far."

"Wow! Did you buy your bike here? How are you managing without gears?" I asked.

"Yes, I picked up this bicycle for twenty-five dollars when I got here from Australia. I do okay. I just go at my own pace. I love it. This is my fourth trip to India, and I thought I'd try to explore the country this way."

We parted ways and wished each other well. Brian gazed after him in awe. "Well, Bruce really puts us to shame. Here we are with our twenty-one speed bicycles and panniers. Then he breezes up the mountain on a one-speed with a backpack and a blissed-out smile."

"It's quite humbling," Dermot agreed.

As we biked through a small village in the mountains, we heard barking and sighted a pack of aggressive dogs behind us, headed our way. They gained on us. Fear pumped adrenaline through our blood. A cyclist's worst nightmare in a developing country is a bite from a rabid dog, especially when finding medical attention could be difficult.

"Hurry! Go faster!" Derm called out to me as he sprinted away.

BICYCLE ODYSSEY

I couldn't increase my speed fast enough, and the snapping dogs were closing in at my heels. I reached for my water bottle and squirted at the closest one. The surprise splash of water stunned him. He and the others fell back, and I managed to speed off out of danger.

Six miles from Ooty, Derm's front tire went flat. Sunset approached, and we needed the remaining thirty minutes of daylight to bike into town. Dusk fell by the time he fixed the puncture, so we turned on our bicycle lights, which worked with a wheel-turned generator. We discovered that our front lights malfunctioned. The back lights worked, though, so at least people could see us from behind. Brian was long gone ahead of us; he hadn't stopped while Derm repaired his tire. A deep darkness descended with three miles to go until Ooty. At one point, I heard several horns behind me and saw flashing lights. I pulled off the road in the nick of time as four trucks headed toward us on the two-lane road. Two of them tried to pass the other two at the same time! They were so close that I thought I would have to dive for the ditch. Amazingly, we managed to make our way safely to Ooty.

Derm and I found Brian at a hotel with a view of a lake, where we had agreed to meet. After dinner, we welcomed the calm offered by the stillness of the water, even though we could see only lights reflected off the surface. The cool mountain air chilled us, so we wore our warmest clothes.

When the three of us left the next morning, still bundled up from the cold, we faced horrible traffic for the first ten miles. But when traffic lightened, we enjoyed gorgeous vistas of mist-shrouded peaks and fertile valleys with undulating, green tea fields. Several hairpin turns revealed waterfalls at the road's edge. We leveled out at around one thousand feet and arrived in the steamy tropics of Mettupalayam. What a difference from three hours prior when we had bundled up in sweaters and jackets!

We shared a modest guesthouse with Brian and a young French couple. The owner's small elephant, tethered behind the guesthouse, munched on grass after a day's work. While shooting footage, Derm

CARLA FOUNTAIN

approached too close for the creature's comfort, and the elephant trumpeted with a warning charge toward Derm, frightening us both.

After giving myself a refreshing wash, I wanted to rinse my socks as well. In the short time I had left them out, the socks had attracted dozens of large black ants, drawn by the salt in my sweat. Thanks to my ant phobia, I cringed and squealed. Brian laughed at me.

I washed out the rest of the day's sweaty clothes and hung them up to dry, our usual routine on the trip. Every few days throughout India we were able to send our clothes out for washing for a few rupees. Sometimes we passed the rivers or streams where industrious people washed garments by hand, beating them on rocks and spreading them over bushes to dry in the sun. We received a neatly folded and pressed bundle of clothes the next day.

Washed and refreshed, everyone sat on the porch in front of the guesthouse to cool off in the breeze. We watched two elephant *mahouts* (elephant handlers) take their tuskers into the river to bathe them. The *mahouts* and elephants reveled in the refreshing cool water at the end of a long day's work in the surrounding forest. I could see the strong and loving bond they shared as they played together in the river.

While we watched the elephants, we discussed our plans for the next day. Brian intended to return to Ooty via train.

"I'm a train buff," he said. "I biked these last three days so that I can take the narrow-gauge steam train on the Nilgiri Mountain Railway back. It will take four and a half hours for the coal-fired steam engine to push the train twenty-nine miles up the mountain. It's the steepest track in Asia!"

"To *push* the train?" I asked.

"Yes! The steam engine is in the back to push the train up the mountain. We'll go through two hundred and fifty tunnels and cross sixteen bridges as we wind through the mountains. The scenery is supposed to be magnificent. I can't wait!"

"Sounds like an amazing experience," I said.

Brian's girlfriend was due to give birth to their first child in less than a month, so he planned to head back to Canada soon. We bought a spare pump from him, and he generously gave us other supplies, including duct tape and antimalarial medication.

Brian headed off to take his train ride in the mountains, and Derm and I set out for Coimbatore. We wanted to change the dates on our plane tickets, so we decided to go to a big city to find a travel or airline agency for help. We needed to push the trip back a month so we could stay in India longer. Cycling to Coimbatore was three hours of torture. It was the most demanding riding we had experienced on the trip so far. Coimbatore, a medium dot on our map, was much larger than we had expected, with a population of one and a half million. Miles before we arrived in the center of town, a madhouse of trucks, buses, and cars honked nonstop and frequently ran us off the road. The drivers blasted their horns without mercy while overtaking, weaving in and out, and cutting each other off. To make things worse, other bicyclists darted in and out of traffic, and pedestrians walked in the street, blocking our escape routes. The dusty air choked us, and the temperature rose drastically. We both started to lose our cool but were determined to escape the urban sprawl, so we pushed through. About five miles before the city center, we pulled over for a chai break to settle our nerves and unclench our tight muscles.

As we continued biking into the city, I noticed I had zoned out to cope with the stress. The overwhelming amount of stimulation numbed my senses. I disconnected from the experience in order to cope. Zombie like, I bicycled on as my system went into overload.

CARLA FOUNTAIN

We managed to locate a travel agent who helped change our tickets. When we left Coimbatore two hours later, the stimulation and chaos reached a fever pitch that jolted me out of my numb state and into pure agony. I kept going with sheer willpower and grit. The knowledge that I would soon be out of the city's madness was the only thing that pulled me through.

Panting and choking on fumes, we paused for a moment by the side of the road. Both of us shook from nerves and exhaustion. I took a sip of water. "This is so hard, Derm."

Dermot's hand trembled as he brought the bottle to his mouth. Drops spilled over his chin and onto the ground as he gulped. "I know. We just have to get through it. We're almost out of the city traffic. At least we were able to change our tickets. Come on, let's push on." He shoved off again into the chaos.

I followed, clenching my jaw in determination and gripping the handlebars.

Outside the city, we stumbled on a small community of people making rope from coir (coconut husk fiber). The family group welcomed us with big smiles and proceeded to show us how they made the rope, from start to finish. The pleasant visit with them made up for the horrors of the earlier part of the day on the road. Once again, after a terrible experience, a positive encounter soothed us and reminded us why we were on this journey. Beaming mothers held up babies for me to photograph. We laughed, chatted, and exchanged addresses. Dermot shot footage of the rope-making process. When we completed our trip, I sent copies of the photos to the family. Later that year, I received a lovely card from them written in Tamil.

14

A Hospital Stay

We spent the night in Pollachi, a large town that was much more manageable than Coimbatore. Exhausted and drained, we collapsed at our hotel. A cold shower had never felt so good. But from Pollachi, we bicycled a miserable and dusty fifty-two miles to Palani. The many trucks on the road made for a tense ride. Pilgrims filled Palani on their journey to several important religious sites and temples. We located a hotel, but the clerk didn't initially want to let us stay there.

"No, sir. We are full. No rooms," he said.

Tired and ill, Derm pressed the issue. "Are you sure you don't have anything?"

"No, sir. Only one large room."

"That's fine. We'll take it."

"No, we are full."

Dermot confronted the clerk about his inconsistencies. "You said you were full, and then you said you had a room. You keep changing

CARLA FOUNTAIN

your mind. I think you don't want to give us a room because we're not Indian. Is that right?"

Within a few minutes, we were checked into a regular room. We suspected that they didn't want us to stay there. That was the first time that had happened or the first time we were aware of it.

We showered off the grime that coated our skin. At the end of every day, a thick coating of road dust stuck to the sunscreen lotion we had applied in the morning. There were many times I was certain I could hear a sizzle as the cool water sluiced off our hot, sunbaked skin.

Dermot collapsed onto the bed after his shower. He wasn't hungry, and a sheen of sweat covered his pale skin. I took his temperature and found that he had a fever of 103 degrees. Concern filled me. At the time, I thought that was too high to be heat stroke. Could it be a malaria relapse? I hoped not, especially since we had never completed our series of malaria pills after we left Africa because we had been unable to find more in India. We hadn't been able to buy water-purification tablets either. I prayed Dermot would recover.

By five o'clock that afternoon, I decided to find a clinic or a hospital after Dermot threw up a few times, and his temperature climbed even higher. The clerk at the hotel directed us to a small nearby building that housed the clinic. A young, female physician in her early thirties examined Dermot. She wore a sari and sandals, and her hair hung in a long braid down her back. Her English was heavily accented. Still, I could understand her perfectly, and she could understand me.

But in his feverish state, Dermot wailed out with half-jumbled words. "I can't understand what she's saying!"

Offended, she replied, "I do not understand him either."

So I interpreted, English to English, for Dermot and the doctor. I tried to soothe both of them. We needed this physician to be on our side.

BICYCLE ODYSSEY

The doctor administered two injections of an antibiotic and medicine for Dermot's fever. Several people walked into the clinic while we were there to have their temperature checked and receive injections. They all used the same thermometer dipped in alcohol in between. I asked about the needles.

"These are disposable needles," she answered. I noted condescension in her voice. "Are you worried about AIDS?" she asked. "India has no AIDS problem. We are more worried about you westerners bringing AIDS to India."

Since Dermot had lost so much fluid that day, the doctor decided he should have an IV for rehydration. She took him to a room, instructed him to lie on a cot, and covered him with a loosely woven cotton sheet. I sat beside him. About halfway through the bag of fluids, Dermot fell asleep. Soon after drifting off, he jerked his arm, ripping the needle out. Blood and IV fluid spilled out onto his hand and the bed. I ran to find the doctor, and she attended to him.

She gave me instructions. "He should stay here a few more hours for observation. Bring him food so he can take more medication on a full stomach. Family members must provide the patient's meals and all provisions."

"What should I bring him to eat? Where do I buy it?" I asked.

"Bring him bread and jam. The marketplace is not far from here."

I left to purchase supplies. As I walked alone through the marketplace and into various shops, my mind filled with fear and helplessness. To hunt down the various items Dermot needed, I walked back and forth through the lines of shops and stalls several times. With each pass through, my fear dissipated as places and faces became more familiar. Merchants smiled as they greeted me a second time and helped me locate the next item on my list. I made my way back to the clinic with food, a water bottle, a T-shirt, and a mosquito coil to light at dusk since the clinic swarmed with mosquitos.

159

CARLA FOUNTAIN

Walking back into the clinic, I passed other rooms and glanced in through the open doors. Whole families sat in most of the patients' rooms. Only a couple of people were alone. The clinic was built with an open courtyard and garden in the center. The run-down building had stained cinder block walls and graffiti scrawled on the benches and cabinets.

Dermot was exhausted, so I hoped he would sleep. But he didn't want to stay overnight at the clinic. When he stood to go back to the hotel with me, a wave of nausea overtook him. He threw up, broke out in a sweat, and collapsed onto the cot.

The doctor entered the room and shook her head. "I want him to stay here for the night. Just one night, for more observation."

The doctor and the nurse were compassionate people, and I had confidence in them. I hoped Dermot wouldn't catch another illness in the clinic during his stay, which is a concern no matter where you are in the world. As night descended and the clinic darkened, the staff fired up a generator. The loud sound of the engine drowned out the street noises.

After I made certain he was settled in for the night, I took Dermot's fanny pack with his money and valuables and made my way back to the hotel. At the hotel restaurant, I picked at a meal of *thali*, which is rice with dal plus several other vegetarian dishes served on a round metal platter. My concern for my husband kept me from eating much or enjoying the food.

Upstairs in my room, I couldn't focus on reading. My stomach knotted with tension and fear. Nausea sent me to the bathroom several times throughout the night. Every time I walked in, I greeted the resident cockroach, who came out to rest in the dark. Waving his antennae at me, he scuttled away when I turned on the lights on. My mind churned with worry. I saw a gaping emptiness stretching out in front of me, should I lose Dermot. I sat up late into the night, scared and shaky. I contemplated our immediate problems and Dermot's illness.

BICYCLE ODYSSEY

My head pounded. I turned to my journal and poured out my distress on a page.

> December 21, 1991
>
> As much as our relationship faces problems, and although I have contemplated the need for a separation, I love Dermot and would be devastated if he didn't recover from his illness. What if he dies? What if he's having a malaria relapse? An American died in five days from cerebral malaria in Lamu last month. Will I become a widow here in Palani? I can't lose him!

That night while Dermot slept alone in his room, he felt a hand pat his buttocks. He woke up, yelled, and turned to see an older man scurry out of the room. Dermot thought the man was a mental patient in the clinic who was trying to molest him, but the next morning the same man walked around with a set of keys tied to his *lungi* while he supervised the cleaning of the clinic. When we later told that story to another traveler, he concluded that the man had most likely tried to check for a wallet in Dermot's back pocket.

Dermot's condition had improved by morning, and he received a clean bill of health from the doctor. She said he didn't have malaria as we had feared but probably had the flu or had ingested bad water. I sighed in relief, and the worry drained from me. Derm was still weak, so we spent another day at our hotel to let him recuperate more. We took advantage of the hotel's restaurant and fortified ourselves with their delicious *dosas* and *thalis*.

15

Kodaikanal—Bliss in the Hill Stations

We decided to take a bus to Kodaikanal since Dermot still needed to recuperate and the town would have been a steep climb on our bicycles. Kodaikanal sat at seventy-two hundred feet in swirling mists with thick pine and eucalyptus forests. Minimal traffic circulated in the quiet town, and the fresh, cool air was pleasant after the high temperatures in the plains below. The town offered a delightful place to settle in for a few days of rest and exploration. We planned to spend Christmas in Kodaikanal, hike in the hills, and take day rides without the constraint of our gear.

During the colonial era, the English had ascended to higher elevations and established hill stations to escape the heat and dust of the plains in the summer. Many of the structures in the town had been built during that time period. The stone buildings, cottages with fireplaces, and old churches reminded us of Scotland. We found our own one-hundred-year-old cottage to rent at Keith's Lodge. Fireplaces in both the bedroom and the sitting room provided cozy and comforting heat in the chilly mountain nights. Because of the eucalyptus forests, we could buy fresh eucalyptus and lemongrass oil. Almost three decades later, I still have the bottle of lemongrass oil. The aroma has stayed potent and transports me back to Kodaikanal with one whiff. Dermot and I took hot, steamy showers and inhaled

BICYCLE ODYSSEY

the eucalyptus oil to clear our respiratory systems. We cleansed and healed from our ordeal in the plains.

Well rested, we enjoyed various local eating establishments. The town had a Tibetan restaurant that made delicious spiced noodles and hot, sweet lemon tea—a perfect setting for warming ourselves in the cool mountain air. Isaac, a friendly Indian man with a long beard, ran a small restaurant in a cottage next to ours. We ate almost all our meals there. Isaac made delicious, wholesome meals of vegetable soup with fresh-baked, brown bread, homemade vegetarian pizza, and a satisfying dessert of apple crumble with hot custard sauce. A wood-burning stove fueled the oven. During our many visits to his restaurant, we met the kind chef; his wife, May; and other local people.

On Christmas Eve, I called home and connected after two attempts. We received more distressing news. Much of our mail at home had been lost: our bills, notices, and checks. The uncle initially in charge of our affairs had sunk deeper into depression. No one had been able to contact him. After the call, I was distraught, but I settled my nerves with a cup of masala chai and popcorn. We cleared our heads with an exploratory ride around the hills. The ride through deep forests and fresh air helped soothe us. Back at our cottage, we cleaned up for our Christmas Eve dinner at Sterling Resorts.

We bought tickets for a Christmas Eve buffet at the resort, which was a short stroll along the lake from our cottage. As we walked over, pangs of homesickness echoed through me. I missed our families and holiday meals together. I knew they worried about us. They received news of our whereabouts and wellbeing only once or twice a month when letters and postcards arrived. We, however, were on this great adventure. The homesickness usually vanished when I focused on the next experience. My thoughts of home melted away at the gathering, where we met people from different parts of India, who traveled to the resort while on holiday.

163

CARLA FOUNTAIN

The menu for the evening included roast turkey, stuffing, dal, rice, and plum pudding for dessert. Our traditional Christmas foods comforted us, but the Indian spices and dal reminded us that we were far away from home. Kodaikanal was a popular vacation destination for Indians. I was excited to finally meet a few professional Indian women at the gathering. It had been difficult to meet and talk to other women during our time in the country. That night and later on in the days that followed, I met and talked to several.

Since I had purchased the silk *salwar kameez* in Mysore, I could wear the proper attire for the dinner. The other women donned elegant saris or *salwar kameez* in striking colors. I fit right in and didn't feel awkward.

Aamani, a female language professor from the Tamil Nadu region, engaged me in conversation. We talked over dessert, which included English Christmas pudding as well as Indian sweets.

"I'm glad to see you like Indian food," Aamani said. I noticed a sparkle in her eyes as she spoke again. "Here, try this *gulab jamun*. It's a lovely Indian sweet."

I bit into the fried dough ball drenched in rose syrup. "Mmm. That is delicious!" I reached for another. "Tell me more about your work at the university. I love languages. I think it would be fascinating to learn Hindi."

Aamani laughed. "It wouldn't do you much good here in Tamil Nadu. I studied Hindi in school, and I teach it. But many Tamils do not speak Hindi. Most prefer to speak English instead. In fact, when representatives from all over India gather in the government, they speak English as their common language. We Tamils have a very rich language and culture, and we are proud of it. The Tamil language comes from a language family that is different from Hindi. It even uses a different script."

I laughed and shook my head. "The more I learn about India, the more I see there is to learn. We have such a one-dimensional view of

BICYCLE ODYSSEY

India in the West. The stereotype is that all Indians are Hindu and speak Hindi."

"Yes! India is a very diverse country." Aamani handed me another dessert. "Now, try this *payasam*. It's a delicious rice and coconut pudding."

I never did study any of the languages in the areas we passed through, though I did master the basics of "please," "thank you," "water," and "hello" in Hindi. While traveling in India, I experienced the kaleidoscope of cultures and languages that make up that large subcontinent. On our two-and-a-half-month journey, we traveled through several states, each with different languages and scripts: Hindi, Kannada, Malayalam, Tamil, and Bengali.

On Christmas Day, we hiked with Vikram, a wonderful nature guide, who led treks in the area. We met him through Isaac at the restaurant. Vikram took us on several hikes during our stay in Kodaikanal. He was a kind and patient man.

While walking along one of the trails, Vikram said, "By the time foreigners arrive in Kodaikanal, they have been traveling for a while and are in shock from the bustle of India. The differences between their home and India can take some getting used to."

Vikram paused while I stopped for a drink of water. "My job is to take people into nature and show them a different side of India, a side they wouldn't see otherwise," he said. "When they land here, they are tired and burned out. My job is to help calm and soothe them with walks in nature."

Vikram told us that he offered multiday treks in the Tamil Nadu Mountains. We were content with the day hikes and loved listening to his stories about the forest and the area. He did, indeed, soothe our weary souls.

Isaac and May, who was English, invited us to their home for a Christmas Day lunch after the hike.

165

CARLA FOUNTAIN

Isaac showed us around with pride. "We built this cottage high in the hills above town so we could have this view." He swept his arm wide to encompass the forest below the rocky cliff.

I looked out the window. "It's stunning!"

Dermot ran his hand over the woodwork. "Your craftsmanship is remarkable. I love the details in your house."

A sweet cinnamon scent filled the air as May pulled out a cake from the oven. "We've been together for ten years. I don't miss England at all."

Three cute children ran into the room, drawn by the aroma of cake. "These are our lovely children." May laughed as she tousled their hair. "They study at an English school in Kodaikanal."

"Thank you so much for having us over. It's really special to be in your home on Christmas Day," I said.

"It's our pleasure!" Isaac twirled the radio dial. "Let me see if I can find seasonal music. We might get a signal from the BBC in Sri Lanka."

The soft strains of carols filled the cabin as we sipped tea and ate cake. We nestled around the fire in their cozy home, grateful for their hospitality.

The sun grew low in the sky, filling the room with a golden light. Dermot and I said goodbye and made our own way back down the deserted road into town to find our cottage. He reached for my hand to help me over a rock. "I love their cabin. They're such a wonderful family," he said.

I squeezed his hand. "Yes. It would be cool to build our own cabin somewhere."

"I've always thought about having a place in Mexico."

BICYCLE ODYSSEY

"We'll see where this trip leads us and what other ideas we get...."
My voice drifted off as we focused on navigating the stony road in the
growing darkness.

During our hikes with Vikram in the days following Christmas,
we walked through deep forests and drank in misty vistas with
spectacular drop-offs. We also added cave exploration to our adventures
in Kodaikanal. One area, the Devil's Kitchen, swirled with fog and
harbored mysterious caves. We explored a cave with Vikram. Our feet
slid on the damp floor as we made our way down the narrow passage.

Vikram paused ahead of us, motioned with his hand for us to stop,
and whispered, "Be very quiet. We need to be careful not to shine the
light on the bats. If we startle them, they will all fly out at once."

We could hear the bats chirping, but we couldn't see them in the
dark. Descending and ascending the slippery cave passages stressed me
out. The primal fear of falling into a dark abyss loomed over me. But
Vikram's calm presence helped. I was relieved and happy to exit into
the sunlight. I wasn't sure that cave exploration suited me. I preferred
the nature around the cave in the open air.

The most extraordinary and magical site we explored was the Devil's
Table, a huge, horizontal slab of rock suspended between two vertical
pieces of rock. We scrambled up an incline and sat under the Devil's Table,
gazing out on a deep valley, which narrowed to a triangle. The entire area,
filled with ferns and moss, formed a misty, natural rock garden. Sitting in
silence for a while, we took in the dreamy beauty of the place.

A few birds swooped down and landed in a tree near us. *Chit, chit,
chit.* Their chatter pulled us out of our quiet moment. Vikram spoke.
"One day, a *saddhu*—a holy man—came to this very spot and meditated
for two months."

"I can picture that. I could stay here forever," I said. "I am so glad
we traveled here to Kodaikanal and met you, Vikram. These forest
walks are so healing."

167

Dermot sighed. "This is just what I needed."

One night Derm enjoyed a "boys' night out" with Isaac's local musician friends. Dermot had sent his travel guitar back home after the first month of our trip when we lightened our load. He missed playing. Derm loved to jam with people when he could. Since I was tired from our hike the day before, I decided to stay near our cottage.

I popped over to Isaac's restaurant and heard the *thunk, thunk, thunk* of dough being kneaded. Delicious smells filled the restaurant. Slanting rays of light from the evening sun streamed through the windows.

Isaac looked over his shoulder to greet me. "Hello! Good to see you! Today I have vegetable pie with roasted potatoes and a salad for dinner. How does that sound?"

"That sounds wonderful! I am dining by myself tonight. Dermot is out playing guitar with the friends you introduced him to."

I ate in the kitchen, savoring every bite. Isaac and I chatted while he finished baking the bread. As his only customer that night, I enjoyed the peaceful calm and conversation. I lingered over my apple crumble and gave a contented sigh as I sipped my tea. I looked forward to my solo evening in the cottage so I could collect my thoughts and write. Alone time on this trip was almost nonexistent. As much as I loved Dermot, his strong personality often eclipsed my own.

Back at our cottage, I lit a fire and sprinkled eucalyptus oil on the wood. A clean, healing scent filled the air while I sat and wrote.

> December 28, 1991
> In spite of our lovely cottage, new friends, and idyllic locale here in Kodaikanal, my mood is low tonight. I'm afraid, tired, and uncertain. There were a few

BICYCLE ODYSSEY

times, about three or four years before this trip, when I almost ended our marriage. At that time, my life seemed empty without Derm yet conflicted with him. The times when a desperation filled me, and I flew into a rage against him, a cloud of depression hung over me.

I don't know if my emotions are due to the dynamics of our relationship or if something is wrong with me. I often depend on him when we are together. But I navigated life easier when I was alone. I was more empowered, confident, and self-sufficient. When we are together, I fall into a more dependent, secondary role. His naturally expressive and outgoing personality contrasts with my quieter and more introverted one. I don't want to be overshadowed by him anymore. I don't want to doubt myself.

The next day over breakfast, I shared some of my thoughts with Derm. "It's been hard for me here at times in India. Males dominate society. We hardly ever see women running the shops or the market stalls. People always talk to you first and to me second. Women stay in the background, and it's difficult for me to meet them."

"I'm sorry. It's hard for me, too. Because it's so male dominated, I feel like I need to be protective of you and step up. If I were on my own, I could be much more easygoing."

"I think we should take a little break and spend some time apart when we return to the States. I know it would help me regain my confidence. I feel smothered by your protection."

Dermot's face fell. "I'm not sure … We'll see …"

Was something wrong with me? Would the problems I grappled with happen again in another relationship? I realized I needed time to find my true center and regain my self-confidence. I needed to recognize my own talents, convictions, and aspirations. Time alone was essential for me to empower myself.

Dermot and I met Dhir, a man our age, at Sterling Resorts one day. We enjoyed talking with each other so much that we decided to meet again. We invited him over to our cottage for dinner. He brought a delicious meal from the hotel where he worked, a bottle of brandy and snacks. We lit a fire and talked until almost midnight. Dhir spoke with an informed perspective on the East and West, having lived and studied recently in New Zealand for two years. While we sat around the fire, we enjoyed a lively discussion about cultural issues, comparing his experiences abroad with ours in India.

Dhir added a splash of brandy to our glasses and settled back into his chair. "I have only been back two months from New Zealand. I feel like I am just about over the adjustment period."

Dermot stretched out his legs and asked, "How did you end up in New Zealand?"

"I took an advanced course in hotel management and business. I was fortunate to obtain my position at the resort. It has excellent growth potential," Dhir answered.

I took a sip of my brandy. "Dhir, what is all the talk I've been reading in the papers about affirmative action here? We have that in the States as well, and it's also quite controversial."

Dhir poked the logs in the fire for a moment before answering. "Last year, our prime minister decided that twenty-seven percent of all government jobs would be reserved in the future for the lower castes. There are also quotas for the universities."

"Isn't it a way of reversing the unjust systems of the past?" Dermot asked.

"People from the middle and upper castes are worried. These quotas put their positions at the university and their future jobs in jeopardy. There have been many student protests and demonstrations all over India against these quotas."

"It's a complicated issue. I hope things work out for the best for all involved," I said.

Dhir frowned. "So do I. But I fear we have a long way to go before this is resolved."

Dermot topped off our glasses. "On a happier note, I'd like to toast to our encounter. Our time in Kodaikanal has been wonderful, mainly because we've met such nice people like you, Dhir."

"Indeed! The people we have met and the gorgeous nature surrounding the town have enchanted us. We have enjoyed the city so much that we plan to stay for a few more days," I said.

The day rides around Kodaikanal reminded us of how the mountains in Southern California must have been in the 1800s. On one of those days, we biked on roads blissfully free of traffic and encountered just a couple of trucks and buses the entire afternoon. The forest grew so thick and deep in the interior that we could hear only the rolling of our wheels against the pavement and the rhythm of our breath. The vistas of pine trees and meadows extended for miles. We glided in the woods in a peaceful, magical calm.

Then we came upon a glen so enchanting that we stopped to rest and savor the surroundings. We set down our bikes and walked under the pine trees on a thick carpet of moss and fallen needles. Tall trees surrounded us. The forest embraced and protected us. I wanted to curl up like a rabbit, burrow in, and sleep. I sat on a mossy rock under the canopy of ancient trees and sensed the vibration—the pulse of the earth beneath me. My heartbeat synced up with the earth's. I could have stayed forever, melding with nature in harmony.

After a while, Derm and I mounted our bikes and moved on. There were still a few hours of quiet forest to bicycle through on the return to Kodaikanal. We rode silently and peacefully together in harmony with nature and each other. Looking back at these highlights of our trip, I can see we were indeed very privileged. We experienced a side of India most visitors don't have time to see and don't even know exists. Our journey by bicycle connected us with the hidden, out-of-the-way places that held exquisite beauty and magic.

Kodaikanal held vast differences from the India we had experienced on the plains. We had acclimated to the coolness of the mountain air and the mists that blew in and swirled around the town every day. The descent into the heat and dust of the lowlands would be a shock when we left the next day. I wasn't looking forward to the traffic, thick crowds, and noise.

After meeting such nice people in Kodaikanal, I was sorry to leave. I guessed the locals met foreigners passing through all the time, so perhaps our departure wasn't as significant for them. Our encounters proved very special for me, though. As we packed to leave, I wondered whether lasting friendships were made on the road. It seemed difficult. Time in any one place was short, even if you stayed for a week or so. (I was proven wrong about that after our travels. Almost three decades later, I still have dear friends we met on our trip.)

16

Coming Down the Mountain

The descent from the mountains on a narrow, rutted road was thirty miles of stressful, downhill riding. We rode the brakes all the way. When a truck or bus rumbled by, we squeezed the brakes even harder and moved over or pulled off the road and stopped. Ten miles out of Kodaikanal, the temperature rose. Tropical air hit our bodies and forced us to peel off our sweaters and windbreakers. We wouldn't need them again until Nepal.

With sore hands from gripping the brakes, we reached the bottom of the descent and reentered the full heat of the plains. We had reveled in the cool weather of Kodaikanal, so the temperature shift was quite a shock. We biked through quiet villages and farming communities and made our way to Periyakulam for a late lunch served by an attentive waiter. We had a long ride ahead of us the following day, so we decided to push on to the next town.

Dust filled the air on the approach to Theni. The outskirts of the market town bustled with the ongoing harvest of millet and rice. All along the side of the road, women spread out sheaves of millet to dry. They heaped piles of grain on the road itself, put the grain in shallow baskets, and threw the kernels into the air so the chaff would blow away. We continued through this arresting pastoral scene until Theni's busy town center. Traffic snarled and jammed because of slow-moving

CARLA FOUNTAIN

oxcarts. At times, four to five carts in a row caravanned to market. Bags of grain and goods covered the sidewalks. Idle carts, oxen, and Nandi bulls lined the side of the road. Trucks weighed down with bags of freshly picked cotton lumbered toward the numerous cotton gins.

At the beginning of town, in the poorer area, we passed a huge slab of concrete, about twenty feet by ten feet wide, a public restroom. The sun dried out the exposed contents of this large, open-air lavatory. I hadn't seen open sanitary facilities on such a large scale before. Three little girls helped each other on the slab, then finished and left as we biked past.

We covered fifty-five miles to Theni, so we stayed there to rest up for the next day's ride. Our hotel swarmed with mosquitoes. Three mosquito coils helped smoke them out. Unfortunately, the smoke from so many coils irritated us just as much as the mosquitoes did. To add to the misery, a number of fleas in Kodaikanal had bitten me, and my skin had become infected. The wounds grew large, scabbing and festering. I was fine until nighttime, when I scratched them in my sleep, making them worse.

Leaving Theni, we passed several groups of men driving their herds of oxen in the road. They waved whips to move the oxen along. One man first cracked his whip at his oxen and then at us, missing me by mere inches. I kept on with a stone face and didn't give him a reaction. But inside, I seethed and boiled, on the verge of exploding.

Our ride from Theni to Kumily took us over hot plains on a rutted, bumpy road. At one point, a gang of children ran after us and reached for our bikes and bags. We sprinted past them, only to hit four miles of a climb so steep that we needed our lowest gear the entire way up the mountain to cross the Tamil Nadu border into Kerala. We arrived in Kumily to the lush Cardamom Hills. To our surprise, we noticed many wealthy, German tourists walking around town. Seeing so many European faces was a shock. We had been off the tourist trail for weeks.

The next day we decided to spend another night and bring in the New Year at a cozy, garden restaurant. A fire pit provided warm ambiance in the back courtyard. After dinner, Derm and I relaxed over cardamom coffee with a few other travelers around the flames. Familiar rock music flowed from the speakers. We grew nostalgic. Thoughts about home and our loved ones filled us with melancholy. That night in the pages of my journal, I wrote my New Year's resolutions for 1992.

December 31, 1991

- Relax more.
- Take things with more humor.
- Shoot more video.
- Stress less about Derm and enjoy the trip together.
- Worry about the future when it comes, not before.
- Stay more in the present.

On our way for a forest ride with our bikes on New Year's Day, we met Kaya, an energetic local woman in a bright pink sari, who talked us into taking a spice plantation trek instead. Originally from Sri Lanka, Kaya exuded independence and resourcefulness.

She guided us on an interesting forest walk and showed us the different spices grown in the area: pepper, cardamom, turmeric, nutmeg, cloves, cinnamon, and ginger. Kaya pointed out the growing plants, tiny cardamom flowers, and long, green strings of pepper seeds. We tasted the fresh pepper pods and learned about uses for the various spices. She also took us to a tribal area to meet a family. On the way, we bought candy at a stand to pass out to the children.

As we entered the small community, we noticed two elder women resting by their small hut in the clearing. A group of children played nearby. Kaya introduced us, and they greeted us with smiles. Hands pressed together, they bowed their heads.

CARLA FOUNTAIN

Through Kaya, I asked for permission to record a video of them.

Kaya translated for the women. "She is seventy-five years old, and the other woman is eighty years old. They still work—they carry wood to the plantations in the village."

"They are strong!" Derm and I said together.

"Yes! They carry the wood on their heads. Today is a holiday for them, so they are resting."

I smiled at the two women. "Kaya, will you please ask what makes them happy?"

"They say their grandchildren make them happy."

Kaya adjusted her flowing pink scarf as we walked back to town. "I married a man from Germany eleven years ago in Sri Lanka. Five years ago, he brought me to India to wait while he went back to Germany for a short visit." Blinking back her tears, she continued, "He never came back. He left me alone with our two children. My boy is eleven years old, and my girl is twelve."

Derm and I murmured sympathetically.

Kaya's tears spilled over. "Ever since then, I have struggled. My family in Sri Lanka cut me off completely because I married out of my caste and community. A few years ago, I had no home. I lived on the streets."

Kaya lived in a bamboo hut near town, which she rented for the equivalent of six dollars a month and shared with another family. She invited us to her home for tea. Kaya boiled the water over a small wood fire in a clay cooking stove. We sat on low stools around the stove with her and drank chai out of little cups. A partition divided the hut down the middle. Her side of the room was furnished with a narrow string cot and a small dresser.

"The roof leaks when it rains, and breezes blow through the walls of the hut. But I am so glad to at least have a home now," Kaya said.

"Thank you for your hospitality," I said.

Kaya poured more chai into our cups and sighed. "I have been trying to track down my husband in Germany. I need him to help support me and the children."

"It must be so hard for you, Kaya. I hope you are able to find him soon," I said.

Her heart-wrenching story moved me. But Kaya possessed a strong survivor spirit. She hustled tours and charged a fair price for a one-hour trek. We empathized with her and liked her, so we gave her extra money and a brass tray we had won at the Christmas party raffle in Kodaikanal.

Kaya looked tired and sniffled with a cold when we said goodbye to her. But she perked up and accelerated into high gear when she spotted more tourists. The last we saw of Kaya, she was talking to a middle-aged couple about a tour.

We had plans to bicycle to Kottayam and needed to begin our journey early in the day. The Muslim call to prayer from the local mosque woke us at four thirty in the morning. With the added sounds of horns tooting and pilgrims singing in the street, we didn't need an alarm clock.

I stepped outside to investigate the commotion. The streets teemed with pilgrims, mostly younger men, who had slept on the sidewalk the night before. Many were still sleeping, wrapped in a cloth, with their bundle of belongings for a pillow. Others awoke and sang or walked around and socialized.

CARLA FOUNTAIN

I approached a pilgrim to inquire. "Namaste. Excuse me, what is going on? Why are so many people in the street?"

He smiled and returned my greeting. "Tamil Nadu has declared a *bandh* starting today. We walked all night to cross the border into Kerala before the authorities closed it."

"Is the strike, the *bandh,* about the water issue?" I asked.

"Yes. Tamil Nadu wants to retaliate for the violence the Karnataka citizens inflicted on the Tamils during their *bandh* last month."

"That was scary! I was in Mysore then."

The pilgrim wobbled his head in a circular, figure-eight motion. "We don't want to become caught up in the trouble in the state of Tamil Nadu, so we traveled here to Kumily."

It was a good day to leave town and the border area. In preparation for our journey, we fueled our bodies with pancakes and cardamom coffee. During our travels around India, the tastes and smells of different spices infused our experiences. Coffee plantations were prevalent, and cardamom seasoned the brew. That flavor has always stayed with me—I still like to season my coffee with cardamom. After breakfast, we climbed a gentle ascent up into the Western Ghats. The first twenty-two miles took us past tea plantations, little villages, and splendid views of the mountain peaks and valleys. After a good lunch in Peermade, we glided fourteen miles downhill. The road surface had deteriorated in many parts, forcing us to squeeze the brakes for much of the descent. When the terrain leveled, we relaxed and delighted in gently rolling hills. We stopped at a hotel near Kottayam to ask about the road ahead. The staff told us the thirteen miles to the next town were all uphill. The heat and humidity had knocked us out, so we decided to call it a day and stay at the hotel.

17

Kerala—The Backwaters and Rest

After spending the night near Kottayam, we bicycled to Cochin (Kochi), one of the largest ports in India, where we rested and looked around the city for four days. We visited Paradesi Synagogue, which had been constructed in 1568. Earlier in our trip, we met a woman from Germany, who said her father had grown up in Cochin. He helped organize a large-scale Jewish emigration from Cochin to Israel in the 1950s. Many in the Jewish community had claimed roots to the city, dating to the time of King Solomon. Others had arrived in Cochin in 1492 after the Jewish expulsion from Spain.

There was much to see and do in the old city. We explored the ports, watched the graceful Chinese fishing nets, toured St. Francis Church (one of the oldest European churches in India), and visited several museums to learn more about the history of the area. We also enjoyed the many murals at Mattancherry Palace. Cochin had been an important center for the spice trade for many centuries and was well known to the Greeks, Romans, Arabs, and Chinese.

I noticed that our moods plummeted when we were inactive for too long. Our bodies were used to expending large amounts of energy

CARLA FOUNTAIN

every day and benefitted from the endorphins the exercise produced. When we paused in our journey for several days, our mood shifted. After our fourth day in Cochin, we fell into a funk. We sat at dinner, filled with irritation about many things, and we dwelled on the hardships of travel.

The doldrums lifted as we biked from Cochin to Alleppey (Alappuzha). The clean and prosperous state of Kerala had courteous drivers and excellent tarmac roads to ride on. Our guidebook said Kerala was the only communist Indian state at that time. Many hammer and sickle emblems covered the sides of buildings along the road. Kerala also seemed to be the most prosperous state we visited during our trip in India. The coastal state boasted the highest literacy rate and the highest life expectancy in India.

We reached a good emotional equilibrium after coming out of our deep funk. Cruising down one of the quiet back roads, I smiled and turned to Dermot. "It feels so good to be on our bikes again! We've gotten so strong. What if we stayed in India longer?"

"We could see if we can change our tickets. Maybe extend the trip by six months?"

I nodded. "I bet the art students would want to keep renting our house."

"But we'd need to earn money. We don't have enough."

"We could teach English for a while somewhere. Then maybe go to China."

Derm smiled as he dreamed. "From China we could take the train back through the Soviet Union to Europe."

Our minds spun with the possibilities, and our attitudes danced with positivity again.

180

From Alleppey to Quilon (Kollam), we took a riverboat trip along the backwaters—a network of rivers, lakes, and canals (both man made and natural) that extend down the state. We loaded our bikes onto the boat with all our gear and set out with twenty other travelers. At times our view opened up to lakes fringed with palm trees. We glided past boats loaded with nets and fishermen. People bathed and washed clothes only yards from where their outhouses hung over the water. Villagers paused their activities to greet us as we passed. Decorated dragon boats waited in enclosures for the next race. Our languid journey lasted nearly nine hours, so our boat made a stop for refreshments at a modest restaurant.

We decided to stay in Quilon for a day to relax in a tranquil place. We thought we could shoot video and take photos in the low-key environment. We stayed in a magnificent mansion built by an English lord 180 years before. Our spacious bedroom with twelve-foot-high ceilings came with a full bath and an old-fashioned, claw-foot bathtub.

Dermot gazed around our antique-filled room. "The concierge assured me that the mansion has ghosts."

"It's certainly old enough to have stories to tell. I've been curious about seeing a ghost, but I'd be terrified if we did see one." I shivered despite the heat.

We slept well in the huge four-poster bed and didn't have any supernatural encounters during our stay.

Preparing to set out again on our journey, I frowned and shook our map in frustration. "It only shows a main road inland, and it looks busy. Let's ask around. There has to be a small road along the coast to Varkala."

CARLA FOUNTAIN

Dermot approached and asked several people before he got an answer. "They said there is a back road. Let's explore and go for it."

The back road took us through dozens of little fishing villages with no traffic for the first ten miles of the ride. Bliss! We stopped at a Kali temple, where a petite lady with a big smile greeted us. She spoke in Malayalam as we walked around the temple and took pictures. She handed us a flyer about her temple, also written in Malayalam. We thanked her and continued on.

Decades later, I look back and see it was no coincidence that the goddess Kali showed up so many times on this trip in festivals, temples, images, and figurines. Her dark-blue body, hanging tongue, fierce eyes, and necklace of skulls looked terrifying. She often held a severed head in one hand and a sword in another. Kali destroys and creates. She cuts away and releases that which no longer serves so that the new can be born in our lives. She transforms. On our trip I was going through my own transformation. I needed to find the Kali energy and harness it. Hopefully, like Kali, I would also be loving and kind. It was a fine and difficult balance.

In Varkala, thick strands of coconut palms fringed the red cliffs above the ocean. We found a hotel room two miles from the stunning beach. Our mood continued to improve. We played and bodysurfed in the warm Indian Ocean, with water so clear we could see our feet. Fresh mineral water flowed from a pipe at the rocks by the clean sand. We could rinse the salty sea off our bodies. Locals said the pure water was beneficial to drink, claiming it held curative properties. But we didn't want to take the risk.

After our rest in Varkala, we continued farther down the coast. When we stopped at a village bank to change money, I stayed outside with the bikes while Derm conducted the transaction. A crowd of thirty villagers stood around and stared at me for the entire half hour Derm did business in the bank. The villagers didn't respond to my greetings. They scrutinized me in stony silence. One little girl has stayed in my

BICYCLE ODYSSEY

mind to this day. She was about eleven and thin with wispy hair. Her pale face held sad and tired eyes. She reminded me of the girl, Durga, in the book *Pather Panchali*. Her ragged clothes were so threadbare, they were transparent. She looked at me intently until we left. As different and interesting as India was to us, so were we, often even more so, to the people in the remote places where we stopped.

In the next village, the road turned to sand. While we tried to find out whether the road stayed that way or improved farther on, a crowd of young boys gathered around. No one spoke English. An older man eventually communicated that the road improved farther on, so we pushed our bikes through the sand. As we walked, I turned and caught several boys unzipping my back bag. Other boys tried to open the bag as well. Fed up, I shook my pump at them. They scattered and left me alone. We pushed the bikes for about half a mile until the path ended at a lagoon, where we needed to cross on a raft. The ferryman hoisted the bikes aboard, and we splashed through the water to board the raft with him. Using a long pole to push against the sand, he slowly moved the raft across the lagoon. Once we reached the other side, we pushed the bikes through more sand to a hard-packed road that led to a much more prosperous community than the one we had left.

I trembled with anxiety after my experience with the boys. They hadn't bothered Derm. That was a frequent occurrence in India—no one harassed Derm. If he stood near me, men and boys left me alone. But if he left my side or I was alone, they viewed me as a target. The day before, on the beach at Varkala, I watched our things while Derm swam. A group of boys shifted over to our beach blanket and boldly tried to touch our things and to touch me. They scattered when Dermot walked back. As a woman, despite being quite tall, the boys viewed me as weak and insignificant. My body boiled with anger and fear. I hated the sensation of vulnerability that swept over me.

In a discussion about our odyssey nearly three decades later, I learned of the extreme stress Dermot had experienced in India's male-dominated culture. Our travel situation pushed him into a fierce protector mode.

He feared for my safety. Looking back with this hindsight moved me to tears and explained a lot about his behavior. While I had perceived his demeanor as smothering and overbearing, he'd viewed it as loving and protective.

We spent five wonderful days at Kovalam Beach near Trivandrum. We splurged and stayed at an upscale place much nicer than we were accustomed to. This indulgence cost the equivalent of ten dollars a night for an airy room with a balcony overlooking the Arabian Sea. The luxury helped us rejuvenate.

The bodysurfing at Kovalam Beach was exhilarating and fun in the clear water. But when we paid for a snorkeling trip, our guide took us to a polluted bay with murky water and few fish. Our eyes stung from pollutants in the water.

Kovalam Beach catered to tourists. Many small open-air restaurants dotted the beach and served dinner while showing pirated videos of American movies. Several of the videos scrolled the words "not for public viewing" across the screen. They had been smuggled into India from Hollywood well before their release in America.

One night we attended a dance recital of the traditional Kathakali dance. The performance included the preparations the dancers took as they applied their elaborate, colorful makeup and costumes. We watched for an hour as they carefully painted their faces bright green, vivid blue, yellow, or black with bold, cherry-red lips, thick black arcs around the eyes, and bright yellow arcs filled with designs on the forehead. The makeup helped to emphasize the dancers' exaggerated eye movements. The colors also identified characters: green for nobles and sages, red for evil characters, black and red for demons, and yellow for monks and women. The actors donned magnificent headdresses, colorful skirted costumes, and long, metal nail extensions. The evening

BICYCLE ODYSSEY

continued as they danced with intricate foot and hand movements and acted out stories from the *Mahabharata* and the *Ramayana* with musical and vocal accompaniment.

When we had first bicycled into town on our way to the hotel, we met a local journalist on the road. He struck up a conversation and asked whether he could interview us and take our photo for the local paper. A few days before we left Kovalam Beach, the journalist stopped by our hotel with a copy of the article written in a graceful Malayalam script. We didn't know what he had written, but we were excited to be featured in a full-page story with a photograph in a foreign newspaper. If we had written our own article, we would have said that India challenged us and rewarded us in equal measure. We rejoiced in surviving the Indian portion of our bicycle trip without any accidents. Even though we endured terrifying moments along the way, India gifted us with warm connections to people who generously shared their culture and religion. The subcontinent stimulated all our senses. The people we met and our captivating experiences would stay engraved in our memories forever.

18

Madras and Calcutta

We took a taxi to the airport and flew to Madras (Chennai) for a few days before stopping in Calcutta (Kolkata) on our way to Kathmandu, Nepal. In Madras, we checked our mail at the American Express office. I savored the letters from friends and family, but there was still no letter from the uncle we worried about. One friend's sister had a baby, and he was excited to be chosen as the godfather. Another friend had given birth to her second child. That day as I read letters from them, I envied their cozy family life. They later told me they had envied my life of adventure and travel.

I reflected on this odyssey, which was the apex of all I had wanted to do for so many years. *Had I anticipated the trip too much?* Homesickness crept in, and I longed to return to California. *But if I look forward to going home, will the buildup and expectations cause disappointment when I return?* I realized I needed to find happiness every day—moment by moment—and not set my sights on faraway things. I vowed to stay in the present and relish the experience instead of waiting for the future to fulfill me. I reflected on the trip and recognized that the low points, the "hell" of the trip, had only sweetened the high points, the spots of "heaven": the weeks in Gokarna and Kodaikanal, the visit with the family of rope makers in Tamil Nadu, the rides across the plains during harvest in Karnataka, and the trek in the Western Ghats with the thick forest, coffee, and tea plantations. Our trip through India wasn't a spiritual-seeking trip or a trip to see sights and monuments. We wanted to meet people and touch the heartbeat of the little villages and places far away from the major sights most people visit in India. In that sense, I would say we were successful.

In Madras, I decided to have my palm read. The practice had intrigued me for a while, and I hoped India would be an interesting place to look into palmistry. The posh hotel down the street from where we stayed displayed a sign that advertised readings for twelve dollars. The fee was a splurge on our budget, but I decided to indulge. My palm reader, a well-dressed man in a white shirt and dark pants, used a room in the hotel as his office. He studied the lines in my palm as he gently held my hand. I didn't ask questions while he told me what he saw.

Still studying my palm, the man said, "When you were fourteen, it was an important year for you. Your father was independent. Between the ages of seventeen and twenty-seven, you had independent thoughts and were serious. You have had two loves, and a third one will be permanent. At twenty-eight, you had extra knowledge."

I nodded but kept silent. *Maybe that was when I pursued my teaching certificate*, I thought.

He continued with the reading. "At thirty-one, you will be traveling."

I smiled. *Yes, I am on this trip!*

After placing my hand on the table, he said, "You are not dependent on your parents. But you haven't made much money so far. You have better contact with one of your parents than the other. The last three months' tensions have been reduced. You will live in three countries and settle in the third country."

CARLA FOUNTAIN

I nodded again, saying nothing. *Hmm. I've lived in America, Spain, and France. I wonder which country I will settle in.*

He paused for a sip of water and spoke again. "You will get two or three different kinds of education. Maybe two degrees. After age thirty-four, you will have no health problems. Before that, you will have some problems. But your health has been better the past two years."

I continued to remain silent as I thought about the different degrees I had earned. He was correct there. I hoped he was right about not having health problems after I turned thirty-four.

He picked up my hand again and turned it slightly. "You will have two children total—one daughter and one son. You will achieve full fame in something after you are thirty-six years old. Until then, there is someone else taking the credit for what you do. After you are thirty-eight, you will receive a lot of money. Many poor and sick will benefit from your work. In six months, there will be big plans. You will know more after March."

I thanked him and mulled over all he had said. He concluded with telling me how long I would live. That rattled me. I didn't think readers were supposed to do that—so I decided to put that number out of my mind.

During our time in Madras, we toured a history museum and visited a movie set, where one of India's biggest stars was filming a scene that day. Several enthralled Indian tourists watched the shoot with us and told us about the movie star. On the way back to our hotel, we accidentally walked into the middle of a large political rally. Men swarmed the streets with not a woman in sight. The scene gave me nervous flashbacks to the demonstrations we had encountered in Mysore.

Near our hotel, we found a good bookstore, Giggles, run by a woman named Nalini Chettur. We spent an enjoyable time browsing. Nalini and I chatted, and she helped me choose more books about

India. She had spent time in the West, and we talked about cultural differences. I lingered in the shop for a long time. It thrilled me to talk to a professional woman. There had been few opportunities to meet and connect with women during our trip through India, other than in Gokarna, Kodaikanal, and Kumily. I had yearned to meet more women during our two-and-a-half-month journey through India. I was grateful to support Nalini's business. It pleased me to see in a recent Internet search that Giggles was still open in 2018, almost three decades after our trip.

Purchases of books, clothes, incense, and handicrafts weighed us down at the end of our India segment. On our last afternoon in Madras, we made our way to the post office with a box to mail home. To prepare our package for shipping, a postal worker sent us around the corner to another office. A clerk sewed our box into a burlap bag, sealed the seams with red sealing wax, and wrapped the parcel with twine. We filled out multiple forms, and the clerk affixed dozens of colorful stamps to the enormous burlap bundle. Our parcel survived its two-month journey to the States and greeted us with the delicious smells of India when we opened it upon returning home.

From Madras, we flew to Calcutta and spent one night there. When we left Kovalam Beach, we made a vow not to bike anymore in India, so we took taxis around the city. Cameras in hand, we set out to explore. Calcutta possessed an ancient beauty. Large structures in the Macintosh style stood in aging splendor. They gave the city a mysterious and haunting charm.

The city of Calcutta is named after the famous Kalighat Kali Temple. Hundreds of pilgrims and devotees thronged in front of the large temple complex. Beggars asked for alms, and tourists gathered at the entrance. About one hundred people waited in line to enter. A priest walked us around and told us about the temple. The devotees needed to first

CARLA FOUNTAIN

bathe in water from the Ganges River, which was held in a large tank inside the temple grounds. They brought flowers and fruit offerings into the temple. Photos were prohibited inside the temple grounds. Priests practiced the ritual animal sacrifice of goats and oxen at this temple.

Mother Teresa opened a free hospice for the poor next to this Kali temple in 1952. The hospice gave people a place to die with dignity. We visited the temple on a Sunday. There were not many people out on the streets. The poverty didn't seem as intense as I had expected. Perhaps bicycling through India's serene back roads and bustling cities for two and a half months put things in a different perspective. We witnessed so much, from poverty to wealth and everything in between. Many people lived on the streets in the cities. They cooked, washed, bathed, and shaved in full view of all.

In the afternoon, we wandered over to the Maidan, the largest urban park in Calcutta, near the white marble Victoria Memorial. Hundreds played cricket on the vast, green fields. The expansive grounds of the Maidan provided a welcome respite from traffic in the city. Other couples and families strolled past us, enjoying their Sunday holiday. Unable to resist the spicy scents from the snack vendors, we bought *jhalmuri* (puffed rice mixed with peanuts, coriander, and other spices). The flavorful treat was wrapped in a paper cone.

Dermot paused under a shady tree. "Why don't we rest here while we eat?"

"That's a good idea." I spread my scarf out for us to sit on.

Dermot plopped down and sighed. "These last two and a half months in India have been intense."

"Yes, they have. I worried about our safety many times. But we met such wonderful people in Gokarna and Kodaikanal. Do you realize how fortunate we were to detour to those towns? I am ready to continue on our trip, but now that we are leaving, I feel pulled to come back here one day."

Dermot arched an eyebrow. "Hmm? I'd have to think about that. Right now, I just need time to recover."

"Our first day here, I was overwhelmed. I thought I had fallen down the rabbit hole. Now that the initial shock of landing in this country and culture so vastly different from our own has worn off, I want to learn and explore more," I said.

We sat in companionable silence, gazing at the activities around us on the Maidan. A wave of contentment washed over me. Faint strains of *"Ilu Ilu"* drifted from a nearby tea stand. I smiled. The music was a fitting send-off for our last afternoon in India.

That night we stayed at a small hotel in a quiet part of town. We enjoyed breakfast outside in the serene garden the next morning before we took a taxi to the airport for our flight to Kathmandu. After our meal, I left to purchase a few supplies. On my way back to the hotel, a band of musicians—with noses, ears, and other bits of extremities missing from their bodies—rushed at me with a loud musical fanfare. They extended a donation basket. The Calcutta Leper Society was scrawled across their banner. Shocked and startled, I threw the last of my rupee change into their basket and hastened back to the hotel. The airport and Nepal beckoned.

Because we didn't have a television anywhere we stayed, we benefitted from a great deal of time to read. Cell phones weren't something travelers carried around in the early '90s, and Internet access wasn't common. I enjoyed that year of sinking deep into books. We exchanged books with other travelers and discussed them. In each country, I liked to read novels by local authors or publications about that country. In

CARLA FOUNTAIN

India I read *Karma Cola: Marketing the Mystic East* by Gita Mehta. She had written the book in 1979 after a big influx of westerners traveled to the East, looking for the spirituality and mystery missing from their lives. The book describes what can happen when the ancient traditions of a society are turned into a commodity and sold to people who don't understand them. She also talked about the ills the westerners brought with them to villages in India, including drug addiction and anxiety. *Karma Cola* gave us a lot of food for thought.

For historical background, I also read *Raj* by Gita Mehta. The novel gave me a sense of the period from Queen Victoria's rule on through India's independence from the British as seen through the life of a maharaja's daughter. Anurag Mathur's *The Inscrutable Americans* was a fun read. Mathur, an Indian who had been an exchange student in the United States, experienced the same culture shock we did but in reverse. *India File*, by Trevor Fishlock, gave us good information about religion, history, and culture. One of the columnists in *The Times of India*, which we read for current events during our trip, was Shobhaa De. She wrote about the Bollywood set and was considered to be an Indian Jackie Collins. I read her column and her novel *Bollywood Nights* for a glimpse into that world. I enjoyed *Pather Panchali: Song of the Road* by Bibhutibhushan Bandyopadhyay. This classic tells about the life of a poor Bengali family from the perspective of the two young children. I had also seen the movie adaptation by Satyajit Ray. To understand the complex caste system in India, I read *Caste: At Home in Hindu India* by Sophie Baker. We also picked up and read many of Ruth Prawer Jhabvala's books, including *Heat and Dust* and *Out of India*.

PART 5
• Nepal—Touching the Sky

January 19 to February 4, 1992

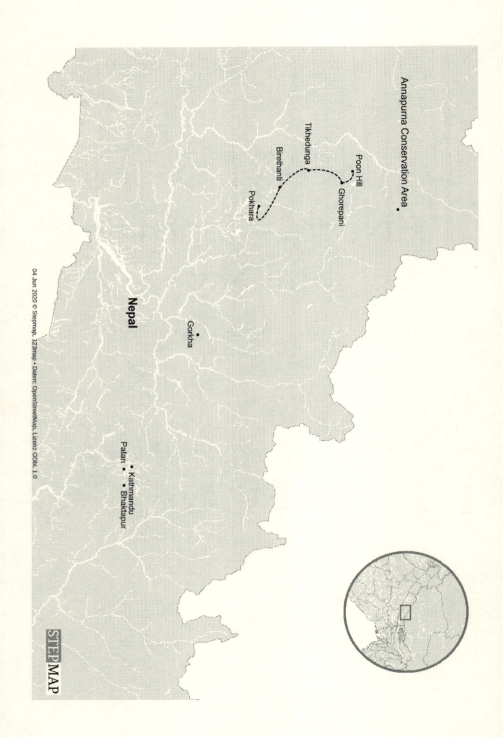

19

Kathmandu Valley and Trekking

A friend of Dermot's, who had traveled in India, told him that people escaped to Nepal and Sri Lanka when India overwhelmed them and they needed a break. We immediately noticed more personal space around us in Kathmandu. A large number of travelers passed through the city, so we weren't a curiosity. We didn't attract the attention we had drawn on the back roads of India.

We biked past majestic buildings and temples constructed with ocher and gray masonry. Stone lions guarded elaborate bronze doors. Children, red cheeked from the cold, played with hoops on the cobblestone squares. Vendors sold a myriad of vegetables and fruit, using ancient brass scales to complete their sales. The smell of wood smoke wafted through the air, promising warmth and coziness. Kathmandu bustled with activity and radiated color. Since fewer cars filled the road, we negotiated the streets with ease.

At the high altitude, Nepal seemed shockingly cold to us after spending so much time deep in southern India. The overcast sky created a dreary ambiance. But the cool weather made the dust more bearable. We wore all our cold-weather clothes and spent hours in restaurants, drinking hot chai and eating steamy bowls of Nepalese *momos* (plump dumplings stuffed with vegetables and meat) served with a spicy dipping sauce.

CARLA FOUNTAIN

The magnificent old town, filled with temples and shops, provided us with hours of exploration. We decided to stay in the Kathmandu Valley for a week and take a few day trips on our bikes to see how we liked cycling in the terrain and get acclimated to the altitude.

After a week in Kathmandu, we couldn't decide whether to stay in Nepal longer or leave for Bangkok. At a restaurant, we met a group of four American bicyclists—young men who had decided to go on a long trip after graduating from college. They had flown in from Thailand and were preparing to continue on to India. They were traveling our trip in reverse. We exchanged stories and information about our itineraries and gave each other helpful pointers.

One of the men, Joe, gave us some valuable information. "If you need your bikes worked on, we found a really good mechanic in Bangkok. He did an excellent job when we needed help."

Dermot slid his notebook over to Joe so he could write down the name and address. "Thanks, Joe. Our bikes could really use a tune-up now. The timing is perfect."

"No problem. Bangkok traffic is crazy, so be careful. It's a fun city, though. While your bikes are getting worked on, you can explore. Then head up to the northeast of Thailand. Very few tourists travel there."

I grinned. "Nothing could be worse than some of our crazy road experiences in India. But we loved the back roads and the little villages. How long will you be in Nepal?"

Joe passed the notebook back to us. "Please write down the places you recommend in India. We plan to stay another week and go to Pokhara in a few days to get out of the city and see the Himalayas. We might do a small trek. Then we'll go on to India. Don't be in a rush to get to Thailand. Why don't you take the bus to Pokhara with us later in the week?"

BICYCLE ODYSSEY

I glanced at Dermot. Our eyes locked in agreement without the need for discussion. For travel and decisions like this, we were on the same wavelength. "I like that idea," I said.

"Yes," Dermot smiled. "Let's all get our tickets together tomorrow morning."

After purchasing the tickets with our new friends, we hopped on the tram in Kathmandu to explore Bhaktapur, a village about forty-five minutes away. When we stepped off the tram, we traveled back in time to a medieval village. Potters worked outside in a courtyard. They used old tires as a base for their potting wheels. Rows of freshly made clay pots stood out in the open air to dry. Lines of handmade copper and brass pots, which hung on the walls, glowed in the sunlight. People used wooden pitchforks to mound stacks of hay on top of the buildings. We walked through the village down narrow, twisting alleyways through a maze of small, enclosed streets, which opened into plazas of various sizes. Gorgeous stone temples and shrines lined the largest plaza.

"I feel like I'm walking through a fairy tale." I sighed. "It's so beautiful here."

"Yes, it is! I love it." Derm pointed to my left. "Look. The boys are rolling hoops with a stick. Children are so creative with the resources they have, just like we saw in Uganda."

Rounding a corner into a plaza, we stumbled on one small Kali temple sacrifice. A few people huddled around the animal's innards, which had spilled onto the ground. Farther on in the main plaza, more people gathered in the center and sacrificed a large ox. Two more oxen stood in line for sacrificing. A person slit the ox's throat so the blood sprayed up from the artery and splattered the shrine. They paraded the severed head around the village, accompanied by a small band of percussions and horn instruments. The sacrifices and rituals continued all day across the town. People approached the altar and dipped their fingers in the blood; they applied a tilak to their foreheads and smeared the blood in the parts of their hair.

During lunch, we sat on a second-story restaurant balcony with a view over the main square. The sacrifice events unfolded in front of us over the course of the afternoon. As we walked through the village later on, we turned a corner and smelled burning hair. We came across a goat or an ox, charred and headless but otherwise intact. After the sacrifice and the removal of the entrails—which people paraded around and carried in bloody buckets, pans, and baskets—the carcass was burned. The ceremony caught us completely by surprise that day. The festival was obviously a time of rejoicing and an important day for the villagers.

We sat crammed into seats built for people much shorter than we were on the seven-hour bus ride to Pokhara. The American bicyclists we had met earlier in Kathmandu squeezed into the bus with us. The tallest one sat behind me, his knees digging into the back of my seat for most of the ride. But Pokhara was worth the trip. The town was nestled in a valley by a large lake. The calm town and the clean air were a welcome relief after the congestion and dust in the city of Kathmandu. While we waited for our bikes to be unloaded from the bus, a familiar-looking young man ran up and greeted us like he knew us. It was Sejun! We had met him in Goa when he worked at the restaurant where we ate most of our meals. We made plans with him to meet for dinner later that night in town.

After a bite of his *thali* meal, Sejun asked, "Do you know about the Gurkha?"

Dermot's face lit up. "Yes! My father told me about the elite Gurkha regiment that the British recruit from Nepal. He admires them. They are considered the bravest and fiercest soldiers in the world."

Sejun sat up straighter and beamed. "My village is in the Gorkha area where the soldiers are recruited from. I tried out to join the regiment. I have many relatives who fought with the Gurkha." Sejun's shoulders sagged, and he let out a sigh. "I didn't pass the test. After that, I was depressed."

"I am sorry to hear that, Sejun," I said. I imagined that he could have supported his family quite well on a Gurkha's salary. Joining the elite unit would have been a high honor.

Sejun smiled again. "I met an Englishman here in Nepal, and he invited me to travel to India with him. That is how I ended up in Goa, where I met you. I was working at the restaurant to earn money before I returned home to Pokhara."

"We sure are glad we had the opportunity to meet you in Goa and run into you here," I said, after we had finished our dinner.

We told Sejun that we had decided to go on a short trek so we could have a glimpse of the Himalayas. Mist shrouded the mountain range in Pokhara Valley, hiding the peaks. Sejun wanted to be our guide. He was disappointed when we told him we preferred to walk alone. We felt bad about not taking him up on his offer, but we needed time to ourselves to be quiet in nature.

We biked about thirty miles to the trailhead at Birethanti to save two days of walking and stored our bikes at a guesthouse. We climbed to twelve thousand feet that day. We thought the first evening's dinner gave us food poisoning because we spent the night vomiting and had diarrhea. After the food poisoning, which we realized much later must have been altitude sickness, I couldn't eat the next day. I collapsed upon arrival at our next destination, Tikhedhunga. My energy flagged, and I lost my enthusiasm. The gray skies and the brown vegetation around us didn't make for a scenic start. I had doubts about continuing on the trek when we turned in for the night. But the next morning dawned with clear skies, and my spirits lifted.

CARLA FOUNTAIN

We pushed on to Ghorepani, where locals said we would be able to see the Himalayas.

That part of the trek challenged us. We climbed vertically up stone steps for two hours. We had developed superb bicycling stamina and strength, but walking up the mountain used different sets of muscles. Trekking was surprisingly hard and humbling for two seasoned bicyclists.

A glimpse of a snow-capped peak in the distance rewarded us. We received even bigger rewards with the view at Ghorepani the next morning. But first we replenished with a hearty meal and a comfortable bed at a lodge. An group of trekkers gathered around a warm fire with us that evening.

Judy, rose cheeked and blonde, was on a ten-day trek. "I come here every year. I work with a nonprofit in Colorado that sponsors a school in Nepal. When I visit, I take a little extra time for a trek."

"That sounds lovely," I said. "I would like to get involved in a project when I return home. We've seen so much on this trip. It makes the world feel very connected, and I want to help where I can."

Derm nodded. "That's a good idea."

Tim loosened his scarf as he warmed by the fire. His numerous silver rings glinted in the light. "I come here twice a year to buy artifacts for my store in London. This country is magical. I opened the store five years ago so I could have a good excuse to visit frequently."

Derm's eyes grew dreamy. "I love art. I've seen some exquisite paintings here. I envy your lifestyle."

Peter, short and stocky with a buzz cut, sipped his after-dinner chai. "Well, I'm here with the Peace Corps. I work with villagers, teaching them about health-related topics: water, sanitation, hygiene, and basic first aid."

BICYCLE ODYSSEY

We talked longer with these fascinating people. Then, with our heads full of ideas, we crawled into bed so we could get up before dawn.

At seven o'clock the next morning, we dragged ourselves out of bed, feeling so tired, groggy, and weak that we hit the trail late. At the top of Poon Hill, the rosy glow of dawn had faded, and everyone else had trekked down to their guesthouses for breakfast and a warm fire. The splendid view and the sounds of nature around us filled me with joy. Snow-covered mountains loomed close to us. Clouds swirled around their crests. After about twenty minutes, a curtain of clouds closed and hid the peaks. The strenuous climb had been worth the effort. Derm and I walked back to our guesthouse for breakfast and slogged down the mountain.

As we trekked along, we often encountered men with trains of donkeys carrying supplies to and from the different villages. The area we were in could be reached only by donkey or by going on foot. The trail was usually wide enough for us all to pass, but sometimes we hikers clung to the side of the hill or stepped to the side so the donkey train could proceed. The donkeys wore bells so we could hear them approaching. Colorful feather plumes waved on their tall headdresses.

Once I stepped the wrong way to let the donkeys pass—to the outside of the trail next to an enormous drop-off. The donkeys' loads swayed with their movements as they walked past us. The last donkey's load swung out and hit my backpack. I lost my balance and tipped toward the precipice. I would have gone over the cliff if the donkey's owner hadn't grabbed me and righted me. We smiled at each other and laughed together. I thanked him. After they moved along up the trail, I looked down the steep cliff and shivered. I would have been severely injured or killed if that man hadn't grabbed me. He saved my life!

Going down the mountain was more arduous than going up. The steep and slippery path forced us to descend slowly. Our knees and muscles strained to keep from sliding or falling. We stopped at Tikhedhunga again to spend the night and bathed for the first time in

CARLA FOUNTAIN

four days. The hostess gave me a quarter of a bucket of warm water and gave Derm two-thirds of a bucket. I questioned the obvious difference.

She laughed sheepishly and shrugged. "The man gets more," she said.

I stifled a chortle. *Of course.*

We took our buckets to the cement bathing cubicle off the courtyard. We undressed, and I saw that unwelcome hitchhikers had feasted on my body. I found a small bite on my stomach that morning at the lodge. I thought a flea had bitten me. But that afternoon when I pulled off my sweater, I looked down to see a small, gray insect clinging to my T-shirt. I feared that the critters were everywhere.

My skin crawled and itched, and my stomach performed queasy flips. "Oh, no! Derm, look! I've got five bites on my chest and torso, and more on my neck. Help me wash, please. I need to rinse any bugs away."

"Wait, look! I've got a rash on my chest and backside."

"Hmmm ... ... I suspect that's from nerves. They don't look like bites."

Dermot's face paled. "I bet something was in the sleeping bags we rented for our trek."

After we collected our bikes at our starting point in Birethanti, we rode uphill for two thousand feet before gliding downhill to Pokhara. Small boys tried to run us off the road, throwing things at us. I was tired and reaching my tolerance limit. But I reflected on our trekking permit guidelines. "Remember Nepal is here to change you. You are not here to change Nepal." I breathed, pedaled on, and didn't react. That incident aside, Nepal's main charm for me lay in the sincere smiles and greetings of the Nepalese we passed on the trail and in the friendly hospitality at the establishments we frequented.

BICYCLE ODYSSEY

My birthday was the next day. I would be thirty-five. I felt old as I limped down the mountain, stiff from the prior days' hikes and the steep descent. The cycling helped stretch and loosen our muscles. I decided to treat myself to a massage. I also planned to undo my braids. I had never caught head lice in all my years of teaching elementary school children, and I hoped I didn't have them now.

Physical and mental fatigue swept over us. My legs cramped from the hike. I stretched them once we relaxed back at our cottage in Pokhara. "That was a beautiful trek. What if we changed our tickets to fly home early from here? That would end our trip on a high note."

Dermot massaged his knees. "Do you have more of that muscle liniment, babe?" He rubbed it in. "Ahhh! Hiking definitely uses different muscles than bicycling. We could fly home after Thailand. I've been thinking about it too." He touched a blister on his heel and winced. "But we probably won't get a chance to take a trip like this for a long time, if ever again. Do we have anything to cover this blister?"

I passed him some antibiotic cream. "Put some of this on first. We do travel well together. I feel like things can only improve. You're right, I don't know when we could do this again. Let's keep an open mind. We might even decide to extend our trip."

We were traveling in harmony, and our relationship showed improvement. I hoped we would work out our problems and could stay together. Our traveling styles synchronized well. Our instincts and ability to adapt meshed. We were confident and comfortable together on the road.

Back in Kathmandu, we applied for visas for Thailand before flying out. The friendly lady at the Royal Thai Embassy handed back my passport and with a teasing smile said, "Be careful. You might lose your husband in Thailand!"

PART 6
• Thailand—Temples and Monks

February 4 to March 21, 1992

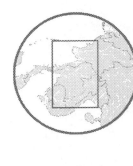
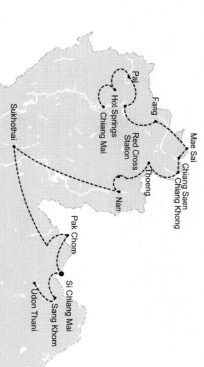

20

Bangkok

In Bangkok, I immediately noticed that people gave each other more personal space than what we had experienced in India and Nepal. No one stared at us, and we didn't attract large crowds. I'd grown weary of being the center of attention everywhere we went. I was relieved to be ignored for once. But going from the medieval villages of Nepal to the bustling freeways and traffic of modern downtown Bangkok required an adjustment period.

Our taxi driver couldn't find our budget hotel the first night in Bangkok, so we stayed at a posh and expensive hotel in a touristy part of town. Two nights later, we transferred to the Bangkok Youth Hostel. The hostel was incredibly clean and airy for only five dollars a night. Cleanliness was a common denominator everywhere we stayed in Thailand.

When we entered Thailand, the customs official handed us a pamphlet with a few cultural pointers aimed at preventing visitors from unknowingly offending Thais. The information provided valuable particulars for our exploration of the country. One tip was to take off our shoes when entering a home or guesthouse. Another was never to touch anyone on the head. The head was considered a sacred part of the body, and many westerners offended the Thais by patting children on the head. Two important feet-related tips were never to use your

CARLA FOUNTAIN

foot to point and never to put your feet up on the seat in front of you at the movies. The foot was considered the lowest and dirtiest part of the body, so you would never want to even point your feet at a person while sitting with your legs crossed. There were several other rules, including that a woman should never touch a monk.

During the first two days, we spent most of our time taking care of necessary business, such as having our bikes repaired at the bike shop our friends had told us about and checking American Express for mail. In Nepal, we hadn't received mail from home, so we felt certain we would have a bundle of letters waiting for us. There was none. We called home, and everyone seemed okay, but I worried that a few people resented our trip. Keeping up with our affairs created more work than anyone anticipated. My parents sounded a little cool. It was somewhat understandable; a check Derm had sent to reimburse my parents for bills they had paid for us never reached them.

After we took care of our business, we spent the next few days in Bangkok, wandering around the city, walking through department stores, and trying to resist the temptation of buying things we didn't need. We did purchase cassette tapes of music we had heard on the road as well as music we missed from home. I loved the street life in Bangkok and that women were out and about, working and socializing. Bangkok was cosmopolitan and sophisticated.

Countless vendors in the streets sold luscious fruits, spicy noodles, tamarind candies, and other goodies. We couldn't identify many foods, but we tried everything. Because cleanliness and sanitation were so good, we could eat from the street vendors and drink the water without becoming ill. We hadn't been able to do that since leaving Europe. Water-purifying tablets made water taste like chlorine, so we were thrilled not to need them.

We toured the Grand Palace and the magnificent Wat Pho, Thailand's oldest and largest royal temple complex. Wat Pho is also home to one of the oldest schools for Thai massage. We received our

208

first-ever Thai massage at Wat Pho. The massage soothed our sore muscles, and we loved the session so much that we returned the next day for another massage. I appreciated that we stayed clothed and could have the massage out in the open air. When I found out that Wat Pho held two-week classes to learn Thai massage, I wanted to enroll. Dermot said he would rather study scuba diving.

"Why don't we take a two-week break? You can go south and become certified in scuba while I study Thai massage," I said.

Dermot frowned. "I don't want us to be apart on the trip."

I shook my head. "A short period of time apart will be good for us. I think it might help our relationship."

His tone sharpened. "No It's not a good idea. I said I don't want us to be apart on this trip!"

"Well, promise me you'll at least think about it. This massage was so good. I would love to learn how to give a Thai massage. It would be a good life skill." I rubbed his shoulder to drive home my point. "You would benefit from my studies also."

Dermot smiled as I kneaded his shoulder, and his tone softened. "It *was* good. It really helped me. Let's go back and get another one tomorrow."

"Yes, let's! I want to try the herbal ball massage. They press into the muscles with a warm compress of medicinal herbs."

After several days in Bangkok, we decided to take the night bus to Chiang Mai. The only difficulty we thought we might face were fewer English-speaking locals. We hoped we would manage in the countryside. Our Thai phrase book helped us with the basic social phrases. Thai is a tonal language, though, so a person can easily say a completely different word from what is intended. To help with the learning, I studied a few phrases every day as we biked. I put the

CARLA FOUNTAIN

words and phrases for my lesson of the day in my front map holder and repeated them.

In the little towns where we stayed, curious children drifted over to talk to us as we sat in the evening breezes after dinner. They enjoyed helping us practice our Thai and laughed as they corrected our tones while we read the phrase book together. Thai has five main tones, so, for example, the word *ma* can mean "dog," "horse," "come," or "the Mama brand of noodles," depending on the tone you use.

21

Chiang Mai to the Northeast— Hill Tribes and Buffalo

Chiang Mai was larger than we anticipated. The city buzzed with continuous activity. We stayed one day and took in a flower festival and parade before heading up north and cycling into the mountains. Leaving the crowded, steamy city and climbing to a higher elevation with fresh, cool air felt wonderful.

We often stopped at Thai Buddhist temples, known as *wats*, along our route, and the monks or nuns frequently invited us in for tea and a chat. Thai temples always stood out and gleamed with gold leaf under the eaves of their tall, swooping, red-tiled roofs. Intricate red-and-gold bas-relief sculptures of Buddha adorned panels on the sides. Often a pair of elaborately stylized *nagas* (serpentine creatures from mythology), large warriors, or massive, curving dragons guarded the entrances.

We met Achara, a Thai woman in her thirties who was sitting outside one of the *wats* we visited. Achara adjusted her nun's robe and patted the steps, indicating that we should sit beside her. "Please sit. Rest and have tea with me. Bicycling in the heat must be hard work."

We happily sat in the cool shade of the temple awning.

She poured a cup of tea for each of us. "I am almost at the end of my stay here," she said.

I took a sip of the light brew. "How long have you been a nun, Achara? Why do you say you are at the end of your stay?" I asked.

"I came here for three months. I was at a period in my life when I needed to take time for reflection. It is quite common in Thailand for people to go into a monastery at some point in their lives." She cradled her cup in her hands. "We shave our heads and wear the monastic robes. People stay in the monastery for three days, three weeks, three months, or even three years. We study and meditate."

The practice sounded appealing to me. We all need time away from our routines for reflection.

In the early mornings, we observed a ritual play out in every town. A parade of monks with shaved heads, clad in saffron robes, walked through the town with their alms bowls. People stepped out from their houses and generously placed food in the bowls, raised their hands in a *wai* (a prayer-like gesture) to their forehead, and bowed as a sign of reverence and respect for the monks.

One day we met a woman named Kulap at the market in a town we had stayed in the night before. Kulap overheard me as I struggled with a transaction. I was using my phrase book without success, and Kulap approached to help. She was married to an American and spoke fluent English.

"Thai language is difficult with the tones! Thank you so much for helping me," I told her as I put the assorted items in my bag.

"No problem. My husband is American, so I understand," she said. "Why don't you come over to my house tomorrow and meet him."

BICYCLE ODYSSEY

We walked outside together. "We can go to a forest *wat* for lunch with the monks. We can take motorbikes to get there. We have two at home." She looked us up and down. "Do you know how to ride a motorbike?"

Dermot assured her that he did. We made plans to meet the next morning. I was excited about the adventure and the invitation.

When we arrived at her house, she gave one motorbike to Dermot for the two of us to ride and then climbed onto hers. For a demure and petite lady, she rode that motorbike like a wild woman, zigzagging through traffic at a fast clip. Dermot managed to keep up. I closed my eyes often and hung on tight.

At the forest *wat*, the monks arranged the donated food they had collected that morning along with the treats we brought them. They sat together in a large, covered pavilion in the middle of a forest glen. Many well-dressed ladies, like our own new friend, came for the lunch. It seemed like a prestigious thing for them to do. After lunch, Kulap introduced us to Geoffrey, a tall, lean Englishman who had been a monk there for many years. Dermot and I wanted to learn more about Buddhism and were happy to be able to converse with a monk, who spoke fluent English.

"I came here several years ago to learn more about Buddhism," Geoffrey explained. "I was looking to understand the big questions in life that I grappled with. I found that studying Buddhism helped me."

"How so?" I asked.

Geoffrey studied my face for a moment. "Buddhism has Four Noble Truths. Suffering exists in life. The causes of suffering are desire and wanting. We can end suffering with the cessation of desire and wanting. There is a path we can follow to accomplish that." He paused, letting us take in his words. "That path is called the Noble Eightfold Path. It includes meditating, right action, right speech, mindfulness, respecting life, right intentions, right livelihood, and truthfulness."

I would have liked to talk more with Geoffrey, but Kulap motioned for us that it was time to leave. I raised my hands in a *wai* and bowed my head. "Thank you for spending time with us, Geoffrey. It was so nice to meet you."

I wished we had been able to meet more fluent English speakers in monasteries during our trip. I studied and read more about Buddhism on my own later.

A rich, green forest surrounded the mountain road on our way to Pai. We never encountered a single vehicle. Heaven! We slogged and sweated up the steep hills in the thick forest and enjoyed the relief of the cooling breeze on the descents. We traveled down dirt roads and finally reached the Pong Dueat Hot Springs. Our attractive wooden cabin on stilts gave us a view of the misty springs and the thick, bamboo forest. The lodge was, however, rather expensive for our budget, and there was no place to buy food. We had only packaged noodles in our supplies. After fifty-five miles of cycling up steep hills, that wasn't enough sustenance.

We unwound at dusk with a good soak in the hot springs to soothe our muscles and our minds. We watched the swirling mists from the hot springs waft up into the tall, leafy, bamboo trees. In the morning, we walked down a forest path to the small pools and soaked again.

I sighed as we relaxed under the sun until I looked over at Dermot. "Yikes! There are little red worms wriggling on your skin."

He jumped up in horror with a huge splash. "You've got them on you too! And a big black one."

That put a quick end to the blissful soak. We ran to where the water cascaded and rinsed off. Derm and I contemplated whether we needed to worry about our exposure to the worms.

That night Dermot couldn't find his wedding ring. He had lost so much weight that the ring had slipped off his finger. Even though I had mixed feelings about our marriage and its future, this loss was terrible. An ominous feeling hung over me. We searched for the ring everywhere, and when we couldn't find it, we decided the ring was lost for good. We both felt glum. I still had my ring and continued to wear it throughout the trip.

Places not accessible by bicycle required a hike. To visit a Karen hill tribe village, we set out on a hot and difficult trek through gorgeous, thick jungle. Their wooden houses were grouped in a clearing in the forest. When we arrived at the small, quiet village, we felt frustrated by our lack of Thai language skills and a bit awkward as well. But we discovered that the Karen, the largest hill tribe in Thailand, have their own language. When we arrived, we observed the villagers as they winnowed grain from their rice harvest and wove bamboo fronds for the roofs of their dwellings.

Two days later in the small and dusty village of Pai, we met Gaëlle and Thierry, who were touring Thailand by car. They walked into the restaurant, where Derm and I were eating a delicious pad Thai dinner. Thierry entered, greeting the room with a polite "*bonsoir*"—as is French custom—and I answered back in French. The friendly exchange led to introductions, and we ended up dining together. I was happy to speak French with them and to compare notes about our journeys. At the end of the evening, they invited us to go with them in their rental car to visit the Soppong caves the next day.

Our guide at the caves was a young Thai woman. She wore simple flip-flops and carried a lantern. To enter the darkness, we walked across a bamboo bridge over a river that flowed into the cave. The cathedral-sized cave glistened with crystals on the stalactites and stalagmites. As we climbed rickety ladders, I started to shake. The height terrified me.

CARLA FOUNTAIN

Our guide's lamp cast the only light, and I could see a dark abyss down below. Thoughts of falling engulfed me with sheer panic. I wanted to go back, but I couldn't because the others were climbing up the ladder behind me. I felt dizzy, nauseous, and full of regret for embarking on this adventure. By the time I arrived at the top, I trembled uncontrollably. I thought a cave adventure would be easier the second time around; however, I was more afraid than I had been in the cave in India. Then, as we walked around the second and third chambers, I began to relax and feel my muscles unclench. The air inside the cave was warm and humid. I imagined curling up and sleeping there. The cave felt secure and peaceful like a womb.

Our guide shined the light on cave drawings of animals, so faded we could barely see them. We continued through a labyrinth of chambers before returning down the ladder. To my relief, the descent was easier. Once we arrived at the riverbed, we took a bamboo raft to the cave's rear exit and observed thousands of swallows flying in to roost for the night. As the light faded, a few bats left the cave. We didn't stay long enough for the mass exodus.

The next day Thierry and Gaëlle proposed that we put our bikes in their car and ride to Mae Sai with them. We accepted and braved the curves and car sickness of the road trip. Along the way, we stopped for a BBQ chicken lunch with honey sauce and rice at a restaurant. The combo was one of our favorite lunches to have on the road throughout Thailand. We stuffed ourselves into the car and zoomed down the hill. It would have taken us four or five days to bicycle the two hundred miles in the hills. But a slow bike ride was much more enjoyable than a fast trip in a car.

Thierry stopped the car in the hills before Mae Sai at an Akha village off the dusty dirt road. The four of us wandered into the village. Thierry strummed his small travel guitar as he walked, and Derm and I followed with our cameras. Gaëlle engaged the head chief in conversation, and he invited us to his house. She must have charmed him. Respectfully leaving our shoes on the ground, we climbed the ladder to the porch of his wooden stilt house. The chief spread a mat

BICYCLE ODYSSEY

out for us and motioned for us to sit down. His wife, who wore a large headdress, brought over hot tea and steamed sweet potatoes, leaving us with her husband, son, and another male guest. The son spoke a little English, so we were able to chat. He taught us the Akha word for *tea* plus a few other words.

"Your accent is good." he said. "Would you like to visit our school and meet our teacher?"

I scrambled to my feet. "I would love to! I am an educator also."

The teacher met us and showed off his cozy, well-maintained schoolhouse. "This is our game room, our library, and a study area."

Two students looked up from their game of checkers and smiled at us.

"What a nice building! May I take a photo to share with my class in the United States? My students would love seeing how children from other parts of the world go to school."

We said our goodbyes and piled back in the car. By the time we drove to Mae Sai on the Burmese border, I was so sick of being in a vehicle that I vowed to bike from there on. We rested in our mini cabins, which were terraced on a hillside overlooking Burma.

That night Dermot and I sat on the porch and looked out at the lights in the small town. Dermot slumped in his chair. "They're such a happy couple. Why can't we get along like that?" he asked.

I didn't know what to say. I gazed at the lights that blurred through my unshed tears. He didn't understand my need for more independence, mistaking it as a sign that I didn't love him. I had grown weary of trying to explain myself.

We looked forward to bicycling again but were sad to leave our new friends. We exchanged addresses as we parted. I kept in touch with

217

Thierry and Gaëlle, visiting them in France many times. I have seen their children grow over the years. Their friendship is a reminder that meaningful relationships can begin anywhere in the world.

Happy to be back on our bicycles, we left Mae Sai. Policemen pulled us over at checkpoints a few times that day. They even searched our bags at one of the stops. They took Dermot's pocketknife out of his fanny pack, opened the blade, and smelled it. I was perplexed and wondered why they did that. Later, I explained what had happened to another traveler.

He laughed at my ignorance. "They were checking for the smell of drug residue. People use their knives to cut heroin," he said. "This is the Golden Triangle area, where the borders of Laos, Burma, and Thailand meet. The Golden Triangle is known for the heroin trade."

Thanks to the advice given to us by the fellow bicyclists we had met in Nepal, we came to a little-visited area of Thailand in the northeast. We were truly off the beaten path and loved the quiet, rural roads and the mountains thick with vegetation. One day between Chiang Saen and Chiang Khong, we traveled thirty-five miles on a dirt road. We had trained every weekend in the Los Angeles mountains for this trip, going up the steep dirt grades on our mountain bikes. I had even bicycled from our home in Altadena to the Mount Wilson Observatory, climbing four thousand feet one afternoon on the grueling dirt switchbacks. But these country roads in the mountains challenged us despite all our training. They were steeper and more isolated than we anticipated. Still, we loved the terrain and rose to the challenge.

We headed east to Nan. We were used to bicycling long distances in a day. The hills, however, slowed us down. Before we knew it, fifty-five miles flew by, and the sun set, leaving us in pitch dark—no moonlight and no town in sight. We crept along with our feeble headlights. There hadn't been any traffic on the back roads for the past couple of days.

BICYCLE ODYSSEY

Not one car, truck, or motorcycle passed us that evening. We were both a little scared and tired. An hour crawled by before we noticed a glimmer in the distance. We crept toward the light in our lowest gears up the steep grade.

When we arrived, I knocked at the door. The small building was a Red Cross station in the Tha Wang Pha District. Three young Thai nurses answered the door and scrutinized us.

"*Sawadee ka.*" (Hello), I said. Pressing my hands together, I bowed in greeting.

"*Sawadee khrap,*" Dermot said as he bowed. "We have arrived here on our bicycles and need to find a place to stay. It's too dark to keep going, and we are very tired. Is there a town nearby?"

The young nurses shook their heads. "There is no town close by." They paused and glanced at each other. "Are you married?"

"Yes," I answered.

They hesitated and repeated, "Are you married?"

"Yes," I said again. I showed them my wedding ring for emphasis.

They talked among themselves and answered, "Okay. You can stay here with us tonight. The town is too far away. But first, come with us to bathe."

They took us to the river down from their station. I used my sarong to wash while covered, as is common for women in Thailand. Dermot bathed in his underwear. Only when we were clean did they show us where we could sleep. They invited us to share their meal of rice and green curry with bamboo shoots. We were grateful for their hospitality. Although the days grew hot in the sun, the nights became cold in the mountains. That night Dermot and I huddled together and held each other close for warmth under the quilt the nurses had given us.

CARLA FOUNTAIN

In the morning we biked thirty miles and hitched a ride on a truck the rest of the way to Nan, where we found a guesthouse. A few other foreigners were staying there also, and we enjoyed talking to them. As proof of just how small the world is, Dermot recognized another guest. A man at the guesthouse had looked at Dermot's car, which he put up for sale in Los Angeles, before our trip. He, like Dermot, was a colorful character, and the two of them enjoyed swapping stories.

Two Thai women ran the guesthouse. They said they planned on taking a trip to visit a tribe called the Mlabri, the People of the Yellow Leaves, and invited us to join them. The two guesthouse owners helped out a small family of Mlabri with medicine. We were keen on going and about three other people from England decided to go with us.

We drove to a small Hmong village for our base camp. The Hmong have a distinctive dress of wide-legged, indigo pants and colorfully embroidered jackets for the men. The women wore mid-calf skirts, colorful blouses, and indigo head wrappings. We spent the night camping alfresco (without a tent) in a field below the cluster of village houses. When we woke up at dawn, a woman worked quietly next to us in the field. She used a slender knife to make small, spiral cuts into a large opium poppy bulb on a plant next to us to gather the resin. I didn't have sweet and crazy dreams like Dorothy when she fell asleep in a field of poppies, but I had a pleasant evening and slept well.

We ate breakfast in the Hmong village and set out on a challenging walk into the hills to find the Mlabri family. One of the Hmong men from the village joined us to lead the way on the hike. He carried his supplies on his back in a cone-shaped, woven basket. The Mlabri are called "People of the Yellow Leaves" because they make a hut with large banana leaves woven onto a bamboo frame. When the leaves turn yellow, they change camp and build a new shelter. They live in small family units and hunt for food using bows and arrows. The family we visited consisted of a man, a woman, a four-year-old child, and an infant. They wore simple clothes. The mother slung the baby on her back with a striped cloth. The patriarch cooked meat encased in a

220

bamboo sheath over a fire. A small, quiet dog and three playful puppies rested with them.

Our group leader gave the patriarch medicine for his infected foot and explained the dosage. The rest of us stood around awkwardly. Dermot and I shared our little family photo book to break the ice. It helped smooth over encounters with border guards and at police checks in Kenya and Uganda. Sharing our lives with those we met gave us an opportunity to engage in conversation. I took out our book to show the patriarch. We jabbered away in English, talking about the photos. The family looked at them and seemed interested. The patriarch nodded. The other foreigners may have thought we were a bit odd. I felt self-conscious as they watched us, but at the time, it felt like the right thing to do.

We stayed in Nan for a few more days. It was located off the tourist trail, and we enjoyed wandering around the quiet, friendly town. We walked to the market for meals, where we sat in the middle of the activity and tried various Thai dishes. One of my favorites was *som tum* (green papaya salad) made from shredded papaya, fish sauce, garlic, peppers, and dried shrimp. The spicy tartness was refreshing with just a pinch of heat from the peppers. Our other staples were pad Thai (the classic Thai dish made with noodles, peanuts, chicken, eggs, tofu, and sprouts) and *gai yang* (Thai BBQ chicken) with a sweet and spicy dipping sauce. I eagerly tried other new dishes we came across. Nothing ever disappointed.

We met Jack, a cyclist from Canada, who stayed in Nan every year for three months during the winter. He was covered in tattoos, which disappeared under his shirt and long pants.

"It is important," Jack explained, "to be able to cover up my tattoos so that I won't be easily identifiable."

CARLA FOUNTAIN

I was fascinated by his tattoos. He had many, and tattoos were not commonplace back then. No one I knew had one at that time, and many people still viewed tattoos as taboo. I loved the delicate pastels and swirls that covered his pale skin. When we set out on the trip, I thought in the back of my mind that I might get a tattoo if inspiration struck me along our journey.

Jack continued, "You need to think long and hard about a tattoo because it lasts forever. I don't think that the delicate pastel colors that you want would show up so well on your darker skin. You are better off using black ink if you get a tattoo."

To this day, I have never gotten a tattoo and probably won't. I never settled on a design that I could be forever attached to. I do feel disappointed about not having those delicate pastels, though. But I'm content to admire and appreciate the ink on others who wear the art well.

Jack bicycled with us and took us to a secret cave near Nan. We stashed our bicycles behind the bushes that hid the entrance. We still had to climb and jump to explore, but this time the drop-offs in the cave weren't as dramatic and scary as in Pai. I enjoyed our adventure without shaking in fear.

Nan's small size made the town easy to negotiate. Dermot and I spent a few afternoons apart, and that filled me with more confidence. The past two months had often forced us into a hyper-vigilant state on the road. We could let our guard down in Thailand. Our demeanors softened, and our bond grew stronger.

Late one morning, I came back from a walk to get Dermot for lunch. "I had the best time at the *wat*. I met a really sweet woman, who showed me around."

Dermot looked up from his sketch pad. "That's great!"

"I feel so comfortable walking around alone to visit the temples and the markets here."

"I can finally let down my guard and relax, too." Dermot went back to his sketch.

"The surrounding nature offers so many possibilities for exploration. I understand why Jack and that couple we met from Japan come back here every year."

"I could see doing that. Nan is slow paced and friendly. It would be fun to come here for an extended stay one day." Dermot put down his sketch pad, stood, and stretched. "Let's go to the market for lunch. I'm starving."

I gave Derm a hug. "I'm obsessed with the green papaya salad."

He gave me a long squeeze before releasing the hug, then locked our door as we set out. "It would be fun to rent a house for a couple of months if we did come back here."

We took a five-and-a-half-hour bus ride from Nan to Sukhothai and biked to Old Sukhothai, the ancient Thai capital. Old Sukhothai, which means "Dawn of Happiness," was the first capital of Siam and was founded by King Ramkhamhaeng in the thirteenth century. We spent a dreamy day wandering around and taking photos of the magnificent temple ruins and the Buddhas strung out over the vast lawns. We biked around the sprawling twenty-seven square miles of tranquility. The next day we visited another historical site at Phitsanulok, one of the oldest cities in Thailand, founded over six hundred years ago. We walked through Wat Yai, built in 1357, home to one of the most revered Buddha figures in Thailand.

In Sang Khom, we found a guesthouse on the Mekong River. It was strange to be with so many *farangs,* what the Thai call foreigners. We thought the area would have fewer tourists. There weren't masses of tourists in air-conditioned buses, but there were at least fifteen

CARLA FOUNTAIN

other *farangs* at our guesthouse that night in the tiny town. Everyone chattered away about politics in their home country. Talking with them was nice for a while, but it made me feel far removed from my reasons for traveling. Most of the other travelers stayed around the guesthouse for the better part of the day. Dermot and I rested there for a couple of hours before heading out to explore the back roads on our bikes. On our little jaunt, we met and talked to local people. I wondered whether the other travelers interacted with the locals.

Most mornings in Thailand, the guesthouses offered two choices for our meal: pad Thai or an American breakfast of two eggs, toast, and butter. We alternated between the two, but I started leaning more and more toward the pad Thai. On the road, we often stopped at little roadside stands that served BBQ chicken or a soup with vegetables and meatballs. Cheerful girls ladled out the soup for us from a big pot that simmered on a burner. We welcomed this nourishment in the middle of a long ride. At this point in our trip, I was ready to eat whatever was available without question. Dermot, who had been reluctant to become a vegetarian when I became one five years before, was now loath to leave vegetarianism. He decided he would add meat to his diet on the trip but wouldn't eat pork. With the little Thai we learned, he became skilled at saying *"My ne mu!"* (No pork!) when we stopped to eat. Most of those meatballs were buffalo meat, though, if I understood correctly.

In Si Chiang Mai, we stayed at a guesthouse run by a Frenchman married to a Thai woman. They had two small children. The man installed innovations, including a solar-heated shower, and was proud of his establishment. He loved the area and put together books with photos and information for his visitors. At his guesthouse, I read about Pearl S. Buck International, an organization that helped mixed-race children who were often abandoned and rejected from society in Thailand. I made a note of the contact numbers for their locations in Bangkok and Udon Thani so we could try to visit one of the centers. Their work struck a chord in my heart—maybe because I was American and because the US presence in Southeast Asia during the Vietnam War was one of the reasons there were so many mixed-race children in the region. Perhaps I was drawn to the organization because of my own mixed-race ancestry; I never felt that I neatly fit into any one category the way society wants us to. Instead, I felt a kinship with many.

We searched for a bank to change money. A man who spoke fluent English conducted my transaction.

"How do you like Thailand?" he asked as he handed me the Thai currency.

"I love it. The people are so friendly. We are bicycling, and this area is beautiful."

The man smiled at me.

"Your English is so good, by the way," I said. "Did you live in the United States?"

"No. But I had many GI friends when the Americans were here. We had a lot of fun. That's why I can speak English."

I nodded and placed the money in my fanny pack.

"Good luck on the rest of your trip. I am glad you are enjoying my country," he said.

"Thank you." I smiled and waved goodbye.

He grinned, thrust his fist in the air, and called out, "Soul, baby, soul! Soul, baby, soul!" as he gave me the Black Power salute.

I saluted back and grinned. Dermot and I shared a chuckle as we walked on. "He must have had a lot of African American GI friends!" I said.

Our French host organized a small boat trip along the Mekong River for a few of us staying at his guesthouse. The river by Si Chiang Mai became so narrow in places that I could practically touch the banks of Laos on the other side. Children played and bathed happily as they cooled off in the water on the Laotian side. They called out to us and waved as our boat glided by.

Another day we rented motorbikes to ride and look for ancient ruins and petroglyphs with a couple from England, who also stayed at the guesthouse. We didn't find much in the way of petroglyphs but enjoyed tooling around the quiet back roads by motorbike. Dermot drove, and I hung on tightly. I enjoyed myself, but at the end of the day, I decided that I preferred my own bicycle.

We left Si Chiang Mai and biked forty miles to Nong Khai. Before we reached our destination, we came upon a large park, Sala Kaew Ku, filled with enormous sculptures of Buddhas, serpentine *nagas*, and dancing Shivas.

At the *wat,* we talked over tea with Niran, a young Thai man. "Luang Pu, a mystic, started building this park and *wat* in 1978."

"I've never seen anything like this," I said, gazing around in awe.

"You'll notice the blend of Buddhism and Hinduism in the statues," Niran said. "Luang Pu started a park like this one in Laos, on the other side of the Mekong, but he had to flee when the Communists took over in 1975."

Dermot sipped his tea. "We just came from India, so it is interesting to see the blend of religions."

BICYCLE ODYSSEY

Niran nodded. "It's too bad Luang Pu is not here today. To be in his presence is very special. He possesses strong powers. He can be in two places at once."

"Wow! Bilocation!" Derm's gaze met mine. "That's fascinating."

"I remember reading in India that Sai Baba also had that ability," I added.

Niran smiled. "Yes, I know Sai Baba."

We spent the rest of the afternoon wandering around the park and taking photos of its fantastical sculptures.

At the next guesthouse, the proprietor was Thai, and his girlfriend was French Canadian. They were the first interracial couple I had encountered in Thailand, where the man was Thai and the woman was *farang*. We saw many mixed couples during our travels through the area—*farang* men and Thai women—but many of those couples were on a vacation arrangement. Men would come over for a month and find a Thai girlfriend. We frequently encountered NO THAI GIRLFRIENDS ALLOWED signs at many of the places we stayed. I often remained outside with the bikes, while Dermot checked us into a guesthouse. With my back turned, all the manager could see was my brown skin, which was the same color as most of the people we had met in Southeast Asia who worked outside. A few times, a manager asked whether I was Dermot's Thai girlfriend because he didn't want them in his establishment. Dermot needed to reassure people on many occasions that I was, indeed, his wife.

We rode through rural Isan in the northeast and passed little villages bustling with harvest tasks. Groups of women, clad in tribal dress and headdresses adorned with silver coins and jewelry, shucked dried corn in front of their houses. The population was more Laotian than Thai, and for the most part, the people spoke Laotian. The proprietor of our guesthouse said that, when he went to Bangkok, the Thai people made fun of the Laotians, calling them "buffalo" or "slow." But the people

227

in the northeast seemed friendlier and more outgoing to us. They were quicker to laugh with us.

During our stay in Thailand, I read *Monsoon Country* by Pira Sudham, a Thai writer from Isan. The buffalo was an important metaphor in the book. The story centered on the life of a boy who grew up with the buffalo, identified with them, and, when he asserted himself, felt the buffalo inside him was raising its horns. *Terre de mousson* was the French translation of the book my new friend Gaëlle read and passed onto me.

We cycled by many herds of buffalo in Thailand, always with a little boy in charge. We often saw a boy on the back of a buffalo, a stalk of grass in his mouth. His head rested on the buffalo's rump, and his legs dangled on each side of the sturdy, placid buffalo's back. The little boy looked relaxed and lost in a pleasant daydream as he watched both the herd and the clouds in the sky—a scene straight out of the book by Pira Sudham.

We met a Frenchman at one of the guesthouses in that area, and I passed *Monsoon Country* along to him. Louis, tall and lanky, had traveled every year for several months and then returned to his home in France, deep in the forest. From every different place he visited, Louis brought back a few seeds of hemp to plant and cultivate when he returned home. He had quite a variety in his harvests.

Because we traveled so slowly by bicycle, when we moved on from a city or town, we wouldn't see other tourists for a few days. They all zoomed away to farther towns on buses, motorcycles, and cars. We always spent a couple of nights in little places where we were the only foreigners. After we left the last guesthouse and the throngs of *farangs*, we enjoyed smooth roads to cycle on and lots of open country.

Udon Thani, the site of a former US Air Force base, had a population of about one hundred thousand people. The city was large enough to

BICYCLE ODYSSEY

explore but small enough not to overwhelm us. A lot of people spoke English, and there were also many Amerasian children in their teens. They were not well accepted by society, and they struggled. I called the Pearl S. Buck International organization, which helped Amerasian children in Udon Thani. We visited their office and received a tour of the orphanage with the director (a Thai woman) and an assistant visiting from Papua New Guinea.

They told us about the hardships mixed-race children faced in Thailand. Many people abandoned babies at the organization. The women took us to the nursery to meet the infants in their care. We played with the babies for a while. The staff also worked to help teach the older children marketable skills, and they offered counseling.

Ed, a bicycle taxi driver, befriended us in front of our hotel on our first day in Udon Thani. He was sweet and always had a huge smile on his face. We gave our bikes and legs a rest and let Ed take us around during our stay in the city. Ed worked a lot with the Americans during the Vietnam War, so his English was fairly good. One night he took us to a special restaurant outside of town where the US officer he used to work for liked to go. Derm and I ate under the stars in the quiet restaurant.

I leaned back and looked at the twinkling lights strung up over our heads. "I'm so glad we traveled to this part of Thailand, Derm. Bicycling here has been wonderful. The roads are smooth and free of traffic."

"And the Thai people have been very welcoming," he added.

"Yes, we were fortunate that the other bicyclists we met in Nepal directed us here."

We held hands in comfortable silence. We were happy and at peace. We had reached a loving equilibrium in our marriage after the rocky patches of discord.

229

CARLA FOUNTAIN

We visited schools in Uganda and wanted to see more schools on our trip. When we told Ed we were teachers, he introduced us to a teacher at the local school. She invited us to visit her classroom and speak to the students in her English class. The students were dressed in neat uniforms and performed their morning calisthenics in straight lines outside before school started. They had a school band of *angkalung* (instruments made out of bamboo tubes attached to a frame). Each instrument consisted of different-sized tubes and produced a unique pitch when shaken. The students shook them in turns to create a song with melodious tones. They used teamwork and impeccable timing to give us a flowing and unique concert. I would have loved a set to take back to my class in the States, but possessions need to be minimal and light when you travel by bicycle.

We strolled around the large market and ate lunch, never ceasing to marvel at the rare food items. A new surprise always awaited us. In Udon Thani, we gazed in fascination at the tubs filled with live frogs of different sizes for sale. Women squatted by the tubs and carefully chose frogs to purchase for the day's meal.

Ed showed up on the morning we left Udon Thani. "Carla and Dermot, I came to say goodbye."

"That is sweet of you, Ed. Thank you. You have been so kind to us," I said.

Ed reached into the basket on his bicycle taxi and pulled out a small bag. "Please, I have a gift for you." He placed a small clay Buddha in my hand and one into Derm's. "I want you each to have one. This Buddha is to protect you, to protect you both," he said.

My eyes filled with tears of gratitude. "*Khob khun ka* [Thank you]. Thank you so much, Ed." I bowed with a *wai*.

"*Khob khun khap*," Dermot said.

"You are welcome. Stay safe on your trip. Keep the Buddhas close to you."

Thailand soothed us and helped our relationship. We were able to relax after the physical and emotional challenges of India. I rarely wrote in my journal during our month in Thailand, a sign that things were going well. I lived fully in the present that month, enjoying the experiences. I had no time to ruminate, focus on perceived problems, or invent new ones.

Before we left Bangkok to start our travels in Thailand, we had a chance encounter on the street with Bob, an American who had recently returned from a trip to Vietnam. At that time (1992), the United States didn't have formal diplomatic relations with Vietnam. There was no US consulate in the country. We didn't even know we could travel there.

"You two are biking in Thailand. That is awesome!" Bob said. "I just flew back from a month in Vietnam. You should really think about going there. It is the most gorgeous country I've ever been in."

I glanced at Dermot. "Really?" I asked.

"Oh yeah. And it would be perfect for biking. There are more bicycles than cars. You would love it. The people are so friendly, and the land is amazing. It's just so beautiful! You need to go now. This is the time to go, when the country is opening up."

"But we thought Americans couldn't go to Vietnam," Derm said. "The United States and Vietnam don't have diplomatic relations. How can we do that?"

CARLA FOUNTAIN

"How did *you* do that?" I asked. I was as intrigued and perplexed as Derm.

"Americans aren't forbidden from traveling to Vietnam. But since we don't have diplomatic relations, you are on your own if you have trouble," Bob explained. "The United States can't help you. I don't think you can even make a phone call to the States from there. There is no American Express in Vietnam. Bring the cash you need for your stay. You won't need much; prices are very low."

I nodded. My head was spinning with the possibilities.

"There is a Vietnamese consulate here in Bangkok where you can apply for a one-month visa. They give you an unattached paper visa, so you don't need to worry about having a stamp in your passport. I can't wait to go back there!" Bob said.

We were intrigued and mulled over the idea during our month in Thailand. The information presented a unique opportunity to travel in a country whose history had been so intertwined with our own country. I wondered how we would be received. Our two countries had such a tumultuous relationship. When we returned to Bangkok at the end of our month in Thailand, we decided to apply for our visas at the Vietnamese consulate. We also purchased inexpensive round-trip tickets to Saigon (Ho Chi Minh City) from Bangkok. So far, our best experiences had come from being open to suggestions and tips from chance encounters. We decided to take a leap of faith.

22

Ko Samet

While we waited four days for our Vietnamese visas to process, we decided to leave the city and visit a beach resort. We took a bus and ferry to the tiny island of Ko Samet so we could rest and swim. No cars disturbed the peaceful island. We found a place right on the beach, where we could rent a tree house or a small bungalow. The bungalow seemed like a good choice because it included a private toilet. But that proved to be a mistake since the island had a water shortage, and the toilet stopped flushing. We filled buckets with water and dumped them into the toilet to manually flush it, but eventually, we resorted to using the public facilities.

The beach sparkled with clean, white sand and clear, warm water. We swam, floated, and read on the beach during the day. At night we watched pirated American movies while dining at the restaurants. The seafood dishes delighted our senses. We had eaten Thai food in Los Angeles before our trip, but this food was on another level. We didn't know exactly what we were eating or the names of the dishes. It all tasted exquisite.

We woke up on our last day in Ko Samet and found the beach inundated by an enormous swarm of jellyfish.

I picked my way across the sand. "There are thousands of them!"

233

CARLA FOUNTAIN

Dermot inched beside me to the water's edge and peered down. "I've never seen jellyfish like this before—small and translucent with a pink center like a flower."

"They are pretty, but do they sting?"

"I don't know. We don't want to risk it. I think our beach time is over."

We steered clear. Walking on the shore or swimming was impossible. It was almost time to leave the island.

Back in Bangkok, we regrouped and prepared for our flight to Saigon the next day. We called home on the eve of our departure to let our families know we were all right and to see how they were. The news distressed us. Our uncle's condition had declined. Other family members had juggled around to help take care of our affairs. Things had become scrambled, and a few bills had gone unpaid. A collection agency had gotten involved, and our credit rating was headed for disaster.

Anxiety filled me. Once again, in the lull between adventures, I worried about the future. I feared I would be trapped when we returned to the States. I wanted to work part time once we were home so I could write about the trip, edit our video footage, and organize my photos. But I worried that earning less money would make it hard for me to be independent and that, out of complacency, nothing would change. I would be too tired to make the extra effort to live on my own and try a period of separation from Dermot. In my heart, I knew we needed time apart. I thought a separation could even save our marriage. But I didn't know whether I had the courage to follow through with that strong desire.

The easy route would have been to go back home, find a job, have a child, and plan my life with Derm. In theory, staying married and starting a family seemed ideal, but inside I recoiled. Fear echoed in my head. I had no one to talk to about my thoughts, so they swirled around until I captured them in the pages of my journal.

BICYCLE ODYSSEY

March 20, 1992

I guess no matter what I do, it's going to be hard to start anew. But I really need time alone. I need to regain my self-confidence and explore my own dreams. I've wanted to end this trip so many times and fly back home. I've stuck it out through the rough patches because I want to complete this trip to its full end. And we've also had phenomenal once-in-a-lifetime experiences because we kept going instead of giving up. I know I won't get the chance to go on a long voyage by bicycle like this again soon, if ever. After Vietnam, I feel I will be ready to return home. I'm not interested in a leisure trip of beaches and good times. I yearn to be educated by this journey through a full immersion in the lives and cultures of the people along the way.

My bank balance was low, and I needed to have money to start over in the United States. I felt ready to go home to create my own environment and lifestyle instead of having life dictated by the travels and the different environments we found ourselves in. After every big trajectory in a country on this trip, I felt ready to go back home to digest the experience. Traveling on to the next country seemed overwhelming after taking in so much. But I always quickly forgot about home as the adventures and discoveries in the next country swept us up.

PART 7

- ## Vietnam—A Warm Welcome

March 21 to April 21, 1992

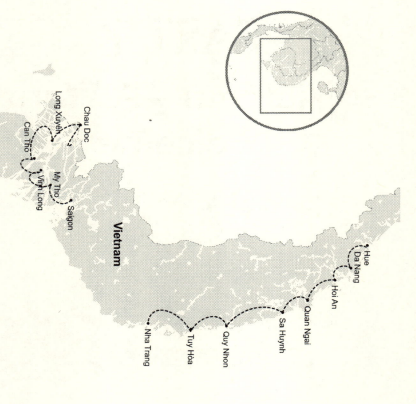

23

Saigon—A Cyclist's City

On the plane to Saigon or Ho Chi Minh City, as it is now called, several Vietnamese men and women our age sat with us. They were on a trip to Vietnam to visit relatives. Most had gone to the United States in 1975 as refugees after our country had pulled out of Vietnam at the end of the war. Many traveled from Little Saigon in Orange County, California. They told us the second largest Vietnamese population outside of Saigon was now in Orange County. The young men and women enjoyed helping us to learn Vietnamese words and taught us how to say a few phrases with the correct tones. For many of them, this was their first time returning to Vietnam since 1975.

At customs in Ho Chi Minh City, the officials dealt sternly with the Vietnamese born who held foreign passports. The women had to declare all jewelry in detail, including wedding and engagement rings. I noticed that several of the travelers slipped money to the officials along with their documents. As foreigners, Dermot and I received good treatment. The official processed us quickly with smiles, not expecting any bribes or gifts. Other travelers had advised us to bring American cigarettes with us to offer as gifts. But the official shooed away the pack Derm offered him and sent us on our way.

The officials' smiles surprised me. I wasn't sure how people would react to Americans arriving in the country. Our two countries had been

CARLA FOUNTAIN

in a brutal, long, drawn-out war. I had been old enough during the conflict to watch the intense drama every night on the news. Although I had been too young to have classmates drafted, I had seen the stricken faces of older acquaintances at school when they received their notices.

Outside the terminal, most of the traffic consisted of other bicycles and a few motorbikes. The slow-moving traffic allowed people to talk with us as they cycled by. People waved and greeted us from the side of the street as we passed. In March 1992, foreigners were a novel sight, especially foreigners on bicycles. Several young men biked alongside Derm and chatted with him. A cheerful older man cycled up to me.

"Where are you from?" he asked.

"America," I replied, unsure how he would react.

He gave me a big thumbs-up and said, "Number one!" His smile broadened. "Where are you going? I will help you find your hotel."

Even without traffic signals and an increasing number of cyclists as we approached the city center, the flow of traffic moved along harmoniously. I wondered what would happen in a few years as more cars filled the country.

At our budget hotel, the staff gave us a non-air-conditioned room for six dollars. A group of young Vietnamese athletes also checked into the hotel. They were in the city for a sports competition, and their lively, healthy energy filled the establishment.

We showered, changed, and set out to explore the city with our Vietnamese phrase book in hand. Sipping a cold drink in the lobby, we soon became caught up in separate conversations with the hotel staff. While Dermot talked with a young man, a young woman looked through my phrase book and helped me pronounce essential phrases in Vietnamese. The lack of personal space surprised me. I had expected that the Vietnamese would be more reserved, but she sat quite close to me. Among women, this proved to be the norm on our trip.

BICYCLE ODYSSEY

"Look," my new friend said as she pointed to a word. "To say hello to a friend, you say, '*Chào bạn.*' And to a young person, '*Chào em.*' To a man older than you, '*Chào anh.*' But to a woman you say, '*Chào chị.*' For an elder woman, like a grandmother, you say, '*Chào bà*' and for a man, '*Chào ông.*' For a—"

"Wait!" I said. "That's a lot to remember! Can I just say '*chào*'?"

"No!" She laughed. "Let's practice." She draped an arm around my shoulder, and we continued with our lesson.

I was dismayed to learn that there was no simple translation for the word *hello*. But the greetings I learned in Vietnamese gave me a sense of connection to people and invoked family ties. For much older people, such as my grandparents' age, the greeting translated to "Hello, Grandmother" or "Hello, Grandfather." To a woman or man my parents' age, I needed to say, "Hello, Auntie" or "Hello, Uncle." To a younger girl or boy, the phrase translated to "Hello, little sister" or "Hello, little brother." I constantly had to estimate the age of the person I interacted with to greet him or her correctly and respectfully.

Modern Vietnamese is written in Latin script, which Portuguese and Italian Jesuits introduced in 1520 to help with learning the language. Before that Vietnamese was written in classical Chinese with a few added Vietnamese characters. By 1910, the modern Latin script was in full use with added markings to show the various tones. This made sight-reading and learning new words easier, even if the tones challenged us.

As we stepped outside the hotel, after my first informal language class, we immediately became immersed in the busy street life. Scores of sidewalk vendors sold hot food. Patrons ate meals while sitting on low stools at little tables lining the sidewalk. The child-sized stools forced us to almost squat on the ground while we ate.

We passed several people with leprosy as well as persistent beggars. In spite of the poverty in some of the areas we walked through, the city exuded elegance. In Old Saigon, French colonial buildings graced

241

CARLA FOUNTAIN

the boulevards: the majestic Hôtel de Ville (Ho Chi Minh City Hall) and old apartments. Wide boulevards in the Haussmann style allowed cooling breezes to flow through the open spaces in the city, and the heat was less oppressive than in Bangkok.

Saigon bustled with activity, and people hustled, trying to make money. Masses of little enterprising businesses lined the streets. A fluent English speaker who owned a lacquerware shop swept us into his establishment to look around. For the next hour, he didn't leave our side until he had taken us to several other shops as well as a travel permit agency, where we finally shook him off. I didn't like his fast talk and hustle, and I feared he would pull us into an expensive deal. Our money was dwindling, and we had to be careful. We needed to rely on the cash we had brought with us.

The sun had already set by the time we left the man. We made our way to the Ho Chi Minh statue and grounds in front of the Hôtel de Ville. Families strolled, kids played, and a refreshing breeze cooled the air. Derm admired the work of a handicapped artist, who drew with his feet while I looked up our position in the guidebook. A man approached with his family in tow to ask whether he could take a photo of *me* with his family. He thrust his baby into my arms. The infant cried at first but gurgled happily as we posed for the picture in front of the Hôtel de Ville. Several other people walked over to talk to us and asked where we were from and what we were doing. They showed so much friendly interest in us that I felt welcome.

We stopped for dinner at a café filled with well-dressed Russians enjoying a French meal. Most of the foreigners in Vietnam since 1975 had been Russian or *Liên Xô,* as the Vietnamese called them. When people sighted us on the road throughout our trip in the country, they called out, *"Liên Xô"* until we said, "American." The friendly correction elicited a broad smile and a thumbs-up from the person, who would then respond with "Number one!" This response was both unexpected and heartwarming. America had been an ally with South Vietnam

242

during the Vietnam War. We might not have encountered the same enthusiastic welcome in Hanoi.

On our way home, we passed several people sleeping on the streets and a group of people going through the trash. But we also saw scores of families sitting out on the sidewalks, enjoying the fresh air.

I noticed that the men we met talked only to Derm when they approached the two of us. Although I would feel inconsequential in those moments, I was grateful for the warm conversation with the woman at the hotel. I would have many more friendly experiences with other women I met throughout our travels in Vietnam.

We weren't allowed to leave Saigon on our own without an official travel permit for the cities we spent the night in. Dealing with the required travel documents at that time in Vietnam was complicated. Officials required us to first register with the police, wait for our registration to clear, and then return in the late afternoon to collect the document. We also needed to find and pay an intermediary to secure a travel permit for us so we could visit other cities. Since we intended to cycle by ourselves without a guide, the paperwork took a few days to organize. While we waited, we explored Saigon.

To avoid the heat, we rose with the sun and ate breakfast early. *Cà phê sữa nóng* (hot, strong, Vietnamese coffee with sweetened condensed milk) revived us. We ate the traditional pho, which is a noodle soup dish cooked in a rich broth, loaded with various vegetables and herbs plus thin slices of meat, sprinkled with peanuts.

We set off to explore Cholon, the Chinese quarter, to see pagodas and the famous Chinese and French colonial architecture we had heard about. We took a cyclo (a bicycle rickshaw) through the city for

CARLA FOUNTAIN

about thirty minutes to reach Cholon. The crowds thickened as we approached the area.

The cyclo driver let us off at the market, and we plunged in to look for hats. The tropical sun seared our skin, and we needed protection. No one in the market spoke English, and several vendors met our attempts at speaking Vietnamese with indifference. I bought a hat but couldn't buy the "sun gloves," long gloves to protect the arms, which ladies wore when they bicycled or rode a motorbike. Either the woman completely misunderstood me, or she wanted to sell only in bulk. Dermot and I enjoyed ourselves, though, and we shared many laughs and smiles with the vendors.

Our hotel provided us with hot water and a tea service to make tea but no tea bags or leaves. After several attempts, I purchased tea at the market. I also wanted to buy classical Vietnamese music cassettes. I picked up a cassette with a picture of a woman playing the zither and asked to hear a sample. But after one minute of ethereal stringed music, the song turned into rollicking pop music. I pointed to the zither and explained that we wanted only that kind of music. The saleslady smiled and nodded. When she returned with another cassette, the front cover had "Music for Lovers" printed on it. But the first track rang out with a military march. We smiled, thanked her, and moved on. She looked bewildered as to why we hadn't bought anything.

In the Cholon district, the hot and steamy day intensified in the narrow streets, which didn't allow breezes to flow. Motorbikes created more exhaust fumes and dust. In that ethnic Chinese neighborhood, people hung signs in Chinese, even though they might have lived in Vietnam for several generations. We passed by old, crumbling mansions, overgrown with weeds. Many single-family homes had been divided into several residences. We wandered through twisting alleyways, with masses of people living in the dwellings that lined them.

Saigon enchanted us and was filled with contrasts. Each district we explored had a unique personality. One night we dined at Madame Dai's restaurant, La Bibliothèque. Madame Dai was a Vietnamese lawyer in her

244

seventies. She had converted her elegant, old house into a restaurant by putting tables in her legal library. During the meal, she strolled around the room and greeted everyone personally with a warm smile. The delicious eight-course French and Vietnamese meal was much more than we could eat, even with our voracious bicycle-induced appetites. We feasted on shrimp paste barbecued on sugarcane sticks, mixed herbs and greens, meat wrapped in mint leaves, spring rolls, and a tasty peanut sauce for dipping. We also ate soup, rice, sautéed vegetables with meat, and a scrumptious shrimp salad with chicken and vegetables. For dessert, they served us a slice of butter cake and fresh strawberries followed by coffee.

As we prepared to leave, the waitstaff directed us upstairs. To our surprise and delight, a Vietnamese traditional dance and music performance awaited us. The female dancers wore the *áo dài* (the elegant national dress of Vietnam), a tight bodice that fell off in long, gracefully flowing strips to the knees, worn over loose trousers. One of the musicians played haunting music on a *đàn bầu* (a Vietnamese instrument with a single string stretched over a hollow bamboo box). As the musician plucked the string, he changed the tension by moving a bamboo rod to create different sounds. According to legend, when men played the *đàn bầu* in markets long ago, women had to be careful because the music was so moving that if they heard it, they risked falling in love with the musician. A *đàn tam thập lục* (a Vietnamese dulcimer) and a *đàn tranh* (an instrument similar to the traditional Japanese koto) joined the *đàn bầu* player that night, enhancing the effect.

Madame Dai, a petite, plump woman with steely gray hair worn in a short bob, presided over the activities. She possessed the forceful energy of a dynamic, independent woman. Her dignified presence radiated with her every move. Madame Dai spoke Vietnamese, French, and English. She was an attentive hostess and gave us a kiss on both cheeks in the French tradition as we departed that night. We left her house, feeling truly pampered and happy. I felt like an honored guest at La Bibliothèque.

CARLA FOUNTAIN

At the Revolutionary Museum, a friendly guide in national dress led us around and explained the exhibits that chronicled the resistance movement in Vietnam from the time of the French occupation to independence and America's departure. We examined manifestos and pictures of executed revolutionaries. We learned about how the party members had hidden secret documents in the seats of stools, the false bottoms of canoes, and compartments in cigarette vendors' boxes. The guide showed us examples of weapons, such as wooden sticks, hoes, and homemade knives people had used in their struggle for independence. The museum displayed various weapons as well as a guillotine the French had used. I'd never seen one up close before. The sight of the weighted, rusty blade held above the slot for a head to go in and the receiving basket below gave me chills. Next to the guillotine stood a large cart used to truck away the bodies.

We also visited the Museum of American War Crimes (War Remnants Museum), which focused on denouncing all the atrocities committed by the United States during the war. When we entered, the docent handed us a pamphlet titled "Some Pictures of US Imperialist's Aggressive War Crimes in Viet Nam." Photos of all the US presidents involved in the war were on display in the museum: Eisenhower, Kennedy, Johnson, Nixon, and Ford. We saw photos of victims with details of the different tortures used. Under photos of US soldiers, we read various captions, including "These soldiers look satisfied with themselves after having disemboweled the enemy."

Outside the museum, we found US soldiers' dog tags on display. There were several for sale, which we thought were from MIAs or POWs. I lamented and wondered about those missing soldiers. I later learned that the US government had investigated many of the dog tags. They found that the tags weren't necessarily from MIAs or POWs.

As we left the museum, we ran into a Vietnamese-born, American man we had met on the flight to Saigon. Ben had left Vietnam as a refugee in 1975 and hadn't returned since. We wanted to interview Ben about his impressions on returning to his home country, but he was

246

afraid to be on camera in front of the museum staff. He was, however, willing to meet with us later at his hotel. When we met again, we sat down over tea for a nice talk with Ben, but he was still reluctant to say anything on camera while he was in Vietnam. He agreed to meet with us back in the States. He lived in Little Saigon in Orange County, California.

Later that afternoon, we walked in front of the former US Embassy. Mass evacuations from the rooftop by helicopter had occurred there on April 30, 1975, when the United States pulled out of the Vietnam War. It felt strange to be so close to the empty building after having seen the chaos and tragedy play out in the news many years before. I thought about the anguish of the many Vietnamese who tried desperately but didn't make the airlift out. I later met several people during the course of our trip who told me about the hardships they had endured after the war because of their association with the Americans before 1975. As a teenager, I knew many Vietnamese in the United States who did leave the country with the Americans at the end of the war. Their hearts were heavy with the sadness of having to leave their homeland, not knowing whether they could ever return.

In 1975, my father, a retired US Air Force officer and Tuskegee Airman, sponsored a young Vietnamese pilot and encouraged our church to sponsor a Vietnamese family. They were evacuated and spent time in a refugee camp before finding sponsors and a temporary home. The pilot lived with my family for four months. I learned a little about Vietnam from him and listened to the music he played on two cassette tapes he'd managed to bring with him. The matriarch of the refugee family treated us to delicious Vietnamese dinners. But I mostly remember the mood of heavy sadness and depression that hung over the pilot. He was deeply grateful for the help to leave and start over because he would have risked torture, imprisonment, and possibly execution if he had stayed. But in the process, he lost his homeland, probably forever.

Sunday night was a big "night on the town" in Saigon. We could barely cross the streets, which swarmed with bicycle and motorcycle traffic. We noticed cultural activity galore, including concerts in parks with traditional Vietnamese music. People loved to be outside at night in the cooler air. The plaza in front of the Hôtel de Ville teemed with little kids playing, families out for a stroll, and vendors selling kites and dragons on a stick.

The next day we visited a pagoda, where a robed priest welcomed us and began a chanting prayer session complete with gongs, percussion, and incense. The sounds and the scents swept us into a meditative state. We said goodbye to the priest with a bow and left the pagoda with clear, calm spirits.

Walking farther to a park by the zoo, we watched a famous water puppet show while enjoying fresh coconut drinks. Puppeteers stood behind a screen in shallow water to manipulate the hand-carved puppets with long poles. The dramatic story unfolded with swoops and splashes. Just watching the figures play in the water cooled me off. The surrounding park also provided a refreshing escape from the bustle and heat of the city. In a nearby art gallery, we started a conversation with the owner, a young woman who was also a painter. The artist on exhibit stopped by, and they invited us to have tea and wine with them.

By our third day, we had collected all our travel permits and were prepared to set out. But our last night in Saigon ended on a sour note when we discovered that instead of gaining eleven dollars on a currency exchange, we had been swindled out of eighty dollars. The men who had approached us on the street to change money played a classic bait and switch move on us and swapped out the five thousand dong bills for two hundred dong bills. We had no way to find the men again. I had felt uneasy about the deal from the start. The men radiated an anxious,

BICYCLE ODYSSEY

nervous energy, and the transaction took place rapidly as they handed off the bills tied in a brown paper bundle under the table in a tea shop.

We both brooded that night at the hotel, distraught over the bad transaction. My head throbbed with a dull pain, and my stomach twisted in knots. I sat on the bed with my head in my hands. "I don't feel well."

"I don't feel well either. I just need to be quiet. My head is pounding." Dermot curled up on the bed, his face to the wall.

My emotions battled within me. I made tea for us, and Dermot fell asleep after taking a few sips. I sat hunched over the tiny desk in our room and wrote.

> March 24, 1992
>
> I'm really shaken by what happened today. We are so vulnerable here on our bicycles. Dermot's so upset. I've never seen him like this. He won't talk about it. That's not like him, and it scares me. I want to go home now in spite of all our great adventures. I'm looking forward to tomorrow's ride with a bit of nervousness and fear. I hope that things work out and we stay safe.

24

The Mekong Delta

We left Saigon at six o'clock the next morning. Even at that early hour, the streets swarmed with traffic for the first seven miles. Derm was plagued with a persistent flat tire, which he had already repaired three times. In frustration he decided to try one of the roadside tire repair shops we frequently passed. The repairman submerged the tube in an old army helmet filled with water to check for air bubbles and found the puncture. He put a piece of rubber on the tube, placed the tube on an anvil, put foil over the tube, clamped it down, squirted kerosene on the foil, and ignited it. It burned for two to three seconds. The man unclamped the tube to reveal a vulcanized seal. We marveled at the clever process.

While Derm chatted with men and boys in the crowd who gathered around to watch the repair job, I talked with a woman in her fifties.

"You are American, right?" she asked.

"Yes, I am," I said.

"I worked for the US government before 1975. Now, I am not doing so well. I have much work and little money. Since I was affiliated with the United States, I cannot work for the Vietnamese government."

BICYCLE ODYSSEY

I reflected on her comment as we biked the remaining miles to My Tho. At the tourist office in town, no one spoke English or French. Afterward, when we changed money at the bank, another customer approached us to chat in English and help us with our transaction. Since the customer had worked for the United States during the war, he couldn't have a government job. He would have been perfect for a position in either establishment. Instead, he labored in the rice fields for ten hours a day. Many skilled people couldn't be utilized where they were needed.

My Tho had been the site of a large center of operations for the US military. The military embarked on their Mekong Delta sorties to search out the Viet Cong from My Tho. The Viet Cong had engineered an extensive network of underground tunnels in the Mekong Delta, which the South Vietnamese and the United States never succeeded in eradicating. The Cu Chi tunnel system, considered the most sophisticated tunnel network ever built, was over seventy-five miles long.

My Tho exuded a laid-back, tranquil feel. The Mekong Delta surrounded the town, and the breezes from the river freshened the air, in sharp contrast to the sweltering heat in Saigon. We tried to check into the hotel the man who had procured our travel permits recommended, but the manager declared that tourists couldn't stay in that hotel. He directed us down the street to a more expensive establishment.

After lunch, we looked for a ferry to visit the Coconut Island Temple. Crowds of people filled the docks. Kids grabbed my arm to pull me toward various food stalls and tweak at my braids. My shoulders clenched and heart raced because they used so much aggressive force. But when I looked down at their faces, my eyes met little girls with huge smiles, so I relaxed and smiled too. I extracted myself from them as best as I could and quickly left to join the line boarding the ferry.

About eighty of us crowded onto the ferry on foot along with two buses and two trucks. The ferry ride was a big social event of the

CARLA FOUNTAIN

day. Hawkers moved among us, selling cigarettes and candies. People talked, socialized, and laughed. They included us in conversations and asked questions. I loved the easy, friendly interactions. Women touched my arm or draped an arm on my shoulder to talk with me. My hair fascinated them, and they often caressed my braids, saying, *"Dẹp,"* the Vietnamese word for "pretty." Their kindness touched me. All through our trip in Vietnam, women approached me and told me how pretty my hair was. I said the same to them. This was especially poignant to me because, as an African American child with tight, curly hair, I had always been told that I had "bad hair." Straight, long hair was the culturally desired norm in the sixties in America as well as in the African American community. When the women in Vietnam told me my natural hair was attractive, they warmed my heart.

From Ben Tre, where the ferry docked, we needed to take a private boat to the island. The boat was small but sturdy. The short, tranquil ride contrasted with the boisterous trip on the ferry. On Coconut Island, we met an older man who spoke French. He led us around and invited us to his house to taste the different fruits that grew on the island. We sampled oranges, sapote, rambutan, pomelo, and a delectable, rosy-pink fruit called "star apple."

We boarded our small boat and admired the sunset as we motored back to My Tho. The ambience that night was what I had pictured Asia to be before I arrived. Soft breezes caressed our skin, lights danced on the water, silent boats glided past us, and rickety, wooden houses leaned over the water on the narrow canals as we floated by.

The departure from My Tho the next day was easier than bicycling out of Saigon. Even though we still traveled on National Highway 1, few vehicles circulated. We cycled past fields and water markets along the river. As we crossed over the numerous bridges, we caught glimpses of the fascinating water life: long canoes mounded with fresh produce slid by, people loaded their boats from the market, and women and men rowed past us.

I marveled at an elderly woman gliding by. "Look, Derm! Do you see how some people row with their feet? And others with their arms while they stand?"

"I've never seen that. It's like a ballet."

I smiled and waved back at a woman we passed. "An elegant water ballet."

We bicycled through a mango cultivation area, passing dozens of stalls lining the road, each selling baskets of ripe mangos. We finally stopped at one, and a woman prepared us two large ripe mangoes for fifty cents. She peeled them and cut the fruit into succulent pieces, which we devoured right there on the side on the road.

Bicycling farther through the Mekong Delta entailed several more ferry crossings. The whole process could take an hour for each crossing. We discovered that Derm had another flat tire when we debarked from the next ferry. Bike repair stands abounded, and we decided to use one. A large crowd of kids and adults gathered to watch. One of the adult men, dressed in green fatigues, pointed to himself and repeatedly cried out, "VC! VC!" in a loud, belligerent voice. I thought he must have been a former soldier. We understood "VC" to mean Viet Cong.

Farther down the road, we passed two people who seemed to have emotional challenges. One elderly man, wearing rags and missing several teeth, waved his arms at us and yelled, "Get back! Go back!" I sprinted by him, but he grabbed ahold of Derm's arm. Derm was going fast so he managed to break free. Later, in the middle of the countryside, we passed a scowling, robust woman, who was walking stark naked in the middle of the road. I gave her a wide berth, but she lunged at Derm and took a swing at him.

CARLA FOUNTAIN

At Vinh Long, we stopped at a bicycle parking lot. We gave our bikes to an attendant, who handed us a claim ticket. His job was to keep the bicycles safe for a nominal fee. As we walked away, we fell into step with a man who wanted to talk to us. When he found out I spoke French, we conversed more.

"I used to teach French at the university, but I lost my job in 1975. They wouldn't let me teach anymore."

"That must have been awful," I said.

The man looked across the street for a moment. "I was sent to a reeducation camp for a month." He grimaced. "Life in that prison camp was very hard. When I came out, I was given a job as a bicycle parking attendant. Now I have a job as a tour guide. I have it better than many others."

We passed several dry goods shops as we walked. "How do you like your job?" I asked.

"It's okay. I make fifteen dollars a month. Food for my family costs ten dollars a month, and we pay two dollars for rent."

"You have children?" I asked as I glanced at Derm.

"Yes. My wife and I have two children. She is a nurse and makes eight dollars a month. In Vietnam now, teachers and doctors make twelve dollars a month."

The former professor proposed to take us on a Mekong River trip for twenty dollars. He guided us down the little canals where people lived and worked on and in the water. We cruised by rice granaries as children swam and played, women washed their hair, old men bathed, and poultry farmers wrangled their ducks. Three enchanting hours flew by with lots of pleasant exchanges, waves, smiles, and greetings. During the trip, we glided past many French colonial villas in good condition, standing amid the lush, tropical

BICYCLE ODYSSEY

vegetation. The buildings, clothing, and quiet transported us back in time to the 1930s.

Americans had built our hotel in Vinh Long during the war. The voltage was 110 with US plugs. Outside, the hotel boasted a tennis court and an assortment of US military hardware on display: a tank, a helicopter, and two jet bombers. I wondered what it must have been like for the Americans stationed there during the war. I knew only what I had seen in the news or in movies about the war. I did know of people who were forever plagued by the terrors they had experienced during that time. One friend's brother couldn't discuss what had happened and withdrew from society.

We biked a short day from Vinh Long to Can Tho, a distance of only twenty miles. There wasn't as much produce for sale as the day before. We'd been looking forward to a refreshing mango break again. No mango stands lined the road, so we settled for a fresh coconut juice break. We drained the shell and ate the tender pulp. The coconut gave us a good energy boost for our cycling.

We biked through another area full of rice paddies during planting season. Workers walked in the shallow water and placed tender, bright-green seedlings in the mud. Most workers wore conical hats, long-sleeved shirts, and gloves to protect them from the fierce sun. They bent over from the hip and worked in a line, advancing steadily down the rows together.

After each ferry crossing, as we traveled through the delta, the road became quieter with less traffic. The ferry crossings didn't faze Dermot, who consumed massive quantities of food amid all the chaos. The minute we approached the docks, my appetite completely shut down from the stress of all the commotion and the press of the crowds.

In Can Tho, the hotel listed in our travel document was hosting a huge wedding party in the dining room. The event included a three-tiered cake and a live rock band, which played the Vietnamese version of "La Bamba" plus other danceable rock songs. While Derm entered to

CARLA FOUNTAIN

secure a room, I waited outside with the bikes. Several curious young people who spoke English approached me. We chatted, and I glimpsed out of the corner of my eye that a man from the wedding party was videotaping me. We were as much of an attraction in Vietnam as the country and people were for us.

Showered and cleaned up, we headed out in search of food. Our first venture into a local eating establishment proved successful. We savored noodles with chicken, vegetables, and garlic for only twenty-five cents a bowl, along with refreshing iced coffee and sweetened condensed milk for fifteen cents. The *cà phê sữa đá* (iced milk coffee) revived us. It became one of our favorite beverages on the trip, even though we knew we shouldn't have ice in our drinks because of the risk of contaminated water. Just hearing the *clink, clink, clink* as the waitstaff chipped pieces from three-foot blocks of ice brought my temperature down and seduced me into living dangerously.

As we explored the town, we stumbled across a Khmer pagoda. A young monk walked over and invited us in for tea. We stayed for about half an hour and enjoyed a friendly conversation with him. The man was twenty-eight and had become a monk when he was sixteen. He told us about his life and what had led him to become a monk.

On our way back to the hotel, we walked through the market. Mounds of produce and foods displaying every color of the rainbow delighted our eyes. The throngs of people shopping were as excited to see us as we were to be there. We made our way through the market, greeting, chatting, and laughing with everyone. I bought a tube of toothpaste with a picture of a Black man with a big, white toothy smile on it. I later found out an American company had used this racist marketing strategy in Asia.

We set out from town at eight o'clock the next morning and covered forty miles in about three hours on shady roads. The day was pleasant and not as hot as we had expected. About five miles out of Can Tho, the traffic disappeared, and we enjoyed a peaceful ride. We stopped

BICYCLE ODYSSEY

more often to snap photos and took a coconut break about ten miles from Long Xuyen. Everyone flocked over to look at us as we sat and drank our coconut water. There must have been seventy-five people standing around us in a tight circle. Several people smiled, but a few of them stared intensely without talking to us.

I caught Derm's eye and chuckled. "Now we know what it's like to be a rock star!"

Derm laughed and made a funny face. The children around him giggled in delight.

We continued along our route. About five miles from town, a young Vietnamese man drove up beside us on a motorbike. Eager to talk to Americans, Sang kept pace with Dermot all the way into Long Xuyen.

Over the hum of his motorbike, Sang said, "I left Vietnam as a refugee on a boat to Thailand when I was twelve. Then I went to America, and I lived with a foster family. Now I am back in Vietnam, visiting my aunts." Sang weaved a little on his bike in the growing traffic. "Come to my house. Have coconut water with me at my home and rest. Then I will show you the way to your hotel. Tonight, we can go out dancing!"

The large town of Long Xuyen boasted several luxury hotels and a huge market area. After our refreshments at his house, Sang led us to a beautiful establishment that was over our budget. We found another lodging in a section of town several blocks from the river, unlike in other towns we had visited. No fresh river breezes cooled the hot and dusty air by our hotel. That section of town had a rough feel to it. Later in the evening, as we walked down a dark street to find a restaurant, we had a few unpleasant encounters—a motorcycle ran us off the road, and a man grabbed Dermot's arm in a tight grip. Dermot wrenched his arm free and yelled. The man hustled off into the shadows. The incidents spooked me. We should have splurged and stayed at the hotel Sang had suggested.

257

CARLA FOUNTAIN

After breakfast at the hotel, Derm headed to the reception to pay, only to find that the police had come by that morning and taken our passports. Derm walked to the police station to retrieve them. Because of the restrictions on independent travel, we could stay only in the cities listed on our travel permit, and the hotels we stayed in had to register us with the police every night. Independent travel by bicycle was uncommon at that time. Most tourists joined a guided group trip.

Dermot came back with our passports and sank into the chair next to me with a heavy sigh. "The police visit was a warning to us. I know we had thought about visiting some other places without a travel permit. But I'm not so sure now."

"That's a bummer. The Vietnamese we talked to said that Dalat is one of their most beautiful cities."

"And I wanted to go to Ha Tien on the Gulf of Thailand to see the limestone formations and cave pagodas. But we weren't able to get a permit for either place. The seizure of our passports made me think that it wouldn't be wise to try to go anywhere not listed on our permit."

Our encounter with the police postponed our departure. By the time we hit the road, the temperature had climbed. The rural area was crowded with people lining the road during harvest season and rice-drying time. Farmers threw rice into the air with baskets, raked the rice out on the road to dry, and loaded the grain into sacks. All the activity on the shoulders of the road made biking difficult at times. The road became quite narrow, and the mounds of rice made it hard to move over when a bus or truck approached. We had a few close calls. Many farmers passed us as they drove their rice-laden ox and buffalo carts to the mills.

The stunning Cao Dai pagodas in rich shades of red, blue, and yellow caught our eyes as we bicycled by in the delta. We stopped to visit two of them on the trip. People took time off from painting and repairing the pagodas to show us around. A large divine eye—which represented God, the universe, and consciousness—gleamed with fresh paint on the front of the temples. Murals at the pagodas showed Victor Hugo writing the message *"Dieu et Humanité; Amour et Justice"* (God and Humanity; Love and Justice) as Sun Yat-sen and Nguyen Binh Khiem looked on. The Cao Dai religion started in 1926 in Vietnam as a universal faith. The religion combined a multitude of major world faiths. Cao Dai's revered saints include Confucius, Buddha, Jesus, Victor Hugo, Muhammad, and Joan of Arc. I wanted to learn more about this religion that strove to embrace all faiths and humanity. A large Cao Dai festival would take place on April 3 at the Holy See in Tay Ninh. I hoped we could travel there and attend the ceremonies.

Chau Doc lay on the border with Cambodia along the Mekong River. Vietnamese and Cambodians had permission to go back and forth across the border, but foreigners couldn't. We met a German woman who had just returned to Vietnam after a visit to Angkor Wat in Cambodia. Her face lit up with excitement and wonder as she told us about her experience. Dermot and I longed to visit the temple complex in Cambodia, but our choice on this trip was slow travel by bicycle with all the rewards that brought. At that time, we would have needed to take an eight-hour bus ride to enter Cambodia. Angkor Wat would be another trip taken in a different way many years later for both of us separately.

As we looked for a hotel in Chau Doc, a local man approached. He seemed eager to talk to us.

"Hello," Dermot said.

"*Chào anh*," I said.

CARLA FOUNTAIN

The man smiled. "Not many Americans have visited Vietnam since the war."

I slowed my pace a bit to maneuver around a street vendor. "No, we haven't been allowed to until recently."

"I spent a year in Virginia training to be a helicopter mechanic for the US government," he said. "Since I worked as a civilian with the United States when they were in Vietnam, I was sent to a reeducation camp after the war."

"I'm sorry," Dermot said.

"Many people spent ten to twelve years in a reeducation camp. I only spent one week there. I am very fortunate."

"What do you do now?"

"I teach English in a junior high school and supplement my work with private lessons. I support a wife and seven children on eight dollars a month."

"We are also teachers. My family is from Virginia," I said.

The man looked pleased with what I said. I felt grateful that I could relate to him.

"Do you know a good place to stay for the night in Chau Doc?" Dermot asked.

"I will take you to a good place, to my friend's guesthouse. He's the number-two man in the police department here."

We walked past noodle stands and cafés set up right on the sidewalk. People drank iced coffee and relaxed in low chairs at tables. The savory scent of lemongrass, basil, and mint on the bowls of noodles in rich broth made me realize I was hungry. I looked forward to reaching our

BICYCLE ODYSSEY

hotel and showering the salt off my body before we set out to eat and explore the area.

Our host greeted us warmly and offered us shots of his homemade tonic as a welcome. "Please have a small glass. I make it with herbs that are very good for your health," he said.

"*Vô!*" (Cheers!). We toasted and chatted. I felt secure and safe in his guesthouse. We didn't need to worry about hassles with the police in Chau Doc since we stayed at a policeman's house. We unloaded our gear and cleaned up.

By the time we found a spot for a meal in the marketplace, my nerves were frazzled. Constantly being the center of attention was fatiguing. A group of children stood around and stared at us while we ate. The market buzzed with activity. I felt the sensory overload I had experienced at times in India.

We bicycled to the pagodas on Sam Mountain about three miles away. I mistakenly thought they would be quiet and peaceful ruins, but the first two pagodas were pilgrimage sites crowded with people. I bought incense from a young girl outside the first temple. She helped me light and place the sticks in front of six different altars outside and inside the temple. I felt self-conscious when Derm decided to videotape me. I carried my money bag under my shirt all the time, and I was sure the bulkiness looked unflattering in the video. Concentrating on spirituality was difficult because the curious people and the lovely art distracted me.

Inside the temple, hazy smoke wafted from the joss sticks burning on the altars. Light streamed through a window near the main altar and pierced the smoke in gentle rays, which illuminated women holding clusters of burning incense above their heads as they bowed repeatedly to Buddha. They placed their sticks in a pot of sand in front of the altar and kneeled to pray. The sweet smell of incense filled my head and calmed me.

261

CARLA FOUNTAIN

Nuns and monks, ranging from young apprentices to elders, filled the pagoda. The nuns approached me to talk and marvel at my hair. Children followed me around. I noticed a European woman enter alone, but no one paid any attention to her. It dawned on me that Derm and I probably received more attention than most other tourists.

The temple across the way overflowed with too many people for us to enter, so we left on our bikes to look for the cave pagoda. As we climbed up the mountain to reach the cave, we met a woman in her seventies who spoke French.

"I will walk with you," she said in a soft voice. "This area is very special and has many important pagodas. I will take you to meet the monks at the cave pagoda."

We paused the steep climb to catch our breath and admire the view. Sweeping her arm out to the west, she said, "See the mountains? Over there is Cambodia."

I shaded my eyes against the slanting rays of the afternoon sun, which bathed the slopes in a golden light. "It's so close!" I said.

We continued our climb. "I was a cook for a French family before independence," she said. Her eyes twinkled. "I cook good French food."

She took us to meet the monks, and they invited us to have tea with them. Afterward, we continued in search of the cave two levels up. The low entrance forced us to stoop, and the cave extended for only two or three yards. Candles illuminated a Buddha, and fragrant incense smoke swirled in the dim light.

We climbed the mountain farther to reach more pagodas. The Mekong flowed off into the Cambodian mountains in the distance. Green fields of tender, young rice plants flanked the river. The scene delighted the senses with its peace and beauty. I would have loved to stay there and not go back to town. We rested while we looked at the

BICYCLE ODYSSEY

view and enjoyed the quiet, broken only by a little boy who stood on the hilltop as he played a flute.

The next morning we took a day trip to Tan Chau. We met only a few other people on bikes and motorbikes. No trucks or buses traveled on that road. We took a short ride with five other people on a small ferry across the river. After we docked, we biked down a quiet road and passed a mosque, the first we had seen in Vietnam. We glided past rows and rows of old French-built colonial houses with dates on them from the 1920s and 1930s. Graceful palm trees framed their elegant, faded-pastel facades. We passed by other styles of houses on stilts with intricately carved woodwork. Antique, hardwood dressers peeked out from entryways, displaying the family altars, joss sticks, and Chinese scrolls.

Farmers worked the rice harvest on the road. They winnowed the rice with straw baskets and raked the grains out on the side of the road to dry. A bit farther on, women worked at huge looms in the shade beneath their stilt houses, weaving colorful and intricate fabric designs. Other women spun thread on their porches. Outside the houses, huge skeins of thread in rich shades of red, purple, and blue dried in the sun. That day's ride was a dream—quiet and peaceful.

The attention we attracted led us to suspect that not many outsiders passed through the area. We stopped for iced tea at a café and soon drew a crowd of over fifty, mostly little children. At first, they stayed outside the confines of the café. But little by little, they inched inside until, within ten minutes, they surrounded us. We drank up and decided to go. As we pushed our way out, a frowning policeman strode up and insisted that we go to the headquarters. We followed him into the small wooden police shack, where he questioned us in Vietnamese. He wanted to see our papers. When we showed him our address in Chau Doc, he relaxed and smiled. He recognized the hotel run by the number two man with the police in Chau Doc. He said we could proceed to Tan Chau.

We continued on our way, but the final three miles of road were rough and didn't have much shade. Tan Chau was charming and tranquil. At a cozy noodle stand, we ran into the European woman we had noticed in the temple the night before. She had rented a motorbike with a driver for the day. Her creative way of exploring more remote places in the country impressed me. We had yet to encounter other foreign travelers outside the cities in Vietnam. We joined her for lunch. She hadn't drawn a crowd at all. Dermot and I, on the other hand, had a small group gather around us. They fiddled with our bicycles while we ate.

On our way back to Chau Doc, we enjoyed a magnificent ride through the rural area again. Huge buffalo ambled by, pulling carts loaded with rice. The river ran alongside us, and rice fields in shades of green and brown stretched out to the horizon. We appreciated and savored those moments on quiet, rural roads.

I was spent and tired from our full day of biking and talking to many people. All I wanted to do was bathe and rest. On days like that, I liked to shower off the road dust and settle in with a good book. That night I continued reading *The Quiet American* by Graham Greene. Set in Vietnam in the early 1950s, the story took place in the midst of the conflict between the South Vietnamese—supported by the French—and the Viet Minh. An American undercover CIA agent, an English journalist, and a Vietnamese woman were the main characters. In that love triangle and murder mystery, Greene described the beginnings of the American involvement in Vietnam. The book hinted at the tragedy to come.

The bus from Chau Doc back to Saigon was a torturous ten-hour haul, with half of that distance spent on bumpy roads. We sat three people to a row in seats built for two. We could have covered the first leg to Long Xuyen by bicycle in the same amount of time. In fact, we wished we

BICYCLE ODYSSEY

had biked back at least to My Tho. Bicycling would have been much more enjoyable than riding that bus.

In Saigon, we exited the bus about four miles from the city center and bicycled toward our hotel through the rush-hour flow of other cyclists and motorbikes. We rode by sense and feel without using a map. About one mile out, an engaging young man approached us on his bicycle and asked whether he could talk to us. Duc biked with us to our hotel, and we invited him for tea at an outdoor café. We ordered tea and settled in for a chat. Duc was so articulate in English that I thought he had lived overseas.

Duc laughed. "Oh no! I have no delusions about my English. I am a medical student here in Saigon, but I am originally from Hue. I have only studied English in school, but I like to read. I've recently read *1984* and *Animal Farm,* and I want to find a copy of *Brave New World.*"

"I enjoyed those books also," I said. "I wish I had a few books to leave with you."

"Occasionally, I am able to see American movies on video. Most people here like to watch movies like *Rambo* and *The Terminator.* I prefer movies like *Dances with Wolves,* which I saw recently."

Derm took a sip of his iced tea. "That was a good movie. You should look out for *The Last of the Mohicans.* It is due to come out this year. I'm sure a copy will make its way here on videotape."

Duc pushed his teacup aside and wrote down the name of the movie. "Thanks!"

"We visited a Cao Dai Temple on our bike ride through the delta to Chau Doc," I said. "The religion is fascinating. I'd like to go to the festival coming up in Tay Ninh. Have you ever been?"

Duc frowned. "I haven't been to the Cao Dai festival."

CARLA FOUNTAIN

"Oh," I said.

His frown turned into a smile. "But if you can travel to Hue, we will have our first Vietnamese-French Festival during the first week of April. You should go to Hue as soon as possible to attend. Hundreds of artists will participate. This is a historic event and a more unique opportunity than going to the Cao Dai Festival."

"Sounds like a wonderful event," Dermot said.

"You need to take the train north to get to Hue in time. It's a twenty-six-hour ride."

Dermot and I took thirsty gulps of our iced tea.

"Why didn't you order hot tea like I did? Everyone knows it's not healthy to have iced drinks in the heat," Duc said. He gestured around us. "If you notice, most people are drinking hot tea."

We thanked Duc for the information about the festival and parted ways. On his advice, we set out to procure travel permits to go north. At the permit office, the official told us we had to go through a tour agency. We tracked down the man who had helped us with our permits before. He said we couldn't officially travel independently. What we had done in the delta was illegal. We hoped regulations weren't stricter north of Saigon.

We spent three days waiting for our travel papers. Dermot was so sick that he had to stay in bed. I also became ill. We had made a bad choice when we'd ordered iced tea at the café with Duc.

25

Hue—Imperial Festivals

We sped north on the express train to Hue and watched the countryside slide past. We were happy to be out of the city, which had started to feel oppressive. We shared our first-class compartment with two Vietnamese men, who changed into pajamas for the duration of our twenty-six-hour trip north. Neither of them talked to us. I suspected they were high-ranking officials. At first, I thought they were hostile toward us until I noticed they didn't talk to each other either.

At mealtime, the porters brought food to everyone but us. They couldn't explain why they didn't serve us. We spent a few confused moments upset that everyone else had a meal except us. Eventually a porter who spoke English told us foreigners had to eat in the dining car at six o'clock.

We had been disappointed to find out from our travel contact that we weren't allowed to go to Dalat, a gorgeous city high in the mountains. The hill tribes around Dalat, the Montagnards, had worked for the Americans during the war and helped them fight the Viet Cong. Americans were not permitted in Dalat at that time because officials feared we would stir up counter-revolutionary trouble with the Montagnards who still remained in the area. Many

CARLA FOUNTAIN

Montagnards had emigrated to the United States as refugees after the war.

We arrived in Hue, tired from our train ride, and found a recently renovated and reopened hotel. It possessed an old-world charm with high ceilings, intricate tiled floors, and spacious rooms. We checked in, showered, and raced off to see the city on our bicycles before sundown. As we crossed the bridge into old Hue, the unhurried bicycle traffic— with zero cars and only a few slow-moving motorbikes—immediately soothed us.

The Tet Offensive in 1968 had partially destroyed the Imperial City in Hue, but what remained exuded wonderful grace and charm. Hue was the cultural capital of Vietnam and was known for its history and poetry.

We attended one of the festival events presented that week, a French play about the pioneer filmmaker Georges Méliès. I felt sorry for the actors performing in the heat and humidity. I was sure they weren't accustomed to it, coming from Europe. The play included films Méliès's granddaughter had restored. I'd never seen such good prints of his films. We sat inside the Imperial City in an old hall with hand-painted frescoes on the walls and ceilings. Bats flitted around the actors' heads. Their moving shadows created a mysterious and moody ambiance.

The next day, we biked out and explored the Forbidden City in the wilting heat. I broke down and bought a traditional conical hat to shade me from the sun.

I held the hat up to the sun. "Look, I bought a poem hat!" Hue is famous for making these. It has a scene from Hue with a poem slipped in between the two layers of woven fibers. You can see the image only when you hold it up to the sun.

Derm smiled as he gazed up at my hat. "That's cool! It's beautiful. I wonder what the poem says."

"The hat will also protect me from stares. I'm getting tired of being a curiosity. At least no one tries to touch my hair anymore since I took my braids out on the train ride."

We biked to the Thien Mu Pagoda close to town. A monk, happy to practice his English, showed us around. "One of the emperor's sons had his wedding ceremony here," he said with pride. "This was an important pagoda for the emperors."

As we stood in the shade of the pagoda, he told us about himself and his daily routine. "I am thirty and have been in the monastery for seventeen years. We all rise at three o'clock in the morning to ring the gong, meditate, and pray before breakfast. I work in the garden, where we grow our own food, until lunchtime." He gestured toward a nearby field.

I followed his gaze and admired the neat rows of vegetables.

"In the afternoons, I work more and interact with visitors. We spend the evenings in meditation and prayer. I taught myself English and want to learn it well enough to help teach the children in the village."

"Your English is very good. The children will be fortunate to have you as their teacher," I said.

He and the head monk radiated with a rich, positive spirit. I felt privileged to meet and talk with them.

Back in town for lunch, we ordered the region's delicious specialty: *bánh khoái* (a panfried crêpe stuffed with sprouts, shrimp, pork, greens, mint, lettuce, and a peanut sauce). By that point on our trip, Dermot had let his no-pork rule slide. Content and full, we sat and enjoyed people watching after our meal. French and Vietnamese women walked by, strikingly elegant in traditional *áo dài*. The long silky material flowed out from the tight bodices of their garments in an array of colors, from soft pastels to vibrant shades of emerald green and deep blue. A father on bicycle passed us. His young son perched on the back rack as he clutched a freshly baked baguette. Both wore red berets. A flock of chattering schoolgirls rode by in matching white *áo dài* that fluttered in the breeze. Ladies bicycled past, protected from the fierce sun with long-sleeved bicycle gloves and poem hats.

To visit the Royal Tombs, we rose at the crack of dawn to bike out before the heat became too intense. We quickly left the bustle of town life and rolled through rice fields and small forests in the cool mist, passing occasional grave sites on the way. Two impressive tombs we examined belonged to Tu Duc and Minh Mang. Minh Mang's tomb, on the west bank of the Perfume River, was my favorite. Devoid of vendors and tourists, the site was still and hushed. The appealing symmetry of the architecture blended well with the surrounding nature.

I sat on a bench to rest and met an elderly woman, who spoke French. She told me about her life and her troubles.

"I had a French husband. But he left me with two children. I was outcast and shunned by society because of our relationship." She paused and took a breath to compose herself. "He went away during the war for independence and never came back," she finished in tears.

I started to cry also and held her hand in sympathy. We sat silently together.

The festival continued with the royal dances at the Forbidden City. The following night we sat next to a local Vietnamese man, who beamed with pride and excitement.

"These dances haven't been performed since 1972. And this is the first time the public has ever seen them. Before then, they only performed these dances for the royal family," the man said.

"We are fortunate to be here now," I said. "The festival is wonderful! I love the dances."

The man returned my smile.

"Are you from Hue?" I asked.

"Yes, this is my city. I am an official and a good party member. But this imperial history is also my heritage."

A dragon dance played out as two dragons flirted, mated, and gave birth to a baby dragon. The trio danced together after the birth. The evening ended with an acrobatic lantern dance. Young girls formed triangles as they held lotus lanterns aloft. I relished the magical evening, wanting it to never end.

Hue was also exciting because we met quite a few artists. A charming man invited us to his studio/gallery/home as we cycled back after the royal dances. I admired half a dozen pieces I would have liked to buy. I loved the work. We also stumbled across an art opening next to our hotel and wandered in. Quite a few of the artists were in attendance, and we met several of them. A friendly Vietnamese man, who spoke French and wore a beret, talked to us.

"A year ago, this exhibit wouldn't have been possible," he said. "The artists here were still censored. Buu Chi is not here tonight because he is still under police surveillance. He doesn't think it wise to meet with foreigners now. He keeps to himself. He is political and was jailed for two years for anti-war protests."

CARLA FOUNTAIN

One painting in the exhibit, *The Triumphant Return of the Mandarins*, was especially bold. A man even showed up to the exhibit dressed in his richly embroidered traditional tunic. We never met Buu Chi. He was a descendant of Emperor Minh Mang and was considered one of the greatest artists of modern Vietnamese painting. The artists and intellectuals we met radiated a strong inner resilience in spite of all the hardships they had endured.

These encounters were a seminal point in Dermot's life. They planted the seed in him to pursue his dreams of working in the art world when we completed our trip.

That night we returned to our hotel, elated from our time in Hue. I sank into a chair under the cool breeze of the ceiling fan and pulled out my journal. I hadn't written much in Thailand. But Vietnam inspired me to write almost every night, even when I drooped from fatigue.

> April 8, 1992
>
> We've met so many interesting and welcoming people here! I wish we could stay longer. One day I hope I can come back for an extended visit. I would love to study Vietnamese and learn more about meditation with the monk we met. I am so glad we met Duc in Saigon. This odyssey has gifted us with an abundance of serendipity!

26

The Central Coast

We needed to head back down the coast toward Da Nang. Several people warned us against bicycling the first leg of the journey because of the steep terrain. We also both felt ill, so we decided to take a bus. Six miles into the bus ride, we realized our hotel hadn't returned our visas and travel permits. We bailed out of the bus and bicycled back to Hue. We debated whether to stay another night and bike out in the morning, but we pressed on and boarded another bus. Two men hammered and did other repairs on the front of the vehicle as we squeezed into the back of the dilapidated bus. We set out an hour later.

Along the way, we passed one of the most gorgeous coastlines we had seen on the trip. I was depressed that we weren't on our bikes. Nausea settled deep in my stomach, caused by the odorous bags of fish cargo on the floor. The bus broke down at least five times, stretching the three-hour trip to five hours. We arrived in Da Nang after dark and checked into a hotel that provided well-deserved amenities and comfort. The owner gave us a room with a fridge and air-conditioning, an unusual luxury for us on this trip.

Before we set out the next morning to bike to Hoi An, we stopped at Da Nang's Museum of Cham Sculpture. We marveled at gorgeous statues and bas-relief sandstone work from AD 500 to 1500, when the ancient kingdom of Champa reigned along the coasts of central and southern Vietnam. The Cham came from Indonesia and traded with India, Cambodia, and China. After the seventeenth century, the ancient kingdom was gone. The Vietnamese persecuted and murdered the Cham, and many fled for Cambodia. We learned that a few small Cham villages are still scattered around South Central Vietnam. We could see Hindu images and Buddhist influences in the sculptures.

As we left the museum, an older man approached us on the street.

Trembling with emotion, he said, "I used to work for the Americans. Can you help me? Could you please take this letter with you to mail in the United States when you go back? I tried to leave Vietnam by boat. But they caught me and sent me to a reeducation camp for several years."

"Of course," I said. I tucked his letter into my book. I wanted to help him. I glanced over at Derm.

The man clasped Derm's hand in both of his. "Thank you. Thank you so much."

I carried the letter back to the United States with me and mailed it. I hoped the person receiving his message could help him.

The bike ride to the Marble Mountains and China Beach was hot, but the caves in the Marble Mountains made the trip well worth the effort. We met an Italian man, who was also biking around Vietnam. He worked for an airline and benefitted from 90 percent off the ticket price when he flew. His story inspired me. I wished we enjoyed more generous vacation times in the States like they did in Europe so we could travel more. At China Beach, we ate lunch and delighted in a cool, refreshing afternoon in the sea with a nice breeze and ocean spray. No one else visited the pristine beach.

After biking the last ten miles to Hoi An, we encountered the alluring architecture that graced the ancient port. The city stood out as one of the most stunning places we visited during our travels in Vietnam. In spite of this, neither of us felt well. Perhaps the heat had sapped my energy. I felt lethargic and nauseous. I decided I wouldn't mind staying in Hoi An for another day to rest. I felt burned out and wondered whether I had the energy to keep going on our trip for another month into Indonesia like we had planned. I recognized that I always felt like this at the end of a month in whatever country we visited. I longed to go home and digest all our adventures. I felt sated, filled to satisfaction. Part of me resented having to push on before I could rest and savor what we had experienced. But that wasn't economically feasible. We didn't have the resources to return home to rest before continuing our journey. I always mustered up the energy to go on and became caught up in the excitement of exploring all over again when we did land in the next country.

Indonesia was our next stop and was one of the places I looked forward to the most. There was no way I wanted to bail out, even if visions of the comforts of home danced in my head and I longed for home-cooked meals. That night, I craved hot apple pie à la mode with a good cup of coffee. The week before, I had craved a crisp salad bar at Souplantation and hot, fresh popcorn with an icy soda at a matinee. I wanted to have my hair done, wear clean clothes, have my teeth cleaned, and stop wearing the money belt and baggy clothes that made me feel so unattractive. I would have loved to sit quietly in a café and not draw a crowd. I thought we had experienced what stardom was like—always being the center of attention, whether a person wanted to be or not.

To recuperate, we spent a day at the beach. We swam, relaxed, and ate fresh, juicy BBQ clams served with rice crackers. A local man approached us and introduced himself while we savored our snack.

CARLA FOUNTAIN

"I'd like to invite you to my home to meet my family," Hanh said. "Many people are afraid to talk to foreigners or to have them in their home. But I am not worried about what the officials will say. Please follow me. It's not too far."

We finished our food and bicycled behind Hanh's motorcycle to a one-story cottage, where he lived with his parents and his wife, Binh. After having tea together, Hanh showed us his garden and bonsai nursery.

"These trees are thirty-five years old," Hanh said. He gestured to a fenced area behind the house. "These are our pigs." Several fat and healthy pigs rooted in the mud.

Back inside, the three of us ate dinner together. Binh, who was six months pregnant, served us rice, tea, a spicy egg dish, a fish dish with three fried fish heads, and a pork dish, which looked like sliced pigs' feet and snout. We made a good effort to eat everything and be appreciative guests. This pleased our host.

"I am glad you like the food," Hanh said. "It is a tradition in our family to always clean your rice bowl."

Over more tea, Hanh told us about his life. "I am a math teacher at the high school. Binh teaches physics. She earns about five US dollars a month, and I earn about six. We want to buy a house and live independently away from my parents, but a house would cost us six thousand dollars. It will take a long time to save for that."

Binh sat with us after dinner and brought out their wedding album. In the photos, she wore an elaborate, Western-style, white wedding gown. For their honeymoon, they had traveled to Ho Chi Minh City. We told Binh how beautiful she looked.

Binh answered, "No!" repeatedly as she blushed and smiled.

We later learned that the traditional response to a compliment was to always deny it to show modesty.

I needed to use the facilities before we headed home. When I asked about the toilet, Binh led me outside to the pig pen. Luckily, they were calm and friendly pigs.

We woke at six o'clock the next morning when Quy, the young man we had hired to lead us to My Son, showed up. We engaged Quy because we could find no clear directions to the site. We all set out on our bicycles for the Cham temple ruins. After a while, we suspected that Quy had never been to the ruins before. The twenty-mile trip turned into thirty miles, and he needed to repeatedly ask directions from people along the way. But Quy was pleasant, and he worked hard on that long bicycle ride in the heat. The first five miles glided by easily as we passed rice paddies and workers in the fields planting seedlings. The next fifteen miles on a side road turned bumpy and unpleasant, especially when a motorcycle policeman stopped us. He demanded to see our passports and insisted that we stop and check in with him on our way back from the ruins.

We biked the final ten miles on a dirt road until we arrived at a river. A man with a small canoe ferried us across the water with our bicycles. We continued on the road for four miles and walked the final mile since the path was so rutted and narrow. At the entrance, a lone museum attendant handed us tickets from the window of his small wooden hut. Quy took advantage of our visit to rest in the shade. The ruins stood in a delightful, quiet setting in the foothills near lush, forested mountains. The area, considered to be one of the greatest Cham sites, had been heavily carpet-bombed by the United States during the war, because the Viet Cong used the ruins as a base of operations. Not much remained. Most of the statues had been moved to the Cham museum in Da Nang,

CARLA FOUNTAIN

which we had visited earlier. We arrived at My Son at high noon when the hot sun blazed overhead.

We walked around the remains of temples from the Champa Kingdom, which dated from the fourth century until the thirteenth century. The Cham constructed the temples, dedicated to the Hindu god Shiva, from fired red brick. Bas-reliefs carved into the brick showed scenes from Hindu mythology. The Champa kings had used My Son for religious ceremonies and for royal burials. Long ago, the important complex had boasted seventy temples. Stretched before us, hidden in the wilds, only a few temples remained. We wandered around the site alone and drank in the beauty. Other than us, no one else visited the sacred grounds.

Weary from the heat, we made our way back to the entrance, where Quy waited. The museum attendant invited the three of us to share his lunch of rice and a handful of peanuts in a sauce. We appreciated the kindness and hospitality he showed by sharing the little he possessed. That sustenance gave us the energy to continue to the road, where we hoped to catch a bus back to Hoi An.

At the crossroads, we found a place to buy cold drinks, where, as usual, we drew a huge crowd. The women delighted in putting their arms next to mine, pointing out that we were the same golden-brown color.

"Same, same," they said.

One of the women asked, "Do you have children?"

"No," I replied.

She smiled at me. "I have seven children," she said. "Do you want to take one of them back with you to America?" Her eyes twinkled as she handed me a toddler. "Here you go!"

The child wailed in fright. She took him back and settled him inside her house to calm his fears. When she returned, she was laughing. She wanted to swap hats with me, and another woman wanted to exchange watches. No bus ever arrived, so we biked all the way back to Hoi An. We didn't arrive at our hotel until six o'clock that night, with barely enough energy left to eat dinner before crashing onto our beds.

Whispers and giggles startled me awake in the middle of a delicious dream about choosing butter cookies to send to my friend Linda in Denmark for her birthday. I could taste them, and they melted in my mouth. Two small boys on their way to school pushed our curtains open to peek at us in our ground floor room. Fortunately, we were both covered with sheets. When the rascals returned after being shooed away, I jumped up. My bicycle shorts were drying on the window grill where they could be snatched by mischievous hands. I thought the boys had taken them. But all was well, and we proceeded to prepare for the day.

We wavered between taking the bus or bicycling to leave town because we were tired from the day before. Eventually we decided to ride our bikes. We wheeled a good eighty miles to Quang Ngai on a smooth, flat road surrounded by countryside. About six miles before town, we noticed a definite reserve in the people we passed. No one called out, "*Liên Xô*" or "Where are you from?" The silence reverberated. The afternoon sun's intense heat elevated. Sweat dripped from our brows. We paused to rest and drink the last of our water. I looked up and noticed several local men on one-speed bicycles approaching us. Their somber faces contrasted with the usual broad smiles and cheerful greetings we received. My stomach clenched with uneasiness. We weren't far from My Lai, and I thought people in the area might, with good reason, be hostile to Americans. We heard that men had attacked two German tourists in the vicinity a few weeks before, so we felt apprehensive.

Dermot spoke to me in Spanish, a language we used when we needed to communicate discretely. "I don't like the vibe I'm getting. Be ready to bike out quickly if we need to."

CARLA FOUNTAIN

The men stopped beside us and scowled. One of them asked, "American?"

Dermot slid his water bottle into its holder and motioned for me to go. "*No! Somos cubanos!*" (No! We're Cuban!) He began singing in Spanish to reinforce his statement. The song's chorus floated back to the perplexed men as we pushed off and dashed down the road.

"That was close! I think you confused them," I said.

Dermot laughed. "Yes! But it would be good to travel to Cuba one day. Imagine a bicycle trip there. That should be our next adventure."

When we arrived at Quang Ngai, we found a hotel built only two years prior. The outside looked luxurious, but the interior was grimy and neglected. We didn't have enough time to bicycle to the massacre memorial in My Lai before dark, so we hired a motorbike taxi and sat three on the bike. We rode fourteen miles round trip through rice paddies fringed with feathery bamboo in the surrounding hills. The beauty contrasted sharply with the violence that had taken place there.

The site commemorates the horrible massacre that occurred in 1968 during the Vietnam War, when American troops brutally tortured, mutilated, raped, and killed between three hundred and five hundred villagers—men, women, infants, and children. Historians called the massacre the most shocking episode of the Vietnam War. Years later, many soldiers who took part in the episode were charged with war crimes. Nevertheless, while we were on the motorbike ride, people seemed friendly. At the memorial, no one hassled us. No one even asked for money. Instead of saying "*Liên Xô*" (Russia), we heard the children say "*Mỹ*" (America).

I didn't feel well the next morning, but we kept bicycling. Thick clouds filled the sky, so we rode the forty miles to Sa Huynh without the blazing sun beating down on us. We couldn't decide whether to take the train to Qui Nhon or to stay the night at a seaside hotel. We checked out both options and decided to take the train. The ticket price

BICYCLE ODYSSEY

was forty cents for both of us to go seventy miles, which would take four hours. The train departure was scheduled for one o'clock, so we raced down the road to look for food. We devoured a nourishing lunch of mango, pineapple, and chicken noodles.

A local man approached us when he discovered we were American.

"I used to work for USAID. Can you please help me?" he asked. "I need to contact my friend in Ohio. I need him to help me with my papers so I can emigrate to America."

We agreed to try, wrote down the necessary information from him, and left to catch the train. He gave us a name but no address. It saddened me that we had a slim chance of succeeding with so little to go on.

While we waited with a small group of friendly people, I tried to find a toilet. They told me there wasn't one in the town. They used the beach behind the graveyard. I walked there, but about twenty young men stood around on the beach. Eventually I found an area on the other side of the railroad tracks. I had suffered from a stomach bug for the past four days. Fortunately, the crowd gathered at the station didn't follow me to the ditch.

The group chatting with Dermot had grown when I came back. "Are you okay, babe?"

"Not really. I should probably look for a pharmacy when we get to a city. Maybe in Saigon. I'm glad you were here as a diversion so I could sneak away in private, though."

By two o'clock, the train still hadn't arrived. The stationmaster told us it would pull in at three o'clock. After a while, he announced that the train would arrive at four o'clock. The crowd grew around us and started to feel oppressive. We decided to wait at the hotel until four o'clock. As we biked out, we spied a truck on the road. On the spur of the moment, we asked the driver for a lift. He agreed to take us for a small fee and left us twelve miles shy of Qui Nhon.

CARLA FOUNTAIN

At the hotel in Qui Nhon, I spread a Vietnamese muscle liniment over my sore shoulders, neck, knees, and ankles. We ate a hearty meal at the restaurant next door to the hotel and talked about our trip and our plans.

"If we ever come back to Vietnam, I want to go north to Hanoi and bike to the border with China," I said.

Dermot nodded. "I hope the border will be open in a few years. I also want to come back and look into more art. I loved spending time with the artists we met."

Once settled in our room for the night, I dove into *Saigon* by Anthony Grey, an epic novel that spanned several decades—from the French colonial era in 1925 through the Vietnam War. We had found many stands along our trek with used books in French and English. I picked up books about Vietnam that helped me learn more about the country's history. I also found many French classics.

The next day we biked on gorgeous stretches of road in the mountains with wild, open land and forest in the distance. Best of all, the population was sparse. We delighted in this peaceful nature experience. When we did pass other people, they either ambled in small villages fringed with thick vegetation or worked in emerald-green rice paddies framed by coconut palm trees. The rich smell of ripe grain intoxicated us as farmers gathered, dried, winnowed, and threshed the rice harvest.

The coastal road followed a bay for a few miles. In a village at the end of the bay, we took refuge from the sun and ducked into a restaurant overlooking the water for lunch. From that point, the road turned inland and climbed over the mountains. After we covered the seventy miles to Tuy Hoa, we stayed at the Tourist Hotel, where we talked with a Vietnamese man.

"I worked for the Americans when they were here. Because of that, I spent ten years in a reeducation camp after the war. Please, I need your help to contact the doctor I used to work with."

BICYCLE ODYSSEY

"Of course. We will try to help you. What can you tell us about the doctor?" I asked.

He gave us a name, a state, and a clinic. With tears welling in his eyes, the man told us a confusing story about his life. His hands shook as he wrote down the information for me. We felt bad because we knew that, with so little to go on, we would have difficulty tracking down his doctor friend in the States. But we would still try.

The road from Tuy Hoa to Nha Trang both delighted and challenged us for eighty-five miles. The first five miles out of town were busy and dusty before we reached quiet hills with dense vegetation and lush palms. We savored the quiet, lack of crowds, and beauty of the overcast morning. We cycled a little slower than necessary to enjoy the experience even more fully. After the mountain pass, the peninsula spread out before us. We arrived at a fishing village with a colorful fleet in the harbor and thatched houses along the water. A bit farther down the road, we found a hotel and thought we might spend the night. The beach looked inviting with white sand and a deserted bay, but we discovered that the hotel had never been completed. The skeleton structure promised to be a luxury hotel in the future. We found a restaurant on the beach and went in for a drink and a bite to eat. To cool off, we took a dip in the deserted bay's clear and placid turquoise water. Thickly forested hills surrounded the beach, and trees shaded the sand. I could have stayed there forever. The waiter offered to let us sleep in the restaurant, and we almost accepted his invitation. But when he told us that a good, smooth road with only two hills lay ahead, we decided to continue on and cover more distance that afternoon.

The next five miles were as promised. We passed bays with white sands stretching as far as we could see. The road surface deteriorated after about six miles, slowing us down to a crawl over rocks. This situation continued off and on for the next five to ten miles. At times we looked up, and all we saw was a rough road to the horizon. We plugged on. We wanted to arrive in Nha Trang before dark. But night fell, and we continued to pick our way through the gravelly road. Thirteen miles

283

later, a mountain pass still lay ahead of us in the darkness. We breathed a sigh of relief when we arrived safely in Nha Trang and found a hotel.

We spent three days in Nha Trang, recuperating from our four-hundred-mile ride down the coast. At the end of that ride, I felt lean and strong, but I still suffered from a bad stomach bug and the beginnings of a cold.

Nha Trang provided a good resting place. We had enough space so no one hassled us. We took full advantage and retreated to the beach, rested in our modest hotel room, or relaxed in the restaurants at the luxury hotels. We could avoid the crowds that usually gathered around us. One day as we finished our lunch on the terrace of a restaurant, a young woman on a motorbike stopped and smiled when she noticed us.

"Where are you from?" she asked.

"America."

"I want to talk to you. I am going to Orange County, California, soon. I am so happy! I'll come back later." She waved as she zoomed away, but she never returned to talk to us.

We took the train from Nha Trang back to Saigon. As we waited to put our bikes in the luggage car, a young man pushed his way to our bikes, fiddled with the gears, sat on my back rack, and nearly tipped over the bikes. Then he sneezed in my face. I glared at him and told him to leave me alone. He moved away a few paces but returned to squeeze the brakes with a smirk. At the same moment I could feel a surge of anger boiling up inside me, another man to my right smiled and asked me questions about America, pulling my attention away. His friendliness and calmness defused the situation and helped me move through my anger. I was grateful for his kindness. We talked until the train arrived.

We found prime seats in the middle of the car with a table in front of us and plenty of leg room. After securely locking our panniers to the overhead rack, following the lead of the other Vietnamese passengers, we settled in to enjoy the ride. But the calm disappeared when, twenty minutes into the trip, an older woman with her teenage daughter and son set up their hot food business and served meals right at our feet. For the next three hours, the mother ran back and forth shouting, barking orders to her children, and soliciting customers. She plopped her pile of warm meat—liver, chicken, steak, pork, and fried eggs—in front of us on the table and placed her huge tub of rice across the aisle. Their business possessed a total of five plates, so they rinsed off plates and spoons in the washroom and polished them dry with a grimy rag for the next round of customers. Any vague stirring of hunger quickly dissipated as I watched her operation. Her son dashed back and forth, sneezing profusely as he served the plates of steaming food.

We had been wise to lock our panniers to the luggage racks. Because of the heat, people opened all the windows to let in a breeze. Deep in the night, when we stopped at a few stations, hands reached inside the windows and tried to grab unattached bags.

A group of young adults hung out at the train station in Saigon as we waited to retrieve our bikes from the luggage area. I noticed many of them were mixed race—Caucasian and Vietnamese as well as Black and Vietnamese. A tall, young woman with hair like mine smiled at me. We laughed and exchanged words in the little Vietnamese I knew. When we received our bikes and I turned to say goodbye, one of the women swatted me playfully on the back. I learned that the mixed-race young adults had a difficult time fitting into society. Like the children we had encountered in the Pearl S. Buck International organization in Thailand, they weren't accepted because of their mixed ethnicity. They faced heavy discrimination, and many were vagrants. People called them *bụi đời*, which means "dust of life."

CARLA FOUNTAIN

As we left Vietnam, I reflected on how fortunate we were to have visited at that point in time. Vietnam remains to this day one of the highlights of our trip. I felt privileged and grateful to have visited when the country first opened up and people were eager to connect. The women I met in the country embraced me into their sisterhood with their friendly and natural interactions. People mainly used bicycles, and few motor vehicles circulated on the roads. That made for an ideal bicycling experience on our journey. Like our month-long detour to Uganda, a chance encounter steered us to Vietnam. After our trip, I agreed with Mr. Gaj in Uganda when he spoke of the natural beauty in Uganda and Vietnam. They were the two most beautiful countries, in his opinion. We couldn't have planned these highlights of our trip. They had happened only because we had stayed open and adaptable, and followed our intuition.

PART 8
• Singapore and Bali—Winding Down

April 27 to May 31, 1992

27

Singapore—A Pause

By the time we left Vietnam, we were merely skin, muscle, and bone. Because of the heat, we never had much of an appetite. Yet we still bicycled tremendous mileage. When we flew back to Bangkok to finish the last leg of our trip and catch our flight to Singapore, we decided to have clothes tailored during our four-day layover. The inexpensive, gorgeous Thai silks and the abundance of tailors were too good to pass up. I envisioned myself stylishly outfitted and ready to start work when I returned home. Unfortunately, because of my emaciated state when I had the items made to measure, none of the clothes, except for the ones made to fit loose, ever fit well once I regained my normal, healthy weight.

Before traveling to our final destination of Bali, we stopped over in Singapore for a couple of days. We gave the bicycles a rest and walked around to the different ethnic areas of the city to fill up on delicious food. An American teacher we met during our trek in Nepal invited us to his international school to talk to his high school class. The students were mostly Americans, children of diplomats and foreign executives. Dermot made a short presentation about our trip and impressed our host with his teaching style. After spending that morning with the students, I considered that teaching in international schools would be an interesting thing to do.

After our visit at the school, we stopped at a pharmacy and asked for advice. Our digestive systems had been acting up for weeks. I had never shaken that stomach bug. The pharmacist sold us Chinese Curing Pills, a traditional remedy to treat stomach problems, bloating, indigestion, and diarrhea. The herbal pills did the trick and soothed our tummies. For years after that, I tried in vain to find them again. They had worked when nothing else helped.

We spent a day exploring different areas of the city. Singapore boasted an interesting mix of several cultures. We marveled at the modernity and cleanliness. The city implemented strict laws and severe penalties against spitting, using chewing gum, and not flushing a public toilet. The country was considered one of the safest and cleanest places in the world. Our tours of Chinatown, Little India, and a mosque delighted us. We sampled food from each area of the city.

I finished Elisabeth Bumiller's *May You Be the Mother of a Hundred Sons*, a book about Indian women from various walks of life. The section on Indian women intellectuals resonated with me. I understood the dichotomy of having a feminist or liberated philosophy and still feeling obligated to duty and tradition. That is a universal feeling and not limited to the Indian women I read about. My desire to take charge and forge ahead in my own direction conflicted with the strong pull of duty and what family and society expected of me.

We would be home soon. I would need to act on what echoed inside me and explore my options. For the time being, I tried to stay in the present to enjoy the trip and our explorations. But I was scared of the future and uncertain about the choices I would have to make. To help me commit to my feelings, I wrote them down.

BICYCLE ODYSSEY

April 27, 1991

My new resolve is to speak my mind, my truth, and not acquiesce out of politeness. I long to affirm myself and my beliefs. I want to avoid taking things personally and worrying about other people's judgments. I'm different; I'm a unique individual. I will celebrate that uniqueness and enjoy it. I hope I have the courage to follow through with my resolve. I hope I have the conviction to follow my heart and gut feelings. I've done that on this trip when choosing where to go. I need to do the same when deciding how to live my life.

28

Bali—Blessings and Balm

Bali soothed our weary, travel-worn bodies. We landed in Denpasar and biked to Kuta Beach, where we rested for two days. We delighted in the feel of the warm waves on our bodies. The water tossed us around in a therapeutic cleanse.

The Balinese said there was no word for *tourist* in their language; they called everyone a "guest." We did feel like guests there. I loved Bali from the start and felt things could only get better.

After relaxing at the beach, we headed for the countryside. We biked to the calm, tiny town of Ubud in the hills. Our small guesthouse lay on a quiet street with a view of fields. Every morning, our guesthouse owner did *puja*, a Hindu blessing ceremony, before each door and left a flower and incense offering. Bali was predominantly Hindu in contrast to the Muslim islands lying on either side. After *puja*, the owner left a large thermos of freshly brewed Balinese coffee on our patio table. We poured the rich, strong brew into our mugs and sipped as we watched the village come to life. A little later, our hostess delivered the breakfast of the day. She often served peanut butter pancakes with sliced pineapple, mango, and banana plus a glass of freshly squeezed juice.

Fueled up, we left on our bikes to explore the quiet roads and countryside in the morning coolness. We glided by emerald-green,

BICYCLE ODYSSEY

terraced rice fields. We passed poultry farms, duck herders, and people going to market with their wares. The farmers transported their ducks by using a large piece of fabric with holes cut out for the ducks' heads to keep them calm and contained together in a basket on their way to market. They trussed pigs up in a basket that completely enveloped them; the large, open weaving allowed for airflow, and the light carrier rendered them immobile. The farmers took the secured ducks and pigs to market by bicycle or by *tuk tuk* (a three-wheeled auto rickshaw frequently used on the island).

For our lunches, we stopped at little open-air restaurants or food stands in the market. We loved the various Balinese dishes we tried. Our taste buds delighted in the fresh, interesting spices and flavor combinations new to our palates. We ate meal after meal of chicken satay (grilled, marinated chicken on skewers with a creamy, spicy peanut butter dipping sauce) and *nasi campur Bali* (a scoop of rice surrounded by various ingredients, such as tofu, fish, fried shrimp, vegetables, peanuts, eggs, and spices). Every restaurant prepared its *nasi campur Bali* in a slightly different way. The dish never disappointed.

In the open-air markets, we bought food for snacks and marveled at the fruit, much of which we had never seen before or even heard of until that year's trip. We knew we wouldn't find them back home, so we stocked up on rambutan, mangosteen, custard apple, mango, and star apple to eat on our day rides.

In the afternoons, we loved to go and have a strong Balinese coffee at an outdoor café. The waitress brewed the locally grown coffee by pouring boiling water over finely ground coffee in a cup. We had to take care not to drink the fine sludge at the bottom when we finished drinking our coffee. We struck up conversations with other travelers and foreigners who had made Bali their home.

Ubud enchanted us, and we decided to spend over a week there while exploring the surrounding area. We planned to seek out and talk to Lawrence and Lorne Blair, two brothers who made documentaries and had written the book *Ring of Fire* about their explorations in Indonesia. They both lived in Bali—one in Kuta Beach and the other in Ubud. We wanted to touch base with fellow documentary filmmakers. But an American woman we met at our local café in Ubud scorned the idea. The woman had lived there for a while and knew the Blairs.

"Why do you want to intrude on people's privacy?" she asked. "They might want to be left alone. People are so presumptuous to come over and think they can barge in and talk to a person they don't know." She tossed her head and stormed off in a huff, her waist-length auburn hair streaming behind her.

Her calm, British husband smoothed things over as we sipped another cup of coffee together. "Don't let that bother you. You really should do what you want. See how you feel about it in a few days. They might be receptive to meeting you." He smiled warmly and brushed back his sandy hair.

He made a special effort to be kind to us to make up for his wife's rude and curt manner. But we lost confidence in how the Blairs would receive us, and we let the matter drop. In retrospect, we both wished we hadn't let her dissuade us.

After staying at our budget guesthouse for five days, another guest gave us a tip. The high-end guesthouse across the street allowed people to use their pool for a small fee. We walked over to the other guesthouse's lush, green garden and floated in the pool to cool off in the hot afternoons. The locals found relief in the many rivers on the island during the heat of the day. We often cycled by cool glens on the side of a river, in which whole families sat up to their chests in the shallow flow. They waved and smiled at us as we bicycled by.

BICYCLE ODYSSEY

Bali boasted over ten thousand temples. We visited several each day, from tiny shrines to massive historical temple compounds. Two temples stand out in my memory: *Pura Tirta Empul* (Holy Water Temple) near Ubud and *Pura Goa Lawah* (Bat Cave Temple). We biked to Holy Water Temple and spent the better part of the day submerging ourselves in the healing waters surrounded by statues of gods and goddesses. Traditionally, people visited Holy Water Temple to cleanse themselves of their sins before visiting other temples to pray. I felt cleansed and rejuvenated at the end of our visit to that calm oasis.

A priest who had helped spread Hinduism in Bali established *Pura Goa Lawah* in the eleventh century. Years ago, priests used the cave for meditation. Bat Cave Temple sat at the mouth of a large cave, which was inhabited by hordes of bats. Thousands of them hung at the entrance of the cave, mimicking society in microcosm. Mother bats nursed their infants. Young bats yawned and dozed. Others cuddled. I observed them in fascination as the cute, furry, winged mammals went about their lives.

We spent time in Ubud, visiting various artists and artisans at their workshops. In Bali, the arts were woven into everyday life. Often a man or woman who cultivated rice by day painted in the evenings, danced at a temple, or played in a traditional orchestra. We attended a temple dance almost every night after dinner. I hadn't seen or heard anything like the music and dances in Bali. The gamelan orchestra hypnotized me. Gamelan is the traditional ensemble music of Java and Bali. The instruments include metallophones (large metal bowls of various sizes with coverings), gongs, gong chimes, xylophones, flutes, and hand-played drums called *kendhangs*. Each night the presentations transported us to another realm as young girls in elaborate costumes gracefully reenacted stories from Hindu and Balinese mythology or heroic romances.

We tried the various little open-air restaurants spread out around town. Many of them offered free entertainment and screened bootleg copies of current US films. We often met and talked with the people at the next table. Our stay in Ubud was quite relaxing and social.

Darkness falls quickly in the tropics with little twilight. On our walks home from dinner in the evenings, we gazed up at the stars in the night sky. Without light pollution, the constellations shone brilliantly. The Milky Way stretched across the center of the sky in a different arc than in the northern hemisphere. I couldn't get my bearings. Admiring the southern hemisphere, I laid eyes on unfamiliar stars and took in a completely different angle on the cosmos. I couldn't find my familiar landmarks of the Big Dipper and the North Star.

A few days after we arrived in Ubud and settled in, we walked into town and saw headlines that Los Angeles was in a state of alert at the close of the Rodney King trial. The year before, the police had stopped Rodney King, an African American man, not far from our home and severely beat him. A neighbor caught the altercation on videotape from his nearby balcony and shared the footage with the news. Rodney had done nothing to provoke the brutal beatings and was badly injured. The police officers involved were on trial for using excessive force during the incident. The Rodney King trial ended, and all the officers involved were acquitted. My heart sank, and I felt a surge of rage as I read more.

The news grew worse the next day. The acquittal ruling prompted widespread protest. Fires and violence broke out across Los Angeles not far from our house. Many people said we were lucky not to have been in Los Angeles at that time. But my first reaction was wanting to return home. *To do what? How could I help?* I didn't know how, but still I had a visceral desire to go back. My city was in turmoil, and I wanted to help in whatever way I could. One of the newspapers featured a map showing problems near the school where I had taught.

I expressed my dismay at the verdict to an American businessman we met at the newsstand in Ubud.

After taking a drag of his cigarette, he shrugged and exhaled in my direction. "Well, if you believe in the American justice system, you have to accept the verdict."

He came from a place of privilege and had never felt the humiliation of being profiled.

"The American justice system institutionalized racism and kept people enslaved for many years. The system is not perfect," I said.

The news brought me down. It was almost time to head home to Los Angeles. I felt ready to wind up our trip after our month in Bali.

I visited the meditation center in Ubud for a lesson with an American woman, who ran the center. She led me through a short but powerful and calming meditation. After we meditated, we had a wonderful talk. Other teachers had introduced me to the practice before, but I hadn't been consistent. I realized I needed regular meditation to improve my mindset and help me find my true center.

I shared the conflicting thoughts that tumbled around in my head with her as well as my worries about the future when I would soon return to the States.

She swept back her long, ginger hair and smiled at me. "In order to find your true calling, you need to find out first, what brings you true happiness, and second, what comes easily to you. Usually it's an interest you had as a child or an activity you did well as a child. We often abandon or dismiss those things. We need to recapture them."

As I walked back to our cottage, I reflected on our meditation session. I thought about how bicycling was a moving meditation. The rhythmic, repetitive movement, combined with breath and mantra, shifted my energy. I am certain that bicycling kept me sane and balanced throughout our year on the road. During our times of inactivity, the lack of movement and meditation caused me to falter, bicker, and become unhappy. Those were the times on our trip when we experienced conflict.

Toward the end of our stay in Ubud, we found a little place that offered massage treatments, body treatments, and even haircuts. I visited for a hair trim. My hair had grown so much that it was difficult to comb out every day. The young woman struggled to comb my hair without pulling it. She usually worked on smooth, straight hair, and my tight curls perplexed her. But the few inches she managed to trim helped to lighten the heavy mass of hair I'd grown, and I felt cooler.

The next day we returned to the spa for our Royal Balinese Princess treatments. Our therapists performed a soothing massage and covered us in a paste made from turmeric, which they scrubbed into our skin. The yellow spice coated our bodies from head to toe for an exfoliating, anti-inflammatory treatment. They took us to large, old-fashioned claw-foot tubs filled with warm water. Pink rose petals floated on the surfaces. Their soft perfume filled the room. I sank into the water and soaked. My mind drifted off into a deep peacefulness. Dermot and I spent a heavenly two-and-a-half hours in the treatments. We sorely needed the care. Our bodies had endured rigorous challenges during the past ten months.

After eight days in Ubud, we cycled to almost five thousand feet to reach Bedugul, a mountain resort near Lake Bratan. During the climb, we enjoyed cooler breezes and quiet roads. After a night in the mountains, we journeyed down to the coast on the north side of the island to Lovina. As we traveled west along the north coast of the island,

BICYCLE ODYSSEY

we encountered few other tourists. We found a small guest cottage and bicycled to the water to snorkel. The reef fell off sharply. As we ventured to the edge, I sighted a reef shark swimming in the murky depths. I shivered in spite of the warm water.

Java wasn't on our itinerary because we had heard that the densely populated island had congested traffic. But we were close and wanted to at least touch the island. We decided to bike all the way to Gilimanuk, the western tip of Bali, and take the ferry across to the Port of Ketapang, Java. The port town didn't look very different except that all the women we noticed wore head scarves, a reflection of the predominantly Muslim population on Java. We ate lunch and took the ferry back, continuing on to Terima Bay to spend the night before making our way back east along the north coast of Bali. We stopped at Lovina again for the night and met Stan and Mary, a couple from Washington State who were traveling around Bali by car. The next day we cycled to Amed Beach, a small fishing village, for the night. People told us about a shipwreck off the coast. A Japanese submarine had torpedoed the USAT *Liberty*, a United States Army cargo ship, in 1942. If you were certified in scuba diving, you could dive the wreck. Dermot expressed interest in becoming certified in scuba diving earlier. I wished we'd done our separate studies in Thailand for two weeks—scuba diving for him and Thai massage for me.

We continued east along the quiet, northern coastline and curved down the coast to Candi Dasa. We found a lovely, secluded guesthouse right on the water. To our surprise, Stan and Mary, whom we had met in Lovina, and another American couple, Tom and Nancy from California, had also checked in. Only the six of us were staying at the guesthouse. We ate our meals together and engaged in lively conversations. Few people we knew in our circle of friends in the States traveled as much as we did. Talking to other people who traveled frequently and learning how they managed filled us with excitement.

"We take a month-long trip every year and finance our vacations with sales from handicrafts we bring back from our travels. We sell the items in the coffee shop we run. The trip pays for itself," Nancy said.

299

CARLA FOUNTAIN

Mary held up an intricate silver bangle for me to see. "I bought handcrafted silver beads here in Bali and plan to sell them at farmers' markets when I return to the States. I found an elderly silversmith in a village yesterday and watched how he made them."

I ran my fingers over the silverwork and admired it. "You'll have to tell us where that is. I would love to visit the silversmith."

Nancy and Mary's ideas excited and inspired me to buy several items to resell. I sold a small amount when I returned home. I also made lovely necklaces to offer loved ones as gifts. But I didn't succeed on the level the two women talked about. I wasn't a natural salesperson and didn't make much money.

Both couples expressed passionate ideas about shared-living communities they wanted to develop. I asked them to tell me about their vision.

"People would live in their own houses around a common green area, so they would still have a level of privacy," Tom said.

"They would all share resources that people only utilize occasionally, such as tools, washing machines, lawn mowers, etcetera," Stan said.

Throughout the evening meal, the two couples expressed their excitement about the communities. Each of them continued to share their visions.

"Right! There is no need for everyone to have their own lawn mower they just use once a week or once a month."

"It's a more sustainable way of living."

"Think of all the money people would save."

"It reduces unnecessary consumption and saves resources."

Their discussions gave us good food for thought.

We took day rides to Tenganan Pegringsingan, an ancient village, and Klungkung, known for classic Balinese paintings. In Tenganan, we visited the elderly silversmith, who showed us how he handcrafted silver beads. I bought several beads to make jewelry with. I also bought several strands of amber beads. I loved the rich, earthy caramel color of the amber and the variations of shades. I got an idea to combine the silver beads with the amber for jewelry. For myself, I fashioned a meditation *mala* I still use today. The thick, solid beads become warm in my hands and are soothing to count with a mantra. They hold special memories for me because of my experiences in Bali.

Along the road, we ran into a man who looked like he was from the Indonesian region of Irian Jaya (West Papua) on the island of New Guinea because of his curly hair and dark skin. His short Afro matched mine. He looked at us with interest, and we stopped to say hello. He wanted to know where we had come from. He smiled and patted his hair, then patted mine, and we laughed together. All through Southeast Asia, local people unused to seeing nonwhite tourists reacted to me. They put their arm up to mine, noting that we had the same warm, brown skin color. But that was the first time my hair matched that of a local person. The encounter made me wish we could continue on to Irian Jaya before our return home.

We left our idyllic spot in Candi Dasa to catch the ferry for the island of Lombok from Padang Bai. The crossing took four hours. When we arrived at Lembar, we stepped off the boat into another culture. Lombok, in contrast to Bali's Hinduism, was a predominately Muslim island. We biked along the north coast of Lombok, stopping at a few temples along the way.

CARLA FOUNTAIN

Jeff, a young American at one of the temples, asked, "Are you going to Gili Air?"

I shaded my eyes from the bright sun to better look at him. "Gili? Where? I haven't heard about it. What is it?" I responded.

"You would love it. Gili Air is a little island about two kilometers in diameter just off the coast here. There are no cars, only sandy lanes. It's surrounded by clean, white beaches and crystal-clear water. You should check it out."

"Thank you. I love places like that. Is Gili Air very crowded?"

We walked together in search of a cooler spot under several trees. "There aren't many tourists on the island yet. It's a word-of-mouth kind of place and very quiet. You should really go now before it becomes too popular. I'm on my way back there for a second visit. Maybe I'll see you."

Intrigued, Dermot and I cycled to find the docks. We loaded the bikes onto a small boat for the short crossing. I needed to lift my fully loaded bike and wade into the water to board. After our short crossing, I lost my balance as I lifted my bicycle out of the boat. I fell backward into the shallow water, soaking my small backup camera. Fortunately, I had two cameras, and we were near the end of our voyage, because the camera never recovered from the dunking.

We found lodging in a little guest hut and enjoyed the quiet island for a few nights. Gili Air was everything Jeff had said it would be. The calm atmosphere offered yet another opportunity for self-reflection. I practiced the meditation techniques I had learned at the center in Ubud. I felt peaceful and at ease as I followed the rise and fall of my inhalations and exhalations. My meditation enhanced my relationship with Dermot. We spent an enjoyable time together on Gili Air and for that month in Bali—free from conflict and in harmony.

On our second evening on Gili Air, we ran into Jeff on the beach. We shared a meal and talked with him and a few other travelers about their journeys.

Jeff pulled back his long, blond hair. "I came to Asia to study martial arts," he said.

"What kind of martial arts do you practice?" Dermot asked.

"*Pencak silat*, a special form practiced in Indonesia. I found an elder master I want to study with."

"That's cool! How long will you stay?" I asked.

"I plan to be here for at least a year, maybe two. Right now, I am just taking a break and resting on Gili Air before the intense studies," Jeff said.

"This is a good place for that," I said. "Thank you for directing us here. On our trip this past year, our best experiences happened when we opened up to deviate from our set path. When we listened to suggestions from people we met, we found amazing places."

Jeff leaned back on his arms and watched the play of light on the water. "That's so true. Life really opens up when we listen to our intuition."

Soft light filled the room at dawn when I opened my eyes. A rooster crowed, and several more joined in. Careful not to disturb Dermot, I reached for my journal and pen.

> May 24, 1992
> Last night on this quiet island, I had vivid dreams. I dreamt I was at a family gathering, and my Aunt Louise,

one of the strong matriarchs of my family, talked with me. I told her about my trip. She's often stern, so she took me by surprise with her warmth and enthusiasm. I expressed my uncertainties about starting in a new direction upon my return home. My aunt took my hands in hers, looked into my eyes, and said, "But you have to do what's best for you." This morning I woke up feeling empowered and supported. I have to trust myself and my intuition in all aspects of my life.

We took the short ferry ride back to Lombok and rode to Ampenan, where we spent two nights at a new guesthouse run by a modern local woman. In the gorgeous setting, she appeared stressed by all she needed to do to run the business. I was reminded that, even in the middle of paradise, life can overwhelm us if we take on too much or let things bother us.

We passed two groups of playful, rowdy boys on the way to the ferry for Bali. The first group smiled and waved at us, but the second rushed me and tried to grab my bags. I pedaled hard and yelled at them. When I caught up to Derm and stopped to catch my breath, I found that one of the boys had managed to unzip a pannier and grab my small flashlight. Incidents like that happened rarely on our trip. The encounter was only the third time in our eleven-month journey that I had been rushed. In retrospect, all encounters were mild and not life threatening. We passed more boys coming in from fishing. They proudly held up their catches for us to see.

We loved Ubud so much that we decided to go back for two more nights. On the last day, we ran into Joe, a young man who had been part of the bicycle group we met in Nepal.

BICYCLE ODYSSEY

Joe grinned. "Imagine running into both of you."

"It's great to see you, Joe! What are you doing here in Ubud?" I asked.

"I left the guys to meet with my girlfriend, Sally, here in Bali. She's on her way to Irian Jaya to spend six months researching culture and plants for her graduate work in ethnobotany."

"Wow! That sounds like an exciting adventure," I said.

"Let's hang out tonight for dinner so you can meet Sally."

"Sounds like a good plan," Derm said. "We can catch up."

During dinner we compared travel notes and future plans. Sally and Joe spoke passionately about their work. They were full of social consciousness and burning with ambition. I admired their robust energy. Their stories and projects fascinated me.

After helping himself to more chicken satay, Joe said, "I'm enrolled in law school for the fall." His blue eyes flashed. "I want to earn my law degree so I can help the African National Congress fight against the apartheid regime in South Africa."

He impressed me. So many Americans had no idea about the struggle in South Africa.

Sally took another sip of her pineapple juice. "I'm excited to go to Irian Jaya. The island's rugged mountains and thick jungles will make travel difficult, though. Did you know that, because many groups remain in isolation due to the terrain, over one thousand languages have developed there?"

I was stunned. "Fascinating!"

We talked long into the night. I envied Sally's adventure ahead in Irian Jaya. We wanted to spend time there as well. The rugged terrain

305

CARLA FOUNTAIN

would have made bicycling difficult, maybe even impossible. But I wanted to learn more about the cultures in Irian Jaya. Indonesia merited a whole other year of travel. The archipelago contained thousands of islands with a myriad of cultures. We touched on only a tiny portion. Because of the mix-up with our round-the-world tickets, we didn't have the stopovers in Biak and Irian Jaya we had initially planned on. That would be for another time, I hoped. I wanted to return and explore more in the future.

Before we parted that night, Sally cautioned us, "I've had problems with intestinal worms here in Indonesia. Since you guys have been in Southeast Asia so long, you probably have them also. The pharmacy sells parasite medication over the counter here. That might be a good idea."

I cringed as I thought about parasites possibly running amok inside me.

Sally chuckled. "You can also buy a sleep aid if you are concerned about the long twenty-three-hour flight home that you have coming up."

The next day, even though we didn't have signs of worms, we bought and consumed our medications so we wouldn't bring any parasites home with us. We said goodbye to Ubud and bicycled down to Legian Beach, where we soaked in the clear waves for two days. We needed time to regroup for our flight home on the last day of May. Tourists filled the beach.

Dermot flagged down a vendor and bought us grilled corn on the cob, drizzled with a sweet and spicy chili sauce. I savored this last snack. One of the delights of our trip had been tasting the different foods and seasonings.

After our snack, I rubbed sunblock on Dermot's back. He had been successful in not getting a sunburn during this entire trip. No small feat with his fair, freckled skin.

306

"After our travels on the back roads and into little towns on the island, Bali already seems far away with so many westerners surrounding us." I sighed. "I feel sad that our journey is coming to an end."

Dermot rubbed more lotion on his face. "Me, too. I'm ready to go home, but I also want to continue our odyssey."

We lay back on our towel, inhaling the tangy salt air and listening to the sounds of the waves. Dermot's wedding ring, now back on his finger, glinted in the sun. The gold band had mysteriously resurfaced that morning from a hidden recess of his pannier after having gone missing at the hot springs in Thailand. My eyes misted when I thought of how symbolic it was. We had almost given up on our marriage and on our trip many times throughout this odyssey. All the same, we had persevered and continued to the end. Lulled by the rhythmic *whoosh* of the waves, we closed our eyes and reflected on our trip.

On our last night at the hotel in Legian Beach, I sat, tense and nervous, while I made my list of things to do back home. I recalled a time before when I had returned to the States, transformed and excited, after studying in France for a year. Once home, I bent to the pressures of expectations and school. I became so obsessed with grades and career that my friends from France told me I seemed like a different person when they came to visit. My life narrowed as I focused on my career path, and I became rigid. I feared falling into the same cycle all over again when we returned home from Bali.

I felt overwhelmed by the tasks that loomed ahead of me. I needed to find a job, make a living, and deal with the mundane aspects of life. It would be difficult to shift gears so abruptly after my year of travel. To accomplish everything, I feared I would have to submerge myself completely in the process of reentry. All the wonder and adventure of the trip would soon fade into the past, and that fact depressed me. But

CARLA FOUNTAIN

I wanted and needed to keep a balance. I realized the importance of holding on to the magic of the trip and the lessons I had learned from the journey. I vowed to keep meeting people and to having stimulating discussions, to go more with the flow but still in my own unique direction. I needed to relax and not take life so seriously. I hoped I would be able to find a balance between all my dreams and the realities of life. After all, to accomplish my dreams, I needed an income.

With those thoughts swirling in my head, I slept fitfully. But when I did finally sleep, a group of strong women visited me in my dreams. They traveled and worked independently. We talked about their work and journeys. Our discussion emboldened me. I woke up, infused with new confidence.

The sky slowly lightened at dawn as the elder of our guesthouse finished his prayers and made fresh coffee for us. We sat on the veranda for our last Balinese coffee before our final bike ride to search for gifts to bring home. We took a taxi to the airport. Both our bicycles and legs could now rest.

The flight from Denpasar to Honolulu was so long that our plane needed to refuel in Biak, a small island northwest of New Guinea. We stepped off the plane and walked through the terminal as a group of young men serenaded us with local music and songs. I felt wistful while listening to them, staring at the gateway that led to a place I wanted to explore more.

I leaned back in my seat when we boarded the plane after refueling. We settled in for the long flight across the ocean. I squeezed Dermot's hand in gratitude. "We did it, Dermot. I can't believe some of the situations we found ourselves in. I am grateful that we encountered so many wonderful people."

Dermot sighed and squeezed my hand back. "This journey will stay with us for the rest of our lives. Thank you for going on this odyssey with me."

BICYCLE ODYSSEY

I blinked back tears of gratitude. "Thank *you*. I couldn't have accomplished this journey with anyone else."

Weary and content, we closed our eyes and slept as the plane winged its way over the Pacific.

We ended our trip on a high note. Uganda and Vietnam remained the unexpected and unplanned highlights of our trip because of their natural beauty and the generosity and friendliness of the people. India had tested our mettle and limits. But our encounters with exceptional and caring people in India had rewarded us richly. Our weeks in Gokarna and Kodaikanal had highlighted our time on the subcontinent because of the connections we made with locals who generously shared their lives and culture with us. Europe was a second home. I would revisit Indonesia and Thailand in a heartbeat for more exploration, even on my own. Both countries were welcoming and filled me with a sense of security and ease.

My parents picked us up at Los Angeles International Airport. They were thrilled that we had completed our trip and were relieved to see us back home safe. They had anxiously followed every postcard, letter, and phone call. I didn't fully grasp until many years later how much they had worried about us.

We still had ownership of our house. Because I had given my father power of attorney, he had been able to straighten things out on our behalf. We had a little money left, enough to tide us over for a couple of months until we found new jobs.

After we arrived at our house, I looked in bewilderment at all the possessions we had stored in the garage. I had lived for most of the trip with only the contents of one bicycle pannier, which included four changes of clothing. *Why did we have all this "stuff" in the garage?* During our year away, I realized how few material possessions I needed to live well. I felt light and liberated—both mentally and physically—with fewer possessions. I resolved to carry that lesson with me in the months and years to come.

309

Afterword

We survived our odyssey with no major illnesses and no broken bones. We felt good. We were alive. We had faced numerous near-death incidents and came out unscathed. One photo, taken as we sat in the departure lounge in Denpasar, shows two gaunt and sunburned bicyclists. Neither of us had ever been that thin in our adult lives, and we probably will never and should never be that thin again. A close friend of ours later told us that, when we returned from our trip, we looked scary: haggard and malnourished.

After our enormous bicycle journey, we gave thanks that we were alive and safe. We hung up our bicycles for a while. I had no desire to bike around town or to go on a long ride after we returned. Urban Los Angeles and spread-out Orange County, California, where I now live, seem more dangerous for bicycling to me than a crowded road in Southeast Asia. In the countries we traveled through on this odyssey, thousands of people biked in the cities. Motorists knew to look out for cyclists. Traffic moved in an organic flow that miraculously worked. Here in Orange County, I feel vulnerable on a bicycle because few pedestrians and bicyclists are on the roads or sidewalks. And there are certainly no cows or goats. Motorists don't pay attention to anything without four wheels; a bicycle or a pedestrian can easily seem invisible to them. I have, however, recently dusted off my bicycle. It's serviceable after a fresh tune-up, but I doubt either of us could undertake the trip again.

Our bicycle odyssey planted the seeds of major life changes for both of us. Dermot decided to follow his passion and work in the art world. Inspired by our visit to the school in Singapore, I taught in an international school in Spain for two years. My Thai massage experience in Bangkok intrigued me so much that I completed massage studies in the United States. The meditation center in Ubud stimulated me to deepen my yoga and meditation. This led me to further my studies and ultimately to teach yoga and meditation so I could share with others the benefits I had derived from both practices. As of today, I've worked in the holistic healing arts for over twenty years.

My palm reader in Madras, India, was uncannily on the mark about many things. My third place to live, France, is now my second home. Many poor and sick benefitted from my studies in massage and yoga because I have worked for hospices and hospitals. When I taught in the United States, I taught in low-income areas. I have yet to see the large sum of money the palm reader predicted, though.

The plight of mixed-raced children in Thailand and Vietnam was a problem I wanted to help with. A year after I returned home, the United States granted citizenship to Vietnamese offspring of American fathers from the time of the war and facilitated their journey to the States. Catholic Charities asked for volunteers to help the new immigrants acclimate, overcome culture shock, and learn English. Excited by the chance to help, I applied and was matched with a young woman in her twenties. I now also help support projects with Pearl S. Buck International in both Thailand and Vietnam.

Dermot and I always traveled well together. Maybe that was the secret that kept our relationship intact for nine years. We usually traveled by bicycle. Hence, we experienced a built-in mood stabilizer, a moving meditation. Our trips held us together.

Our troubles began and grew when we stopped bicycling. We separated and divorced in 1993, a year after our trip. The divorce marked a period in our lives filled with hurt, misunderstanding, and bitterness that lasted for many years until, almost two decades after our trip, we reconnected to share photographs and videos from our odyssey. We realized this voyage would always remain a glorious chapter in our lives. Our trip ultimately helped heal the bitterness of our divorce after nearly twenty years. The memories of our odyssey healed our conflict and pain. I'm grateful that we learned from the trip and now see each other with respect and love after going through the fire and turmoil of our separation. Perhaps, like the cycles of events on our trip, the fire, hardships, and agony serve only to make the taste of reconciliation sweeter.

I longed to see the world by bicycle because I wanted to move close to and connect with all I expected to encounter on our travels—to breathe in the air and the dust, and have them blend in with me, to drop my sweat on the ground and connect with the earth, to meet face-to-face with people in the places I journeyed. After our bicycle odyssey, I felt a kinship with so many more of the people on the planet. I studied their languages, traveled their streets and back roads, shared their food, and participated in their sacred ceremonies. My compassion and empathy grew because they became part of me.

Throughout our trip, we wanted to record people's answers to questions about life: What makes you happy? What would make the world a better place? Most answers to the latter surprised us.

People both poor and well off said, "The world is fine the way it is. I am happy."

Our Western upbringing causes us to want to change, move forward, improve. Sometimes that drive causes us to lose sight of the beauty in the present moment. Losing touch with the present can be a big source of discontentment and unhappiness. I hope we can move forward while still maintaining our focus and awareness of the existing beauty around us.

Women I met on the road and after the trip inspired me. Several weeks after our trip, I met Dorothy Hosmer, who had read about my journey in the local paper. She told me her own fascinating story. She had traveled alone by bicycle in Europe from 1937 to 1939, which included five months of bicycling from Poland down into the Balkans before the beginning of World War II. I reflected on her story, on the two women cyclists I had met in Kenya, and on Dervla Murphy, the author of *Full Tilt,* the book that first inspired me to plan our bicycle odyssey. These women had bravely set out alone and bucked tradition. I admire them and thank them for their inspiration.

I have found a corner of France with quiet farm roads that call out for me to explore. Breathing in the fresh air, I rhythmically cycle alone through undulating vineyards and hills for hours. I have my sights set on an extended journey along a lesser-used path of the Camino de Santiago de Compostela through France and Spain. This time I might journey on foot. But whether by foot or on bicycle, I plan to have stretches when I travel alone.

I hope this recounting of our odyssey inspires others to fearlessly venture out and connect with nature and the many people in our vast, beautiful world. I hope that, like I did, they will find the depth and magic inherent in the many places between the major dots on a map, the places off the main roads. By staying open to chance encounters along the way in life and being receptive to new experiences, we are steered to hidden gems and to the sublime. We also discover ourselves.

Budget and Sample of Expenses

One of our mentors, a fellow bicyclist who inspired us, said he spent about $12,000 on his five-year journey around the world in the mid to late 1980s. We spent about $15,000 for our eleven months of travel in the early 1990s. We racked up most of our expenses in Europe in the first three months. Cities—whether in Europe, Africa, or Asia—ate up the bulk of our budget. Once we reached the countryside, costs dropped dramatically. For the curious, I include a sample of our expenses.

The round-the-world tickets for two people were $4,484. In Europe, we mostly camped or stayed in hostels. We averaged between thirty and fifty dollars a day for meals and lodging. In Kenya and Uganda, we averaged ten dollars a day for meals and lodging. We had one splurge day at fifty-five dollars. Our budget hotels in India—all clean and decent but basic—were one to two dollars a night. The luxury hotel we treated ourselves to in Kovalam Beach, India, was ten dollars a night. Food was so inexpensive that I stopped keeping track of money spent on meals after Europe. All accommodations in Thailand were pristine and comfortable, even at the low price of between two and five dollars a night. All hotels in Vietnam were eight to ten dollars a night, which was the foreigner price. (Locals paid the equivalent of one to two dollars a night at that time.) In Bali, we averaged two to five dollars a night for attractive and clean bungalows.

Trip Itinerary

I estimate that we biked about seven thousand miles in all. Since our odometer broke early on in our trip, this list is an underestimate of our mileage and includes what I could record using maps and road signs along the way and after the fact. I didn't record the many detours, meanderings, and day trips.

Date	From—To	Transport	Miles
7/7/91	Los Angeles to London, England	Plane	
7/16	London to Halifax	Train	
7/18	Halifax to Arnside to Grange-over-Sands	Train/bike	35
7/19	Grange-over-Sands to Ambleside/The Lakes	Bike	20
7/20	Ambleside to Penrith to Glasgow, Scotland	Train/bike	24
7/21	Glasgow to Buchlyvie	Bike	23
7/22	Stirling, Bridge of Allan day trip	Bike	38
7/23	Buchlyvie to Tyndrum	Bike	50
7/24	Tyndrum to Oban	Bike	36
7/25	Oban to Iona	Ferry	
7/27	Iona to Isle of Mull to Tobermory	Ferry/bike	20
7/28	Tobermory to Armadale/Isle of Skye	Ferry	
7/29	Armadale to Uig	Bike	57
7/30	Uig to Tarbert/Isle of Harris	Ferry	
	Tarbert to Callanish	Bike	40
7/31	Callanish to Stornoway	Bike	17

Date	From—To	Transport	Miles
	Stornoway to Ullapool	Ferry	
8/1	Ullapool to Contin	Bike	38
8/2	Contin to Whitebridge	Bike	38
8/3	Whitebridge to Spean Bridge	Bike	31
8/4	Spean Bridge to Rannoch Station	Train	
	Rannoch Station to Carie	Bike	40
8/5	Carie to Crieff	Bike	33
8/6	Crieff to Edinburgh	Bike	51
8/9	Edinburgh to Paris, France	Plane	
8/12	Paris to Saint-Martin d'Étampes	Train	
8/12	Saint-Martin d'Étampes to Chartres	Bike	38
8/14	Chartres to Blois	Bike	80
8/15	Blois to Amboise	Bike	22
8/16	Amboise to Chinon	Bike	44
8/17	Chinon to Vouvant	Bike	66
8/18	Vouvant to La Rochelle	Bike	45
8/19	La Rochelle to Royan	Bike	44
8/21	Royan to Bordeaux via Carcans Plage	Bike	75
8/22	Bordeaux to Meilhan-sur-Garonne	Bike	48
8/23	Meilhan-sur-Garonne to Verdun-sur-Garonne	Bike	92
8/24	Verdun-sur-Garonne through Toulouse	Bike	25
	Toulouse to Montesquieu-Lauragais	Bike	20
	Montesquieu-Lauragais to Molleville	Bike	20
8/25	Molleville to Carcassonne	Bike	33
8/27	Carcassonne to Cerbère, Spain	Train	
	Cerbère to El Port de la Selva	Bike	16
8/28	El Port de la Selva to Cadaqués	Bike	10
8/31	Cadaqués to Llançà	Bike	14
8/31	Llançà to Paris	Train	
9/3	Paris to Orry-la-Ville	Train	
9/3–8	Orry-la-Ville to Zele, Belgium	Bike	205
9/8	Zele to Amsterdam, Netherlands	Train	

Date	From—To	Transport	Miles
9/9	Amsterdam to Apeldoorn	Bike	56
9/10	Apeldoorn to Bad Bentheim, Germany	Bike	58
9/11	Bad Bentheim to Copenhagen, Denmark	Train	
9/13	Copenhagen to London	Plane	
9/14	London to Nairobi, Kenya	Plane/bike	10
9/24	Nairobi to Kikuyu	Bike	22
9/25	Kikuyu to Naivasha	Bike	44
9/26	Naivasha to Fisherman's Camp	Bike	13
9/27	Hell's Gate National Park day trip	Bike	20
9/29	Fisherman's Camp to Nakuru	Bike	60
9/30	Nakuru to Molo	Bike	33
10/1	Molo to Kericho	Bike	40
10/2	Kericho to Kapsabet	Bike	62
10/3	Kapsabet to Eldoret	Bus	
10/4	Kapsabet to Kakamega Forest	Bike	30
10/7	Kakamega Forest to Mumias	Bike	32
10/8	Mumias to Tororo, Uganda	Bike	48
10/9	Tororo to Jinja	Bike	80
10/11	Jinja to Kampala	Bike	62
10/15	Kampala to Mityana	Bike	56
10/16	Mityana to Mubende	Bike	55
10/17	Mubende to Fort Portal	Bus	
10/19	Fort Portal to Kasese	Bike	46
10/20	Kasese to Parish house	Bike	40
10/21	Parish house to Ishaka	Bike	25
10/22	Ishaka to Ntungamo	Bike	34
10/23	Ntungamo to Kabale	Bike	50
10/24	Kabale	Bike	
10/25	Kabale to Bwindi Impenetrable Forest	Bike	52
10/26	Kabale to Tororo	Bus	
10/27	Tororo to Malaba	Bike	8
	Malaba to Nairobi	Train	

Date	From—To	Transport	Miles
10/28	Nairobi to Mombasa	Train	
10/31	Mombasa to Kilifi	Bike	40
11/1	Kilifi to Watamu	Bike	35
11/2	Watamu to Malindi	Bike	18
	Malindi to Lamu	Plane	
11/12	Lamu to Malindi	Plane	
11/13	Malindi to Nairobi	Bus	
11/15	Nairobi to Bombay, India	Plane	
11/16	Bombay to Vasco da Gama/Goa	Plane/bike	5
11/17	Vasco da Gama to Benaulim	Bike	20
11/22	Benaulim to Palolem Beach	Bike	30
11/25	Palolem to Karwar	Bike	28
11/26	Karwar to Gokarna	Bike	36
12/1	Gokarna to Murdeshwar	Bike	50
12/3	Murdeshwar to Kundapura	Bike	44
12/4	Kundapura to Mangalore	Bike	64
12/5	Mangalore to Hassan	Bus	
12/6	Hassan to Belur Halebid	Bus	
12/8	Hassan to Krishnarajanagara	Bike	50
12/9	Krishnarajanagara to Mysore	Bike	25
12/13	Mysore to Kadakola to Mysore	Bike	20
12/14	Mysore to Mudumalai and through game park	Bike	60
12/17	Mudumalai to Ooty	Bike	44
12/18	Ooty to Mettupalayam	Bike	35
12/19	Mettupalayam to Coimbatore to Pollachi	Bike	70
12/20	Pollachi to Palani	Bike	52
12/23	Palani to Kodaikanal	Bus/bike	4
12/26	Kodaikanal day trip	Bike	30
12/27	Kodaikanal day trip	Bike	20
12/29	Kodaikanal to Theni	Bike	55
12/30	Theni to Kumily/Kerala	Bike	40
1/2/92	Kumily to Kanjirappally	Bike	45

Date	From—To	Transport	Miles
1/3	Kanjirappally to Kottayam	Bike	25
1/4	Kottayam to Cochin	Bike	42
1/7	Cochin to Alleppey	Bike	40
1/8	Alleppey to Quilon	Boat	
1/10	Quilon to Varkala	Bike	25
1/12	Varkala to Kovalam	Bike	55
1/16	Kovalam to Madras	Plane	
1/18	Madras to Calcutta	Plane	
1/19	Calcutta to Kathmandu, Nepal	Plane	
1/23	Kathmandu to Patan day trip	Bus	
1/24	Kathmandu day trip	Bike	15
1/25	Kathmandu to Pokhara	Bus	
1/26	Pokhara day trip	Bike	13
1/28	Pokhara to trailhead at Birethanti	Bike	30
1/29	Trekking to Poon Hill	Hike	32
1/31	Birethanti to Pokhara	Bike	30
2/4	Kathmandu to Bangkok, Thailand	Plane	
2/7	Bangkok to Chiang Mai	Bus	
2/10	Chiang Mai to Pong Dueat Hot Springs	Bike	55
2/11	Pong Dueat Hot Springs to Mae Sae village	Bike	13
2/12	Mae Sae village to Pai	Bike	32
2/14	Pai to Fang	Car	
2/15	Fang to Mae Sai	Car	
2/16	Mae Sai to Chiang Saen	Bike	22
2/17	Chiang Saen to Chiang Khong	Bike	35
2/18	Chiang Khong to Thoeng	Bike	48
2/19	Thoeng to Tha Wang Pha Red Cross station	Bike	60
2/20	Tha Wang Pha District to Nan	Bike/hitch	30
2/21	Camping trip to visit Mlabri tribe		
2/24	Nan cave day trip	Bike	15
2/25	Nan to Sukhothai	Bus	
2/26	Sukhothai to Old Sukhothai	Bike	20

Date	From—To	Transport	Miles
2/27	Phitsanulok	Bus/bike	6
2/28	Loei	Bus	
2/29	Loei to Pak Chom	Bike	55
3/1	Pak Chom to Sang Khom	Bike	40
3/3	Sang Khom to Si Chiang Mai	Bike	35
3/6	Si Chiang Mai to Nong Khai	Bike	42
3/9	Nong Khai to Udon Thani	Bike	36
3/13	Udon Thani to Phimai	Bus/bike	6
3/14	Phimai to Bangkok	Bus/bike	3
3/16	Bangkok to Ko Samet	Bus/ferry	
3/20	Ko Samet to Bangkok	Ferry/bus	
3/21	Bangkok to Saigon, Vietnam	Plane/bike	6
3/25	Saigon to My Tho	Bike	45
3/26	My Tho to Vinh Long	Bike	47
3/27	Vinh Long to Can Tho	Bike	20
3/28	Can Tho to Long Xuyen	Bike	40
3/29	Long Xuyen to Chau Doc	Bike	35
3/30	Chau Doc day trip	Bike	25
3/31	Chau Doc to Saigon	Bus	
4/4	Saigon to Hue	Train	
4/6	Hue Royal Palace	Bike	10
4/7	The Royal Tombs	Bike	20
4/9	Hue to Da Nang	Bus	
4/10	Da Nang to Hoi An	Bike	20
4/11	Hoi An day trip	Bike	10
4/12	Hoi An to My Son to Hoi An	Bike	62
4/13	Hoi An to Quang Ngai	Bike	80
4/14	Quang Ngai to Sa Huynh	Bike	40
	Sa Huynh to Qui Nhon	Truck/bike	12
4/15	Qui Nhon to Tuy Hoa	Bike	70
4/16	Tuy Hoa to Nha Trang	Bike	85
4/19	Nha Trang to Saigon	Train	

Date	From—To	Transport	Miles
4/21	Saigon to Bangkok	Bike/plane	6
4/27	Bangkok to Singapore	Plane	
4/29	Singapore to Denpasar/Bali, Indonesia	Plane/bike	6
5/1	Legian Beach to Ubud	Bike	22
5/9	Ubud to Bedugul	Bike	27
5/10	Bedugul to Lovina	Bike	20
5/11	Lovina to Gilimanuk	Bike	44
5/12	Gilimanuk to Ketapang Port/Java	Ferry	
5/13	Gilimanuk to Terima Bay	Bike	9
5/14	Terima Bay to Lovina	Bike	40
5/15	Lovina to Amed Beach	Bike	55
5/16	Amed Beach to Candi Dasa	Bike	30
5/17	Candi Dasa to Tenganan	Bike	10
5/19	Candi Dasa to Klungkung	Bike	30
5/20	Candi Dasa to Denpasar	Bus	
	Denpasar to Lembar/Lombok	Ferry	
5/21	Lembar to Mangsit	Bike	22
5/22	Mangsit to Gili Air	Bike/ferry	13
5/24	Gili Air to Ampenan	Bike	27
5/25	Ampenan day trip	Bike	25
5/26	Ampenan to Lembar to Bali	Bike/ferry	16
5/27	Ubud		
5/29	Legian Beach		
5/31	Denpasar to Biak to Honolulu to Los Angeles	Plane	

Packing List

Bicycles, Parts, Tools, and Supplies

- Two Trek 520 touring bikes
- Front and back panniers
- One tent
- Two sleeping bags and liners
- One small hand-pump water purifier
- One camp stove, which could run on any imaginable fuel
- One travel guitar
- One retractable defense stick
- Water purification tablets
- Two helmets
- Four water bottles

- Assorted nuts, bolts, and screws
- Pannier hooks
- Gloves
- Two bike locks
- Baling wire
- Extra batteries
- Gloves
- One extra freewheel
- Cables
- Two spare rear derailleurs
- Four spare inner tubes

- One link extractor
- Lubricant
- Pliers
- One Allen wrench
- One adjustable wrench
- Spanners
- One spoke wrench
- One crank bolt wrench pin
- One headset wrench
- One tire gauge
- Vise grips

- One cyclometer (which promptly broke)
- Four patch kits
- Long-nose pliers
- One compass
- Two pumps
- One file
- Two sets of bike lights
- Two extra chains
- One screwdriver
- Candles
- One spare tire
- One front derailleur
- Two flashlights
- Electrical tape
- Hose clamps
- Duct tape

Medical Supplies

- Antibiotic pills
- Acetaminophen
- Lip salve
- Vitamins
- Ibuprofen
- Bandages
- Malaria pills
- Antiseptic cream
- Insect repellent with deet
- Diarrhea pills
- Sunblock

Clothing and Personal Items for Each

- Two pairs of bicycle shorts
- One wool sweater
- One chamois towel
- One pair of casual pants
- Four sock and underwear changes
- One pair biking/walking shoes
- One skirt for me
- One pair of sandals
- One Gore-Tex rain jacket
- One pair of Gore-Tex rain pants

- Three shirts to bike in
- One bathing suit
- Chamois towels
- One bandanna
- One visor
- Spare glasses
- One long-sleeved shirt
- Extra passport photos
- Pocketknife
- Toothbrush and paste
- Camp soap
- Lotion
- Notebook, pens, and pencils
- Business cards with our names and P.O. box
- Postcards and photos of family and home
- Addresses
- Passports
- Money belts
- American Express cards (one for each of us)
- Travelers Cheques for the first leg of the journey
- Checks from our bank accounts at home
- One fanny pack
- Plastic zip bags
- Binoculars
- Maps
- Guidebooks
- Needle and thread

Photo and Film Equipment

- 35mm pocket camera with flash
- 35mm SLR camera with zoom lens
- 35mm slide film (80 rolls)
- Hi8 camera
- Lens-cleaning kit
- Hi8 tapes (30 hours)

Gift Items

- Postcards of home
- Mexican woven friendship bracelets

Acknowledgments

As the saying goes, it takes a village. Here is a big thank-you to all who encouraged me to write this book, especially to my husband, Scott. Thank you to Anand Mehrotra, whose wisdom teachings helped me to finish processing this journey, which took place almost three decades ago, and to see it with fresh eyes lit with love and gratitude. How we remember and recount our past can bring about great healing. As I am, so is my world. Thank you to my first beta readers, who helped me with their questions. Thank you to my first editor, Jennifer McGrath, and to the author Jennifer Asbenson, who led me to her. My appreciation goes out to all the writers who shared their stories with me at the Los Angeles Times Festival of Books. Thank you to Susan Katz for your valued input, extra polishing, and encouragement. Thank you to Linda, Harsha, Janet, Priti, Carl, Steen, Per, Brigitte, Lee, François, Bernard, Françoise, Janet, Vivek, Raghu, Vijay, Keith, Israel, Raj, Gaëlle, Thierry, and the Caffertys. And most of all, thanks to the wonderful people we met who shared their lives with us throughout our journey—you are forever in my heart.

Printed in the United States
By Bookmasters